The Service Economy

NATIONAL BUREAU OF ECONOMIC RESEARCH

NUMBER 87, GENERAL SERIES

The Service Economy

VICTOR R. FUCHS

The City University of New York

Assisted by Irving F. Leveson

NATIONAL BUREAU OF ECONOMIC RESEARCH

NEW YORK 1968

Distributed by COLUMBIA UNIVERSITY PRESS

NEW YORK AND LONDON

RELATION OF THE DIRECTORS TO THE WORK AND PUBLICATIONS OF THE NATIONAL BUREAU OF ECONOMIC RESEARCH

1. The object of the National Bureau of Economic Research is to ascertain and to present to the public important economic facts and their interpretation in a scientific and impartial manner. The Board of Directors is charged with the responsibility of ensuring that the work of the National Bureau is carried on in strict conformity with this object.

2. The President of the National Bureau shall submit to the Board of Directors, or to its Executive Committee, for their formal adoption all specific proposals for research to be instituted.

3. No research report shall be published until the President shall have submitted to each member of the Board the manuscript proposed for publication, and such information as will, in his opinion and in the opinion of the author, serve to determine the suitability of the report for publication in accordance with the principles of the National Bureau. Each manuscript shall contain a summary drawing attention to the nature and treatment of the problem studied, the character of the data and their utilization in the report, and the main conclusions reached.

4. For each manuscript so submitted, a special committee of the Board shall be appointed by majority agreement of the President and Vice Presidents (or by the Executive Committee in case of inability to decide on the part of the President and Vice Presidents), consisting of three directors selected as nearly as may be one from each general division of the Board. The names of the special manuscript committee shall be stated to each Director when the manuscript is submitted to him. It shall be the duty of each member of the special manuscript committee to read the manuscript. If each member of the manuscript committee signifies his approval within thirty days of the transmittal of the manuscript, the report may be published. If at the end of that period any member of the manuscript committee withholds his approval, the President shall then notify each member of the Board, requesting approval or disapproval of publication, and thirty days additional shall be granted for this purpose. The manuscript shall then not be published unless at least a majority of the entire Board who shall have voted on the proposal within the time fixed for the receipt of votes shall have approved.

5. No manuscript may be published, though approved by each member of the special manuscript committee, until forty-five days have elapsed from the transmittal of the report in manuscript form. The interval is allowed for the receipt of any memorandum of dissent or reservation, together with a brief statement of his reasons, that any member may wish to express; and such memorandum of dissent or reservation shall be published with the manuscript if he so desires. Publication does not, however, imply that each member of the Board has read the manuscript, or that either members of the Board in general or the special committee have passed on its validity in every detail.

6. Publications of the National Bureau issued for informational purposes concerning the work of the Bureau and its staff, or issued to inform the public of activities of Bureau staff, and volumes issued as a result of various conferences involving the National Bureau shall contain a specific disclaimer noting that such publication has not passed through the normal review procedures required in this resolution. The Executive Committee of the Board is charged with review of all such publications from time to time to ensure that they do not take on the character of formal research reports of the National Bureau, requiring formal Board approval.

7. Unless otherwise determined by the Board or exempted by the terms of paragraph 6, a copy of this resolution shall be printed in each National Bureau publication.

(Resolution adopted October 25, 1926 and revised February 6, 1933, February 24, 1941, and April 20, 1968)

To Nancy, Fred, Paula, and Kenneth

CONTENTS

TABLES

CHARTS

PREFACE

The Service sector, also known as the "tertiary" or "residual" sector, has long been the stepchild of economic research. This was unfortunate but tolerable during the 19th and early 20th centuries when the shift from agriculture to industry was in full swing and services were of lesser importance. Since the end of World War II, however, the Service sector has become the largest, and, in many respects, the most dynamic element in the U.S. economy. Furthermore, most of the industrialized nations of the world appear to be following, with some lag, the pattern set by the United States. Thus, the emergence of this country as the first "service economy" has created a new set of priorities for economic research.

In recent decades, pioneering studies at the National Bureau by Friedman and Kuznets, Fabricant, Barger, Stigler, and Kendrick,[1] have done much to meet Colin Clark's challenge that "The economics of tertiary industry remains to be written." [2] Nevertheless, the paucity of data on this large and rapidly growing sector of the economy left unanswered many questions concerning service output, employment, productivity, and wages.

This book describes the growth of service employment in the United States and quantifies the major reasons for this growth. It also examines intersector and intrasector differentials in productivity change, describes and analyzes industry patterns of hourly earnings, develops measures of sector differences in cyclical behavior, and explores the implications for society and for economic analysis of the growth of a service economy.

[1] See Milton Friedman and Simon Kuznets, *Income From Independent Professional Practice*, New York, NBER, 1945; Solomon Fabricant (Assisted by Robert E. Lipsey), *The Trend of Government Activity in the United States Since 1900*, New York, NBER, 1952; Harold Barger, *Distribution's Place in the American Economy Since 1869*, Princeton University Press for NBER, 1955; George J. Stigler, *Trends in Employment in the Service Industries*, Princeton for NBER, 1956; *Employment and Compensation in Education*, New York, NBER, 1950; *Domestic Servants in the United States 1900–1940*, New York, NBER, 1946; John W. Kendrick, *Productivity Trends in the United States*, Princeton for NBER, 1961.

[2] Colin Clark, *The Conditions of Economic Progress*, London, 1940.

In carrying out this project, which was begun in 1963 with the financial assistance of the Ford Foundation, important new bodies of data were utilized, including the first official series on real gross product by major industry group, the *Censuses of Business* for 1963, the *1960 Census of Population and Housing,* and the one-in-a-thousand sample of that Census. Utilizing these and other materials, such as input-output tables and the Bureau of Labor Statistics Survey of Consumer Expenditures, we have attempted to increase our understanding of the service industries, and of the ways they are related to and differ from the rest of the economy.

Several papers and articles reporting some of the results of the project have already been published.[3] A number of other studies are in preparation.[4]

In this book, the growth of service employment is examined in detail in Chapter 2, following a first chapter which presents a summary of the major findings. Trends in recent decades receive primary attention, but longer-term trends are also considered. The growth of the Service sector's share of employment in individual states and in foreign countries is discussed. Greatest emphasis is given to the distribution of employment by industry and sector, but some occupational data are also presented.

The growth of service employment is found to be related primarily to differential trends in output per man. These are explored in Chapter 3. Comparisons between the Service and Industry sectors are made for output per man, output per unit of labor input, and output per unit of total

[3] Victor R. Fuchs, *Productivity Trends in the Goods and Service Sectors, 1929–61: A Preliminary Survey,* New York, NBER, Occasional Paper 89, 1964; *The Growing Importance of the Service Industries,* New York, NBER, Occasional Paper 96, 1965; *Productivity Differences Within the Service Sector* (with Jean Alexander Wilburn), New York, NBER, OP 102, 1966; *Differentials in Hourly Earnings by Region and City Size, 1959,* New York, NBER, Occasional Paper 101, 1967; "The Growth of Service Industries in the United States: A Model for Other Countries?" *Manpower Problems in the Service Sector,* Supplement 1966-2, OECD, Paris, 1966; Irving F. Leveson, "Reductions in Hours of Work as a Source of Productivity Growth," *The Journal of Political Economy,* April 1967; David Schwartzman, "The Contribution of Education to the Quality of Labor, 1929–1963," *American Economic Review,* September 1968. In addition, a Conference on Production and Productivity in the Service Industries was held in Ottawa in 1967 under the sponsorship of the Conference on Research in Income and Wealth; the conference papers will be published by the National Bureau shortly.

[4] David Schwartzman, "The Growth of Sales Per Man-Hour in Retail Trade, 1929–1963," in *Production and Productivity in the Service Industries,* V. R. Fuchs, ed., NBER, in press; Reuben Gronau, "The Value of Time: The Demand for Air Transportation"; David Schwartzman, "Retail Trade in the United States, 1929–1963; An Analysis of the Growth of Sales Per Worker"; Irving F. Leveson, "Nonfarm Self-Employment in the U.S."; Auster-Leveson-Sarachek, "The Production of Health, An Exploratory Study," NBER manuscripts.

factor input; and some interesting differences are noted. Trends for each major industry group are also examined and intergroup differences are analyzed.

Considerable emphasis is given to intersector comparisons, but this is not to posit some bland homogeneity for all the service industries, or to deny the existence of conflicting trends within the sector. Chapters 4 and 5 are devoted to analyses of productivity in detailed service industries. Chapter 4 uses correlation and regression techniques to analyze inter-industry differences in productivity change across seventeen selected retail trades and services. Chapter 5 presents case studies of three important service industries: barber and beauty shops, retail trade, and medical care. Considerable attention is given to the conceptual and statistical difficulties encountered in measuring and interpreting trends in output and productivity in these industries.

The trends in employment and the trends in productivity are, of course, related. The relation is not a simple one, however, but involves consideration of trends in capital formation, quality of labor prices, wages, and other variables. Sector differences in the growth of the quality of labor prove to be of particular importance, as is the related question of differential trends in earnings in the Industry and Service sectors.

The availability of the one-in-a-thousand sample of the *1960 Census of Population* permits an intensive examination of interindustry and intersector differences in hourly earnings, presented in Chapter 6. This analysis, which includes consideration of demographic characteristics, location of industries, unionization, and other variables, contributes to an understanding of changes in earnings over time as well as in cross section.

Although this book deals primarily with long-term trends, the growing importance of the service industries also has important implications for short-term movements. These implications for cyclical fluctuation in employment, output, and productivity are examined in Chapter 7. Monthly data for 1947–65 are used to calculate measures of cyclical amplitude in various industries and sectors.

The final chapter considers some other aspects of the growth of a service economy. This growth is shown to have important implications for the labor force, the role of women, unions, education, and industrial organization. In addition, Chapter 8 discusses some problems and challenges to economic analysis that are implicit in the growing importance of the service industries.

With few exceptions, this study is concerned only with the U.S. economy. The shift to services has proceeded further in this country than anywhere else. Too, the available data, though far from adequate, are richer and more reliable than those for other countries. Fortunately, a number of investigators in other countries have carried out studies along lines similar to those laid down in two preliminary NBER reports.[5] Thus, readers of this book will find it possible to make comparisons between some aspects of the U.S. experience and that of Western Europe, the United Kingdom, Japan, Australia, and Canada.[6] Studies of service industry employment are also available for Israel, the U.S.S.R., and Latin America.[7]

The time span covered in this book is, with some exceptions, 1929 through 1965. The earlier year marks the beginning of many of the most important time series, and the later year was the most recent with data available in time for inclusion in the analysis. Some of the analyses are limited to more recent periods because of the lack of available data.

The level of industrial detail is largely determined by the availability and reliability of the data. For some purposes, such as measurement of trends in physical capital, only broad sector comparisons are attempted. For others, such as the analysis of interindustry differences in earnings in 1959, it is possible to include over 100 detailed industries. Because data were taken from a variety of sources, different industry classifications are used in different parts of the study. Thus, the analysis of interindustry differences in earnings in 1959 utilizes the industry detail found in the *1960 Census of Population,* whereas the analysis of industry growth, 1929–65, uses the industry detail developed by the Office of Business Economics.

This study does not, for the most part, break new ground in the measurement of employment or output. The emphasis is on the analysis

[5] Victor R. Fuchs, *Productivity Trends* (OP 89) and *Growing Importance* (OP 96).

[6] Maurice Lengellé, *La Revolution Tertiaire,* Editions Genin, Paris, 1966, and *The Growing Importance of the Service Sector in Member Countries,* OECD, Paris, 1966; B. M. Deakin & K. D. George, "Productivity Trends in the Service Industries, 1948–63," *Economic Bulletin,* No. 53, London and Cambridge, March 1965; "The Growing Service Industries—Their Productivity and Price Formation," Japanese Economic Research Institute, Intermediate Report, May 1967; B. D. Haig, "The Measurement of Real Expenditure and Product of Goods and Services," pp. 520–535, and J. A. Dowie, "Productivity Growth in Goods and Services: Australia, U.S.A., U.K.," pp. 536–554, both in *The Economic Record,* December 1966; David A. Worton, "The Service Industries in Canada, 1946–66," in *Production and Productivity in the Service Industries,* V. R. Fuchs, ed., NBER, in press.

[7] Gur Ofer, *Service Industries in a Developing Economy,* New York, 1967, and "The Service Industries in the U.S.S.R.," unpublished Ph.D. dissertation, Harvard University; J. R. Ramos, "The Labor Force in Post-War Latin America," unpublished Ph.D. dissertation, Columbia University.

of existing data, on the explanation of clearly perceived trends, and on the estimation of the magnitude of observed relationships. This emphasis is the result of personal research interests and aptitudes; it does not reflect a judgment that problems of measurement are inconsequential.

It has long been known that the measurement of real output in the service industries is in an unsatisfactory state. This book does not alter that basic situation, although the discussion of the direction and likely magnitude of biases may shed some new light on the problem. Also, alternative estimates have been presented where applicable, and some effort has been made to indicate the degree of confidence that can be placed in the various findings. Many of the conclusions presented in this book are not dependent upon the particular output measures used; they would be equally relevant if some different, and presumably superior, output measures become available.

The need for more and better quality data concerning the service industries is urgent. These industries now account for well over half of all U.S. employment, and their share has been increasing every year. The trends discussed in this book suggest that a substantial change in emphasis on the part of data gathering agencies is required in order to provide the information necessary to solve the problems raised by the growth of a service economy.

Acknowledgments

The service industry project involved many persons at the National Bureau, and my debt to my colleagues, collaborators, and assistants is great. A staff reading committee, consisting of Gary S. Becker, Solomon Fabricant, and Robert E. Lipsey, reviewed the first draft of this book and made many helpful suggestions. Solomon Fabricant was Director of Research when the project began, and he retained a strong interest in it throughout the period. John R. Meyer and Geoffrey H. Moore read portions of the manuscript and contributed several useful comments. Jacob Mincer has been a valued source of advice throughout the study. Charlotte Boschan developed the computer program used to analyze earnings and other information from the 1/1,000 sample of the *1960 Census of Population*. Others who contributed to the study include: F. Thomas Juster, Anna J. Schwartz, David Schwartzman, and Jean Wilburn. I am also indebted to Francis M. Boddy, Wallace J. Campbell, and Douglass C. North, members of the National Bureau's Board of Directors, for their helpful comments on the manuscript.

Research assistants frequently play an important role in National

Bureau projects, and this one has not been an exception. Irving F. Leveson was my chief assistant until the project was almost finished; his dedication and perseverance more than justify his inclusion on the title page of this book. Michael Grossman joined the project at a late stage but made many contributions, particularly in connection with the chapter on cyclical fluctuations. I am happy to acknowledge also the assistance of Marietta Aloukou, Richard Auster, Henrietta Lichtenbaum, Judy Mitnick, Linda Nasif, Elizabeth Rand, Regina Reibstein, Robin Ringler, Harriet Rubin, Deborah Sarachek, Katherine Warden, Kay Wilson, and Lorraine Wolch; they served for periods ranging from one summer to two years. Sophie Sakowitz checked most of the tables and provided advice concerning business cycle turning points.

Lorraine Lusardi was administrative secretary to the project, typed the manuscript, and, in addition, was a most efficient and conscientious personal secretary. I am also grateful to Joyce M. Rose for secretarial assistance during the early stages of the study. The charts were drawn with skill and care by H. Irving Forman. Some of them were plotted by computer in collaboration with the electronic data processing group at the National Bureau. Thanks are due also to Joan R. Tron for a careful and empathic editing of the manuscript.

Several persons outside the National Bureau have also provided helpful comments concerning this manuscript or the preliminary reports. At the risk of inadvertently omitting some, I would like to thank Daniel Creamer, Edward Denison, Jack Gottsegen, A. Gilbert Heebner, H. Gregg Lewis, and Albert Rees. It is also a pleasure to acknowledge the splendid cooperation received from the U.S. Office of Business Economics, The Bureau of the Census and other government agencies.

Financial support for the project was provided primarily by the Ford Foundation. A grant of computer time from the International Business Machines Corporation is also gratefully acknowledged. Certain data used in this book were derived from punch cards furnished under a joint project sponsored by the U.S. Bureau of the Census and the Population Council, and containing selected 1960 Census information for a 0.1 per cent sample of the population of the United States. Neither the Census Bureau nor the Population Council assumes any responsibility for the validity of any of the figures or interpretations of them published herein based on this material.

VICTOR R. FUCHS

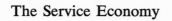

The Service Economy

1

SUMMARY OF FINDINGS

The United States is now pioneering in a new stage of economic development. During the period following World War II this country became the world's first "service economy"—that is, the first nation in which more than half of the employed population is not involved in the production of food, clothing, houses, automobiles, or other tangible goods.

In 1947 total employment stood at approximately 57 million; by 1967 it was about 74 million. Virtually all of the net increase occurred in institutions that provide services—such as banks, hospitals, retail stores, schools. The number of people employed in the production of goods has been relatively stable; modest increases in manufacturing and construction have been offset by declines in agriculture and mining.

Numerous dramatic examples of the growth of services are readily available. For instance, the *increase* in employment in the field of education between 1950 and 1960 was greater than the total number employed in the steel, copper, and aluminum industries in either year. The *increase* in employment in the field of health between 1950 and 1960 was greater than the total number employed in automobile manufacturing in either year. The *increase* in employment in financial firms between 1950 and 1960 was greater than total employment in mining in 1960.

This book, which reports on the results of more than four years of investigation of the transition from an industrial to a service economy, has the following objectives. First, it delineates in considerable detail the growth of service employment. Second, it attempts to explain this growth, paying special attention to the relatively slow increase in output per man in services. Third, it describes and analyzes differences in productivity change among the service industries, and explores some of the conceptual problems encountered in measuring service output and productivity. The fourth objective is to compare the service industries with the rest of the economy with respect to such critical matters as earnings, behavior over the business cycle, industrial organization, and labor force characteristics. These comparisons lead to a consideration of the implications of the growth of a service economy. The transition from an agricultural to an industrial economy, which began in England and has been repeated in most of the Western world, has been characterized as a "revolution." The shift from industrial to service employment, which has advanced furthest in the United States but is evident in all developed economies, has proceeded more quietly, but it too has implications for society, and for economic analysis, of "revolutionary" proportions.

Service Employment

The first major finding, plainly in evidence but not sufficiently appreciated,[1] is that the balance of employment in the United States has shifted dramatically (and probably irrevocably) in favor of the service industries. The Service sector's share of total employment has grown from approximately 40 per cent in 1929 to over 55 per cent in 1967.[2] Between 1947 and 1965 alone, there was an increase of 13 million jobs in the Service sector compared with an increase of only 4 million in Industry and a decrease of 3 million in Agriculture.

The increase in service employment was distributed widely through the sector; most service industries had above-average growth rates, and only a few experienced declines. Moreover, if service employment is equated with white-collar and service occupations, the shift away from goods production has been even greater than the industrial classification statistics suggest. This is because there has been a shift of employment within the Industry sector from direct production of goods to activities which, if they were not carried out within the firm, would be classified as services.

Although the relative growth of service employment has been particularly rapid in the past few decades, the trend has been evident for at least the past century in this country, and can also be observed in most

[1] So prominent an observer as J. K. Galbraith seems to have missed this development; c.f. his book, *The New Industrial State,* Boston, 1967.

[2] The Service sector is defined to include wholesale and retail trade; finance, insurance, and real estate; general government; and the services proper, including professional, personal, business, and repair services. The Industry sector is defined to include mining, contract construction, manufacturing, transportation, communications and public utilities, and government enterprise. For a discussion of these and alternative definitions see Chapter 2. Capitalization of the initial letter indicates that the sector as defined is being discussed; when services are being referred to in general terms, the initial letter is not capitalized.

Employment is measured in full-time equivalents, including the self-employed and military personnel, but excluding unpaid family workers.

growing economies. The pervasiveness of the trend to services is also observable within individual states; almost all have shared in the growth of service employment. Until about 1920, the increase in the Service sector's share of total employment was simply part of the general shift in the United States from agricultural to nonagricultural pursuits. Since then, and especially in the past two decades, a sharp divergence in growth rates between Service and Industry has become evident.

Reasons for Growth of Services

When we seek an explanation for this drastic shift of employment, three principal hypotheses are explored: (1) a more rapid growth of final demand for services; (2) a relative increase in intermediate demand for services; and (3) a relatively slow increase in output per man in services.

The first explanation involves the relation between spending patterns and levels of income. As income rises, it has been argued, the demand for goods tends to rise less rapidly than the demand for services; hence, the importance of services in the economy will rise. The relationship between income and demand for various outputs (the income elasticity) is difficult to measure, and precise estimates are beyond our grasp. The available evidence suggests that the growth of the Service *and* Industry sectors relative to Agriculture was related in considerable degree to a low income elasticity of demand for farm products. As Adam Smith noted in the *Wealth of Nations:* "The desire of food is limited in every man by the narrow capacity of the human stomach." Whether there is a similar limitation for goods in general is less clear. The demand for any particular good—such as automobiles or radios—may reach a point where further increases in income do not trigger much additional buying, but new goods—such as pleasure boats or T.V. sets—frequently appear to take up the slack.

Examination of cross-sectional buying patterns, and of trends in output over time, suggests that the growth of income and a consequent shift in demand has not been a major source of the relative growth of service employment. Measured in dollars of constant purchasing power, the Service sector's share of output was the same in 1965 as in 1929. Measured in current dollars, it grew only from 47 to 50 per cent. As a share of nonagricultural output in constant dollars, the Service sector actually declined over the same period, while in current dollars its share rose by less than 1 percentage point. If gross product is classified by type of final output rather than by industrial origin, the share accounted for by "services" increased only slightly between 1929 and 1965, whether measured in current dollars or after adjustment for changes in price.

The second explanation that has been explored is the growth of intermediate demand for services by goods-producing industries as a result of increased division of labor. As an economy grows, there is some tendency for specialized firms to be organized to provide the business and professional services that were formerly taken care of within manufacturing and other goods-producing firms or were neglected. An analysis of the input-output tables for 1947 and 1958 indicates that there has been some shift in this direction, but the employment change attributable to this source is less than 10 per cent of the total change.

The major explanation for the shift of employment is that output per man grew much more slowly in the Service sector than in the other sectors. In other words, the amount of labor required for a given amount of output fell more rapidly in Agriculture and Industry than in Service. The average annual rates of change, 1929–65, were Agriculture 3.4 per cent, Industry 2.2 per cent, and Service 1.1 per cent. The differential between Industry and Service, slightly over 1 per cent per annum, was similar in several subperiods that were examined. Although there are serious questions concerning the measurement of real output, especially in Service, it does not appear that the differential in output per man is attributable to biases in the measures of output. For one thing, the differential is almost as large if Industry is compared with a Service subsector which excludes government, households and institutions, and real estate—the industries that present the knottiest problems in measuring output.

The lag of output per man in the Service sector is explained by many factors. First, there was a greater decline in hours worked per man in Service than in Industry. Thus, the differential trend in output per manhour was not as large as that in output per man.

A second, and more important, explanation was the much more rapid increase in the quality of labor in Industry than in Service. This differential is suggested by the much faster growth of wages in Industry (.5 per cent per annum faster in 1929–65). The growth of unions explains part of the differential trend in wages, but the major part probably reflects an upgrading of skill levels in Industry. This inference is supported by changes in the demographic characteristics of the labor force in the two sectors. The level of schooling, the percentage male, and the percentage of prime working age have all been rising more rapidly or falling more slowly in Industry than in Service. The upgrading of labor quality in Industry is also revealed by the faster growth of professional and managerial occupations in that sector. Thus, substantial evidence points to a more rapid rate of growth of human capital per worker in Industry as a major factor explaining the more rapid growth of output per man.

A third explanation, more tentative and based on less reliable data than that for human capital, points to a differential trend in physical capital per worker, also in favor of Industry. This difference in physical capital has probably been quantitatively less important than the difference in human capital in explaining the lag of output per man in the Service sector.

The differential trends in hours, human capital, and physical capital do not account for all of the sector differential in growth of output per man. The residual, which is about .5 per cent per annum, suggests that there was probably more rapid technological change in Industry than in Service, or that Industry benefited more from growing economies of scale.

Although the hypothesis of a sector differential in productivity change is supported by the data, it is not true that output per man was static in services. Except for those service industries where output is assumed to always equal labor input, there was usually some positive growth of productivity.

Productivity, Growth, and Wages

The relationships between productivity, growth, and wages have received considerable attention from economists. Hypotheses derived from previous studies limited to or heavily concentrated on manufacturing were tested in this study in two ways. First, correlations between the variables were examined across the ten major industry groups.[3] Second, similar correlations were run across seventeen detailed retail trade and service industries.

The hypothesis of a strong positive relation between growth and productivity was not supported when tested across the ten major industry groups. There was no correlation between growth of output and productivity, and there was a negative correlation between changes in employment and productivity in the 1929–65 period. The slowest-growing industry group (measured by output or employment), agriculture, had the fastest rate of increase of output per man, and many similar dis-

[3] These groups are: agriculture; mining; construction; manufacturing; transportation; communications and public utilities; government enterprise; wholesale and retail trade; finance, insurance, real estate, and services; and general government.

crepancies are observed. These findings provide some support for the view that disparate rates of change of productivity may involve major structural changes in employment patterns.

The analysis of detailed industries, on the other hand, reveals a significant positive relationship between industry growth rates and changes in productivity. The correlation found among the seventeen service industries is of the same order of magnitude as that found by other investigators in studies of manufacturing industries. The way productivity stimulates growth, and growth stimulates productivity, is illustrated in the case study of the barber and beauty shops (see Chapter 5). Rapid changes in beauty shop techniques have stimulated growth through decreases in price and improvements in quality. An increase in the demand for beauty shop services has raised productivity through the stimulation of technological change, an increase in the average size of transactions, and a decrease in idle time. Barbering, by contrast, has been relatively stable in technology and in demand.

Analysis of the relation between changes in productivity and wages among the seventeen service industries also supports previous findings based on manufacturing; no correlation between changes in output per man and changes in compensation per man is observed. On the other hand, a significant positive relation between these two variables is observed among the ten major industry groups. To the extent that earnings reflect human capital, this finding supports the view that differential trends in output per man among major industry groups have been related to differential trends in labor quality.

Sector Differences in Hourly Earnings

An examination of hourly earnings for a single year (1959) reveals that persons employed in the Service sector earn significantly less than those employed in Industry. The average hourly rates as calculated from the one-in-a-thousand sample of the *1960 Census of Population* were $2.31 and $2.70 per hour, respectively.

The sector differential was examined first in broad terms and then through a systematic analysis of differences in earnings among 138 industries. The richness of the data made possible more comprehensive comparisons than those based on economic censuses or sample surveys. All industries in the Service and Industry sectors were included, and the earnings examined included those of salaried employees and self-employed workers as well as production workers. This is particularly important in Service because more than half of the persons employed in that sector are either salaried or self-employed.

"Expected" earnings for each industry were calculated, based on the demographic characteristics of the workers in each industry and the national earnings rates for each of 168 color-age-sex-education groups. To the extent that labor quality is associated with these characteristics, differences in average "expected" earnings across industries measure differences in labor quality; differences between actual and "expected" earnings measure differences in wages, holding labor quality constant.

This adjustment for demographic characteristics explains almost three-fourths of all interindustry differences in hourly earnings, but it does not explain any of the intersector differential. The "expected" earnings for each sector (Service and Industry) were both $2.50 per hour, indicating that the labor mix on average was about equal. Average hourly earnings in the Industry sector exceeded those in the Service sector for males and for females, for whites and nonwhites, and at every age and level of education.

The sector differential is also evident among industry groups. Every group in the Industry sector except one had actual earnings higher than "expected." Every group in the Service sector except two had actual earnings below "expected." Hourly earnings in construction, for example, were $2.87, although "expected" earnings were only $2.58. Hourly earnings in durable manufacturing were $2.79 although "expected" earnings were only $2.54. In the Service sector, the lowest standardized earnings were found in retail trade and personal services. Based on the demographic characteristics of the workers in retailing, hourly earnings should have been $2.37, but in fact were only $1.96. For personal services the "expected" earnings were $1.82 and the actual earnings were only $1.36.

The differences in hourly earnings among 138 industries were analyzed in order to explain the sector differential in earnings. The degree of unionization proved to be the most important variable after demographic characteristics in explaining interindustry variations in earnings in 1959. Unionization was found to have a strong and consistent relationship to hourly earnings after allowing for demographic characteristics, location, size of establishment, and other variables. The union effect seems to be strongest between 20 and 60 per cent unionization. Below and above that range, changes in unionization do not show much systematic relation to earnings. Within that range, a change of 10 percentage points in unionization is associated with a change of about 8.5 cents per hour or about 3.7 per cent.

More than half the persons employed in Industry are union members; the Service sector is only about 10 per cent unionized. According to the analysis of interindustry differentials in earnings, the greater unionization in Industry explains about two-thirds of the sector differential in hourly earnings. The larger size of establishments ranks after unionization as an explanation of the higher earnings in the Industry sector.

Other findings from this portion of the study are that, within the Industry sector, average earnings of the individual industries tend to be similar. The weighted (by man-hours) coefficient of variation across 81 industries in that sector is 13.7 per cent. The labor force mix as measured by "expected" earnings also is very homogeneous. The coefficient of variation is only 8.5 per cent. The industries in the Service sector, on the other hand, tend to be much more heterogeneous. The coefficient of variation for 57 service industries is 29.3 per cent for actual earnings, and 16.1 per cent for "expected" earnings.

Sector Differences in Cyclical Fluctuations

Although this report is primarily concerned with long-term trends, several tests of hypotheses concerning cyclical fluctuations were carried out. Monthly data covering the period 1947–65 were analyzed with the aid of the NBER cyclical analysis program. The results were checked and confirmed by analysis of deviations from long-term trends.

The principal findings are that output and employment are more stable over the business cycle in the Service sector than in Industry, but productivity tends to be more unstable in the Service sector. The stability of Service output is attributable to the fact that services cannot be stored. Thus, this sector avoids the swings in output that result from changes in the rate at which business firms and consumers add to or diminish their inventories of goods.

The stability of Service employment over the business cycle is even more striking than the stability of output. For the sector as a whole, the average rate of change of employment during expansions was $+2.9$ per cent per annum, and during business cycle contractions it was $+.7$ per cent per annum. Thus, in absolute terms, Service employment continued to increase even during periods when general business activity was declining. By contrast, the average annual rates of change of Industry employment were $+3.2$ per cent in expansions and -8.3 per cent in contractions.

The stability of employment in services can be explained in part by the stability of output. Even for equal cyclical changes in output, however, there is evidence that Service employment is more stable. This can be explained by the large numbers of self-employed and salaried employees, and by the substantial number of service industry employees classified as "wage and salary workers" who are actually compensated on a "piecework" basis. The latter group includes real estate, insurance, and security brokers, waiters and waitresses, barbers and beauticians, and most salesmen of durable goods. Their wages, in whole or in part, are determined by their output and take the form of commissions, tips, or a share of "profits." Because their earnings are more sensitive to cyclical fluctuations in spending than are their hours of work, we can think of these workers as having "flexible" wages, and this increases the stability of their employment.

The stability of service employment over the business cycle results in considerable cyclical instability in output per man. Between business cycle peaks and troughs in 1947–65, the average rate of rise and fall (net of trend) was 2.8 per cent per annum for retail employment compared with a rate for manufacturing employment of 13.3 per cent per annum. On the other hand, deflated sales per man-hour in retailing show an average cyclical amplitude of 3.8 per cent per annum, compared with only .5 per cent per annum for deflated sales per man-hour in manufacturing. As the relative importance of the Service sector grows, we can expect more stability in employment, but probably more instability in productivity for a given amount of cyclical fluctuation in aggregate economic activity.

Implications for Industrial Organization and Labor

In addition to its effect on cyclical fluctuations, the growth of service employment has important implications for industrial organization and for labor. To be sure, a shift in the relative importance of different industries is only one of many changes that are occurring simultaneously in the economy, and these other changes may tend to be offsetting in nature. Also, the sum total of these shifts and changes may itself set in motion further developments whose implications are at present indecipherable. Nevertheless, it is useful to note several major differences between the service industries and the rest of the economy, and to speculate about some possible consequences of a "service economy."

In the production of goods, for instance, with some notable exceptions such as agriculture and construction, most of the output is accounted for by large profit-seeking corporations. Ownership is frequently separate from management, and significant market power is often held by a few firms in each industry. In the Service sector, on the other hand, and again with some exceptions, firms are typically small, are usually owner managed, and are often noncorporate. Furthermore, nonprofit operations, both public and private, account for one-third of the Service sector's employment.

One statistic that epitomizes what has been happening to the American economy is the percentage of the national income originating in business corporations. Ever since the development of the private corporation, its role in the economy has tended to grow, but its relative importance apparently reached a peak about 1956 when corporations accounted for over 57 per cent of total national income. Since then there has been a tendency for this fraction to remain stable, or even to decline, despite changes in the tax laws which encourage the incorporation of small firms.

As these and other facts become better known, we may see an end to the myth of the dominance of the large corporation in our society. Most people do not work and never have worked for large corporations; most production does not take place and never has taken place in large corporations. In the future, the large corporation is likely to be overshadowed by the hospitals, universities, research institutes, government agencies, and professional organizations that are the hallmarks of a service economy.

As stated above, many services are produced by nonprofit institutions. The growing importance of such organizations poses some disturbing questions about efficiency and equity. As the problem of sharply rising costs in nonprofit hospitals illustrates, we may need new instruments of regulation and control to supplement the present system which relies upon competition and a drive for profits as the primary spurs to efficiency in production and distribution.

Some of the most startling comparisons between the Industry and Service sectors concern the characteristics of their respective labor forces. One simple, but profound, difference is that many occupations in the Service sector do not make special demands for physical strength. This means that women can compete on more nearly equal terms with men, perhaps for the first time in history. In the Service sector, we find women holding down almost one-half of all jobs, compared with only one-fifth in Industry.

The ultimate effects of this simple change could be very far reaching. To be sure, man's superior economic position is partly attributable to his more continuous attachment to the labor force and to other factors. To the extent that higher earnings are based on strength, however, the advent of a service economy should make for greater equality between the sexes.

We also find a disproportionate number of older workers in services, despite the rapid growth which favors new entrants to the labor force. In addition to making more modest demands for physical strength, the Service sector attracts women and older workers because it provides greater opportunities for part-time employment. The use of part-timers contributes significantly to the efficient operation of service firms because demand in many cases comes at particular hours of the day and particular days of the week.

Given the importance of females, part-timers, and the self-employed in the Service sector, it is not surprising to find a large difference in the extent of unionization in the two sectors. Unless there are strenuous new efforts at organization, the continued growth of services may mean a decline in union influence in the United States. On the other hand, if the unions become successful in organizing the Service sector to the same extent as the Industry sector, we may see significant changes in the nature of the union movement and in the reaction of the public to strikes and other forms of union activity.

Still another implication concerning labor which may be of considerable importance (although it is difficult to quantify) is a trend toward "personalization" of work. The transfer from a craft society to one of mass production was said to depersonalize work and alienate the worker. The advent of a service economy implies a reversal of these trends. Employees in many service industries are closely related to their work and often engage in a highly personalized activity that offers ample scope for the development and exercise of personal skill. It should be stressed that the possibility of deriving satisfaction from a job well-done and of taking pride in one's work are only prospects, not certainties. At their best, however, many service occupations are extremely rewarding, and in some the line between "work" and "leisure" activity is often difficult to draw.

This view runs counter to the assertion that automation results in the depersonalization of work. It may be true that the initial impact of automation is the substitution of machinery and controls (highly impersonal) for work that was formerly done by human labor. Given full employment, however, the major impact of automation is to eliminate relatively routine, impersonal work entirely, with the result that if one looks at the kind of work people are now doing—the type of work that is growing most rapidly—it is typically of a much more personal character than before.

Implications for Economic Analysis

Considerable rethinking of economic concepts may be required, as a result of the growing relative importance of services. One problem arises because the consumer frequently plays an important role in the production of services, but not in the production of goods. This unmeasured input can have significant effects on productivity in retailing, health, education, and many other service industries. In the supermarket and laundromat the consumer actually works, and in the doctor's office the quality of medical history the patient gives may influence significantly the productivity of the doctor. Productivity in banking is affected by whether the clerk or the customer makes out the deposit slip—and whether it is made out correctly or not. Thus, the knowledge, experience, honesty, and motivation of the consumer affect Service productivity, but the tools and data necessary to incorporate these factors into our analysis do not exist.

A second concept that may require further development is that of labor-embodied technological change. When, as in some services, formal education is important and there is job security, the rate at which advances in knowledge affect productivity will depend in part on how fast labor embodying these new advances can be added to the work force. Moreover, it is not true that physical capital is always a fixed factor and labor always variable, as is usually assumed in models based on manufacturing. In many service firms the reverse assumption is closer to reality.

Another set of concepts requiring re-examination are those concerned with productivity and demand. The flow of production in many service industries is uneven, with sharp peaks at particular hours or on particular days separated by periods of slow activity. Also, the size of the production run (i.e., the individual transaction) is often very small. For these reasons the analysis of the relation between output and productivity in services will probably have to pay more attention to changes in the timing of demand and to changes in transaction size.

A final implication is the likelihood that current estimates of real gross national product are becoming less useful for studies of productivity and economic growth because, at high levels of GNP per capita, a large fraction of productive effort is devoted to services (where real output is often very difficult to measure) and to other activities, such as those of the "do it yourself" type, that are not measured at all. In the future, we shall probably find it necessary to develop auxiliary measures of "output" and economic welfare to be used in conjunction with the estimates of real gross national product.

Suggestions for Further Research

The preceding section suggested some of the conceptual problems posed by the growth of a service economy. These represent only a portion of the tasks that lie ahead for economic research. Numerous analytical questions require investigation. For instance, what is the relation between growth and productivity across industries? If there is a positive correlation, does the causality run primarily from productivity to growth or from growth to productivity? If the latter, what are the relative contributions of economies of scale, induced innovation, or still other factors to this relationship? Why has labor quality grown more rapidly in Industry than in the Service sector? Have unions been a major cause of this shift? Is it the result of sector differences in elasticities of substitution between capital and labor or between skilled and unskilled labor? Or has technological change proceeded differently in the two sectors? What are the current income elasticities of demand for various goods and services? Are they changing? What is the elasticity of substitution between goods and services with respect to price?

One area of research with much promise concerns greater attention to the diversity that exists within the Service sector. This study is primarily concerned with intersector differences, but throughout the book, and especially in Chapters 4, 5, and 6, significant intrasector differences are noted. These variations among Services with respect to skill levels, wages, productivity trends, capital intensities, and other factors should be explored.

Perhaps the most urgent need of all is for more and better-quality data concerning the service industries. Although the United States is now a service economy, the statistical reporting system largely reflects the interests and conditions of an economy dominated by agriculture and industry. We need more analysis, but we also need the factual basis that will make the analysis more fruitful. One unmistakable finding of this study is that there are significant gaps in our statistical information concerning service output, employment, prices, wages, investment, and profits. These gaps must be filled if we are fully to understand this sector or, indeed, if we are to understand the economy of which it is the major part.

2

THE GROWING IMPORTANCE
OF SERVICE EMPLOYMENT

In 1947 U.S. employment stood at 58 million. The comparable figure
for 1965 was 71 million, an increase of 13 million over eighteen years.
Nearly all of this net growth occurred in the Service sector; modest increases in manufacturing and construction have been almost completely
offset by declines in agriculture and mining. Between 1929 and 1965
Service sector employment grew by 20 million. The Industry sector increased by only 10 million and Agricultural employment declined by
5 million. This chapter is primarily concerned with delineating the
growth of service employment from several different points of view.
Trends in recent decades are examined in detail, but longer-term trends
are also considered. The growth of the Service sector's share of employment in individual states and in foreign countries is discussed. Greatest
attention is given to the distribution of employment by industry and
sector, but some occupational data are presented as well. The chapter
begins with a discussion of the sector definitions. It concludes by examining some of the reasons for the shift to service employment.

Sector Definitions

More than a decade ago George J. Stigler wrote, "There exists no author-
itative consensus on either the boundaries or the classification of the
service industries." [1] A careful review of subsequent studies provides no
basis for challenging this conclusion. Some studies include transportation,
communications, and public utilities in the Service sector; others exclude
these industries.[2] David Worton, in his study of the service industries in

[1] George J. Stigler, *Trends in Employment in the Service Industries,* Princeton
University Press for National Bureau of Economic Research, 1956, p. 47.
[2] These industries were included in the Service sector by Gur Ofer in *The
Service Industries in a Developing Economy,* New York, 1967. They were excluded
by Maurice Lengellé in *The Growing Importance of the Service Sector in Member*

Canada, includes transportation and communications, but excludes public utilities. This definition is also used by Deakin and George in their study of the U.K., and by J. A. Dowie in his study of services in Australia.[3]

Even within the work of a single author, variations in definition are evident. Simon Kuznets included transportation, communications, and public utilities in the Service sector in much of his early work, but excluded them in his most recent study.[4] Gur Ofer also worked with the narrower definition in his recent study of Soviet services.[5]

The differences to be found among empirical studies reflects the absence of any clear theoretical basis for grouping industries. The two criteria most frequently mentioned are closeness to the consumer and the presence or absence of a tangible product. The notion of primary, secondary, and tertiary industries, for instance, as developed by Allan Fisher and Colin Clark,[6] is related to the degree to which the particular activity is distant from, or close to, the ultimate consumer. There are, however, several industries that service business firms—wholesale trade, commercial banking, advertising—but are nevertheless usually classified in the service or tertiary sector.

A strict application of the intangibility criterion also presents problems. A dentist who makes a false tooth and places it in the patient's mouth is certainly delivering a tangible product, but dentistry is invariably classified as a service. It is difficult to make a sharp distinction between the activities of an auto assembly plant and those of an automobile repair shop, but the former is invariably classified in Industry and the latter is usually regarded as a service. Alfred Marshall sharply pointed up this

Countries, Organization for Economic Co-operation and Development, Paris, 1966. Stigler, himself (*op. cit.,* p. 47), excluded these industries partly on the grounds that "they have been treated in earlier National Bureau studies." But he adds that "the characteristics of transportation and public utilities are sufficiently peculiar so that in any event they deserve separate analysis." (*Ibid.,* p. 47, fn. 1.)

[3] See David A. Worton, "The Service Industries in Canada, 1946–66," in *Production and Productivity in the Service Industries,* V. R. Fuchs, ed., New York, NBER, in press; B. M. Deakin and K. D. George, *Productivity Trends in the Service Industries, 1948–63,* Cambridge, England, 1965; and J. A. Dowie, "Productivity Growth in Goods and Services: Australia, U.S.A., U.K.," *The Economic Record,* December 1966.

[4] Compare, for instance, Simon Kuznets, "Quantitative Aspect of the Economic Growth of Nations; III, Industrial Distribution of Income and Labor Force by States, United States 1919–21 to 1955," *Economic Development and Cultural Change,* July 1958, with his *Modern Economic Growth,* New Haven and London, 1966.

[5] "The Service Sector in the Soviet Union." Unpublished Ph.D. dissertation, Harvard University, 1967.

[6] Allan G. B. Fisher, *The Clash of Progress and Security,* London, 1935, and Colin Clark, *The Conditions of Economic Progress,* London, 1940.

dilemma by noting that in one sense all industries provide services. "Man cannot create material things." [7]

A third basis for classification is revealed in the term "residual" sector, which is sometimes applied to a miscellaneous collection of industries that clearly are not in agriculture, mining, or manufacturing. Just why these industries should have become a residual is in itself an interesting question. The greater attention that has been given by economists to the primary and secondary industries might be explained by many factors: (1) Tertiary employment becomes of major importance only when high levels of income per capita are reached. (2) Some early economists, notably Adam Smith, believed that only the primary and secondary sectors were "productive" and that the other industries were in some sense "parasitic." (3) It is usually much more difficult to obtain data for the service industries, many of which are characterized by small-scale operations. This is also true of agriculture but, in that case, at least the output tends to be standardized and thus more easily measured. (4) Much tertiary production is nonprofit; economic analysis has concentrated on market activities.

In this book the Service sector has been defined to include wholesale and retail trade, finance, insurance, and real estate, general government (including the military in most instances), and the services traditionally so designated, including professional, personal, business, and repair services. The reasons for this definition are very similar to those mentioned by Stigler (see footnote 2). This is, in part, a residual sector; it is a collection of industries that have not received much attention in the past from economists concerned with productivity analysis. There is much heterogeneity to be found in this sector, and part of the book is devoted to an exploration of this heterogeneity. It can be said, however, that most of the industries in it are manned by white-collar workers, that most of the industries are labor intensive, that most deal with the consumer, and that nearly all of them produce an intangible product.

The most questionable decision was to place transportation, communications, and public utilities in the Industry sector because of their dependence upon heavy capital equipment and complex technology. Fortunately, investigation of the impact of this decision revealed that the major con-

[7] Alfred Marshall, *Principles of Economics,* 8th Ed., London, 1929, p. 63. For an interesting discussion of some of the conceptual problems and of the special difficulties involved in translating definitions from English to French, see Maurice Lengellé, "Growth of the Commerce and Service Sector in Western Europe," in *Manpower Problems in the Service Sector,* OECD, Manpower and Social Affairs Directorate, Social Affairs Division, Paris, 1966.

clusions would not be altered significantly if these industries had been classified in the Service sector.

In our preliminary reports, trends in the Service sector were contrasted with those in the so-called "goods" sector. In this book, the "goods" sector is usually divided into Agriculture and Industry. Comparisons between the Service and Industry sectors are of primary interest. They permit an analysis of the shift to services which is relatively independent of the change from agricultural to nonagricultural pursuits.

In addition to dividing the total economy into Agriculture, Industry, and Service, I usually include measures for a group of services designated "Service subsector." This subsector excludes government, households and institutions, and real estate. It corresponds roughly to the private enterprise portion of the Service sector.[8] The measures of real output for the Service subsector are generally regarded as more reliable than those for the excluded industries, and therefore more reliable than those for the total Service sector.

I do not believe that the major conclusions of this study would be significantly affected by any reasonable changes in sector definitions. It may be readily admitted, however, that the sector boundaries are very difficult to draw with precision, and that no division based on allocating major industry groups is likely to be completely satisfactory. It is possible that the best definition for one set of problems is not the best for another set. In recognition of this, and of the heterogeneous character of the sectors, the study presents industry detail where possible.

Sector Trends in U.S. Employment

Tables 1 and 2, and Charts 1 and 2 show the absolute and relative trends in the industrial distribution of employment in the United States since 1929.[9] The years selected for the tables were all marked by relatively high levels of business activity, although cyclical elements in the year-to-year changes are not completely absent. This is particularly true for 1937 when unemployment stood at 14.3 per cent. In all the other years unem-

[8] Real estate does contain some private enterprise, but the large owner-occupied component is more properly classified with households.

[9] Unless otherwise stated, the employment concept used is the Office of Business Economics measure "persons engaged." This consists of full-time wage and salary workers, plus workers converted to full-time equivalents, plus proprietors. The importance of part-time employment has been growing rapidly in the Service sector; therefore, the figures presented in this chapter understate the growth of service employment relative to those that would be obtained from a simple head count of persons employed full or part-time.

TABLE 1

Persons Engaged, by Sector and Major Industry Group,
Selected Years, 1929–65
(thousands)

	1929	1937	1947	1956	1965
Agriculture	9,205	8,864	7,006	5,425	4,039
Industry	18,356	17,125	24,294	27,464	28,194
Service	18,655	21,167	26,400	32,515	39,011
Service subsector [a]	12,263	12,596	16,718	18,836	22,141
Industry					
Mining	1,017	993	973	884	670
Construction	2,306	1,738	3,007	3,700	3,971
Manufacturing	10,556	10,686	15,406	17,702	18,443
Transportation	3,034	2,333	3,045	2,803	2,486
Communications and public					
utilities	1,034	901	1,190	1,492	1,513
Government enterprise	409	474	673	883	1,111
Service					
Wholesale trade	1,744	1,857	2,625	2,953	3,362
Retail trade [b]	5,955	6,095	8,020	8,955	9,767
Finance and insurance	1,207	1,065	1,290	1,825	2,318
Real estate	368	455	576	733	766
Households and institutions	3,249	3,060	3,017	3,995	5,076
Professional, personal, busi-					
ness and repair services	3,357	3,579	4,783	5,103	6,694
General government (includ-					
ing armed forces)	2,775	5,056	6,089	8,951	11,028

Source: U.S. Office of Business Economics: *The National Income and Product Accounts of the United States, 1929–1965 Statistical Tables,* Table 6.6.

[a] Excludes real estate, households and institutions, and general government.

[b] Automobile services and repair are included in repair services, and are excluded from retail trade. Automobile services and repair estimated for years prior to 1948.

ployment was below 5 per cent. The war years are omitted from the tables and charts because the changes in employment patterns caused by the war are largely irrelevant for the study of long-term trends.

In 1929 the Service sector's share of total employment was slightly over 40 per cent. By 1965 this had increased to almost 55 per cent.[10]

[10] Preliminary data for 1967 indicate that the Service sector continued to increase its share of total employment and nonagricultural employment between 1965 and 1967.

TABLE 2

Shares of Total Persons Employed, by Sector and Major Industry Group,
Selected Years, 1929–65
(per cent)

	1929	1937	1947	1956	1965
Agriculture	19.9	18.8	12.1	8.3	5.7
Industry	39.7	36.3	42.1	42.0	39.6
Service	40.4	44.9	45.8	49.7	54.8
Service subsector	26.5	26.7	29.0	28.8	31.1
Industry					
Mining	2.2	2.1	1.7	1.4	0.9
Construction	5.0	3.7	5.2	5.7	5.6
Manufacturing	22.8	22.7	26.7	27.1	25.9
Transportation	6.6	4.9	5.3	4.3	3.5
Communications and public utilities	2.2	1.9	2.1	2.3	2.1
Government enterprise	0.9	1.0	1.2	1.4	1.6
Service					
Wholesale trade	3.8	3.9	4.5	4.5	4.7
Retail trade	12.9	12.9	13.9	13.7	13.7
Finance and insurance	2.6	2.3	2.2	2.8	3.3
Real estate	0.8	1.0	1.0	1.1	1.1
Households and institutions	7.0	6.5	5.2	6.1	7.1
Professional, personal, business and repair services	7.3	7.6	8.3	7.8	9.4
General government (including armed forces)	6.0	10.7	10.6	13.7	15.5

Source: See Table 1.

Sometime during the past decade the United States thus became the first country in history to have more than half its employment in this sector. The tables and charts clearly delineate the broad trends underlying this dramatic shift: (1) the steady decline of agriculture throughout the period; (2) the rapid growth of employment in government; and (3) the relative stability of employment in manufacturing, especially since the mid-1950's.

Some other developments that worked in the same direction were the absolute declines in employment in mining and transportation and the sharp growth in importance of private nonprofit service institutions such as hospitals and universities. In 1929 the Industry and Service sectors

CHART 1

Persons Engaged, by Sector, 1929–40, 1946–65

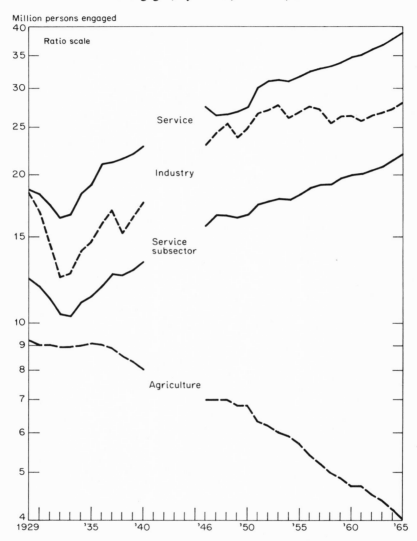

Note: See Table 1 for sector definitions.
Source: U.S. Department of Commerce, Office of Business Economics.

CHART 2

Sector Employment as a Percentage of Total Employment, 1929–40, 1946–65

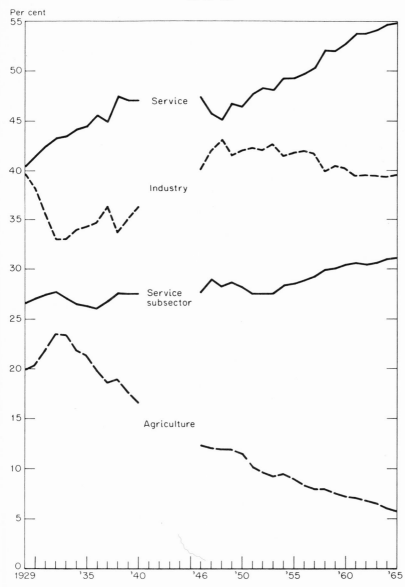

Source: See Chart 1.

were approximately the same size. By 1965, the Service sector was 40 per cent larger than Industry.

Detailed Industries

Table 3 shows that the more rapid growth of service employment is also evident at the detailed industry level.[11] We see that a large percentage of the service industries had rapid rates of growth and only a very few had negative or slow rates. For the Industry sector the reverse is true. More than one-fourth of the industries in this sector showed an absolute decline in employment between 1929 and 1965, while fewer than one-sixth of them had rates of growth in excess of 3.0 per cent per annum.[12] Only two of the service industries showed declines in employment, and almost one-third of them grew at rates exceeding 3.0 per cent. The median rates of growth were 1.96 and 1.41 per cent per annum for the Service and Industry sectors, respectively.

Long-Term Trends

The shift of employment to services does not represent a sudden departure from previous long-term trends. For as long as we have records on the industrial distribution of the labor force, we find a secular tendency for the percentage accounted for by the Service sector to rise. Table 4 shows two sets of estimates of sector shares for census years from 1870 to 1930. Variant 1 estimates shares of "gainful workers"; variant 2 refers to employment.[13] Services grew more rapidly than the rest of the economy throughout the period; the average *differential* in rates of growth was approximately 1.4 per cent per annum. Since 1929 the differential between the Service sector and the rest of the economy has been slightly larger—1.6 per cent per annum.

Until 1920 the shift to services could be explained entirely by the movement from agricultural to nonagricultural pursuits; employment in Industry rose as rapidly as in Service. After 1920, however, the non-agricultural sectors' rates of growth diverged; Industry's share of total employment tended to decline, and the Service sector's share rose sharply.

[11] The most detailed source of employment data providing comparability between 1929 and 1965 is the U.S. Office of Business Economics. The level of detail here is between the SIC two-digit and three-digit classes.

[12] Of the eleven industries in the Industry sector with rates of growth above 2.0 per cent per annum, five are in the transportation, communications, public utilities and government enterprise group. As noted above, these industries have been classified in the Service sector by some investigators.

[13] The concept "gainful workers" includes all employed persons, paid or unpaid, and those unemployed who are not new entrants to the labor force.

TABLE 3

Frequency Distribution of Detailed Industries, by Rates of Growth of Employment, 1929–65

Average Annual Rates of Change	Number of Industries		Per Cent of Industries		Per Cent of 1929 Employment		Per Cent of 1965 Employment	
	Industry	Service	Industry	Service	Industry	Service	Industry	Service
3.0 and over	5	7	14.3	31.8	4.4	12.7	13.0	29.6
2.0 to 2.99	6	4	17.1	18.2	12.8	16.9	19.8	21.6
1.0 to 1.99	10	6	28.6	27.3	45.0	47.7	49.4	38.6
0 to .99	5	3	14.3	13.6	10.0	9.1	7.7	6.0
Negative	9	2	25.7	9.1	27.8	13.6	10.0	4.1

Note: Commercial and trade schools and employment agencies; instruments; miscellaneous manufacturing; and miscellaneous repair services and hand trades are excluded because of incompara- bility over time. Definitions of other industries were not always strictly comparable throughout the period.

Source: Appendix, Table C–6.

The Service Economy

TABLE 4

Distribution of Employment, by Sector, 1870–1930
(per cent)

	1870	1880	1890	1900	1910	1920	1930
Variant 1, gainful workers							
Agriculture	50.8	50.6	43.1	38.1	32.1	27.6	22.7
Industry	30.0	30.1	34.8	37.8	40.9	44.8	42.1
Service	19.2	19.3	22.1	24.1	27.0	27.6	35.2
Variant 2, employment [a]							
Agriculture	47.3	47.1	39.7	34.7	28.4	23.8	21.9
Industry	27.1	27.1	31.2	33.7	37.8	41.4	35.8
Service	25.6	25.8	29.2	31.7	33.8	34.8	42.3

Source: Variant 1: Solomon Fabricant, "The Changing Industrial Distribution of
Gainful Workers: Comments on the Decennial Statistics, 1820–1940" in *Studies in Income and Wealth,* Vol. II, National Bureau of Economic Research, New York, 1949, p.
42. Variant 2: 1900–30: Stanley Lebergott, *Manpower in Economic Growth,* New
York, 1964. A Sector: Table A–6 includes unpaid family workers. I and S Sectors:
Table A–5-Employees, Table A–4-Domestic service, and Table A–7-Self-employed
The "other" category of Table A–7 was distributed among Mining, Finance and Transportation, and Communications using the 1929 percentage distribution of these three
categories from Table A–9. Lebergott's levels for 1900 were used to extrapolate to 1870
by assuming that the percentage change in employment was the same as the actual percentage change in gainful workers (variant 1).
    [a] Values for 1870–1900 are estimated by extrapolating changes from variant 1.

Sector Trends by State and in Foreign Countries

The pervasiveness of the growth of service industry employment is also
evident if we look at changes in sector shares of labor force by state (see
Table 5). Between 1930 and 1960, there was an increase in the relative
importance of the Service sector in every state in the country. In 1930,
the median percentage for the Service sector was 32.8; by 1960 it was
49.8. Between 1950 and 1960 there was an increase in the Service
sector's share in every state except Alabama and California; the decline
in each of these states was less than one percentage point.

Even when the comparison is limited to the nonagricultural labor force
we find only seven states in which the Service sector's share failed to
increase between 1950 and 1960, and only one state (Alabama) for the
entire 1930–60 period.

The growth of services has not been exclusively a United States phe-
nomenon although it has proceeded further in this country than anywhere

else. Inspection of trends in Western European countries for which comparable data can be obtained reveals that the Service sector's share of total civilian employment increased in all countries in the post-World War II period (see Table 6).[14] What is perhaps even more significant, the Service sector's share of nonagricultural employment increased in every country except Switzerland. In none of these countries, however, did the relative gain of the Service sector in total employment come close to matching the shift that took place in the United States between 1920 and 1930.

It is of some interest to ask whether the trends that have been observed in the United States during the past century can also be observed in cross section among countries at different stages of economic development. Table 7 shows sector shares of employment for twenty OECD countries ranked, in descending order of per capita national income in 1960. The U.S. figures for Census years 1870–1960 are inserted at corresponding levels of real per capita income.[15]

We see that the percentage in Agriculture declines as real per capita income rises, and the percentage in Industry and Service tends to rise, but the pattern for the United States is somewhat different from that evidenced thus far by the twenty OECD countries. This divergence is easily seen in Chart 3 where curves have been fitted through the observations for the twenty OECD countries, and the observations for the U.S. Census years have also been plotted. For each sector a curve of the form $X = a + b\frac{1}{Y}$, (where X equals the sector share of employment and Y equals per capita income in 1960 dollars) has been fitted by least squares. These curves are mutually consistent in the sense that at any given level of income the sum of the three sector shares is equal to 100.[16] Each of the curves approaches an asymptote at high levels of income. The asymptote values are the constant terms (a) in each

---

[14] Simon Kuznets's broad study of economic growth reveals a few instances of declines in the Service sector's share of the labor force—in Belgium from 1880 to 1910 and in Sweden from 1870 to 1910—but the general trend is clearly upward in countries experiencing economic growth. See Simon Kuznets, *Modern Economic Growth,* New Haven and London, 1966, pp. 106, 107.

[15] Because official exchange rates were used, a downward bias may have been introduced into the income levels for the foreign countries. See Milton Gilbert and Associates, *Comparative National Products and Price Levels,* OEEC, Paris, 1958.

[16] Linear regressions of X or Y would also give shares that sum to 100, but would imply negative values for agriculture at high levels of income, and values of over 100 for the other sectors. Also, the function chosen was found to give better fits (higher R^2) than the linear function.

TABLE 5

Sector Shares of Labor Force, by State, 1930, 1950, 1960

State	Total Share of Total Labor Force									Service Share of Nonagricultural Labor Force		
	Agriculture			Industry [a]			Service [a]					
	1930	1950	1960	1930	1950	1960	1930	1950	1960	1930	1950	1960
Maine	21.0	10.6	6.0	46.1	48.9	46.0	32.9	40.5	48.0	41.6	45.3	51.1
New Hampshire	13.0	6.2	3.1	56.4	53.6	51.8	30.6	40.2	45.1	35.2	42.9	46.5
Vermont	28.3	17.9	11.8	40.8	39.4	39.1	30.9	42.7	49.1	43.1	52.0	55.7
Massachusetts	3.6	1.8	1.4	55.9	50.5	48.2	40.5	47.7	50.4	42.1	48.6	51.1
Rhode Island	3.4	1.4	1.3	62.7	54.0	49.0	33.9	44.6	49.7	35.1	45.2	50.4
Connecticut	5.7	2.7	1.9	58.2	54.5	52.8	36.1	42.8	45.3	38.3	44.0	46.2
New York	5.2	2.8	1.9	48.7	45.3	44.1	46.1	51.9	54.0	48.6	53.4	55.0
New Jersey	4.1	2.3	1.5	55.6	52.5	51.1	40.3	45.2	47.4	42.0	46.3	48.1
Pennsylvania	7.1	3.9	2.7	59.5	55.2	52.7	33.4	40.9	44.6	36.0	42.6	45.8
Ohio	12.3	6.7	3.8	53.1	51.4	51.5	34.6	41.9	44.7	39.5	44.9	46.5
Indiana	20.7	11.4	6.6	47.8	49.1	49.4	31.5	39.5	44.0	39.7	44.6	47.1
Illinois	11.6	6.8	4.6	49.1	47.9	47.8	39.3	45.3	47.6	44.4	48.6	49.9
Michigan	13.9	6.5	3.5	53.6	53.7	51.1	32.5	39.8	45.4	37.7	42.6	47.0
Wisconsin	27.0	18.5	11.5	42.5	42.8	45.4	30.5	38.7	43.1	41.8	47.5	48.7

Minnesota	32.0	22.4	14.5	31.8	32.5	35.7	36.2	45.1	49.8	53.2	58.1	58.2
Iowa	37.5	28.4	20.7	29.0	28.7	32.0	33.5	42.9	47.3	53.6	60.0	59.6
Missouri	26.5	17.5	9.7	37.7	37.7	40.4	35.8	44.8	49.9	48.7	54.3	55.3
North Dakota	57.2	44.2	32.0	15.4	16.4	17.9	27.4	39.4	50.1	64.0	70.6	73.7
South Dakota	54.1	40.1	30.1	17.4	18.1	20.4	28.5	41.8	49.5	62.1	69.8	70.8
Nebraska	40.1	29.5	20.9	25.1	25.5	27.6	34.8	45.0	51.5	58.1	63.8	65.1
Kansas	34.2	22.4	12.9	31.7	31.6	33.5	34.1	46.0	53.6	51.8	59.3	62.0
Delaware	18.6	8.6	5.2	48.6	49.4	47.0	32.8	42.0	47.8	40.3	46.0	50.4
Maryland	13.9	6.1	3.5	46.3	41.4	39.5	39.8	52.5	57.0	46.2	55.9	59.1
Virginia	32.8	13.6	7.3	35.6	35.6	35.8	31.6	50.8	56.9	47.0	58.8	61.4
West Virginia	22.2	9.6	4.5	52.8	54.9	51.6	25.0	35.5	43.9	32.1	39.3	46.0
North Carolina	45.3	24.0	12.7	30.6	38.4	42.5	24.1	37.6	44.8	44.1	49.5	51.3
South Carolina	51.2	25.5	11.5	26.0	37.6	41.3	22.8	36.9	47.2	46.7	49.5	53.3
Georgia	43.9	21.1	9.0	27.1	35.0	38.9	29.0	43.9	52.1	51.7	55.6	57.3
Florida	25.3	12.1	6.9	32.0	27.6	30.6	42.7	60.3	62.5	57.2	68.6	67.1
Kentucky	40.6	25.1	13.8	33.4	36.6	39.7	26.0	38.3	46.5	44.1	51.1	53.9
Tennessee	40.6	21.3	10.8	30.6	36.6	41.2	28.8	42.1	48.0	48.5	53.5	53.8
Alabama	49.2	23.9	9.7	27.4	36.3	51.2	23.4	39.8	39.1	46.1	52.3	43.3
Mississippi	67.6	40.8	21.2	14.1	22.9	32.1	18.3	36.3	46.7	56.5	61.3	59.3
Arkansas	59.6	34.9	17.9	18.9	27.2	34.7	21.5	37.9	47.4	53.2	58.2	57.7
Louisiana	38.9	17.4	8.0	29.3	34.8	37.2	31.8	47.8	54.8	52.0	57.9	59.6
Oklahoma	38.5	20.1	9.4	29.3	30.3	32.9	32.2	49.6	57.7	52.4	62.1	63.7
Texas	39.5	15.3	8.8	27.3	33.1	34.3	33.2	51.6	56.9	54.9	60.9	62.4

(continued)

TABLE 5 (concluded)

State	Total Share of Total Labor Force									Service Share of Nonagricultural Labor Force		
	Agriculture			Industry [a]			Service [a]					
	1930	1950	1960	1930	1950	1960	1930	1950	1960	1930	1950	1960
Montana	39.1	24.7	17.2	32.3	30.9	29.5	28.6	44.4	53.3	47.0	59.0	64.4
Idaho	45.5	26.6	18.7	26.6	29.8	31.0	27.9	43.6	50.3	51.2	59.4	61.9
Wyoming	35.2	19.2	13.4	34.7	34.3	35.3	30.1	46.5	51.3	46.5	57.5	59.2
Colorado	27.6	14.6	7.6	33.7	31.5	33.0	38.7	53.9	59.4	53.5	63.1	64.6
New Mexico	43.9	17.8	7.1	29.0	30.0	30.5	27.1	52.2	62.4	48.3	63.5	67.2
Arizona	24.7	14.5	8.3	38.7	30.5	32.8	36.6	55.0	58.9	48.6	64.3	64.2
Utah	25.4	12.2	6.1	39.1	35.1	36.2	35.5	52.7	57.7	47.6	60.0	61.4
Nevada	21.6	9.4	4.5	45.4	30.1	25.2	33.0	60.5	70.3	42.1	66.8	73.6
Washington	21.9	9.3	6.6	39.6	38.0	38.9	38.5	52.7	54.5	49.3	58.1	58.4
Oregon	26.0	12.2	8.1	36.9	40.2	39.3	37.1	47.6	52.6	50.1	54.2	57.2
California	14.4	7.0	4.7	38.0	35.6	38.1	47.6	57.4	57.2	55.6	61.7	60.0

Source: 1930 and 1950 figures, Simon Kuznets, "Quantitative Aspects of the Economic Growth of Nations, III, Industrial Distribution of Income and Labor Force by States, United States, 1919–1921 to 1955," *Economic Development and Cultural Change,* Vol. VI, No. 4, Part II, July 1958, Appendix Table 14. 1960 figures from U.S. Bureau of the Census, *Census of Population:* *1960,* Vol. I, Parts 2–50, Table 126 (Experienced Labor Force).

Note: For New York and California the 1950 figures for Industry and Service have been adjusted for changes in the grouping of Radio broadcasting, and T.V. in the 1960 Census publications.

[a] Government enterprise is included in Service rather than Industry.

TABLE 6

Change in Service Sector's Share of Civilian Employment,
Seven Western European Countries, 1950–62
(percentage points)

	Total Civilian Employment	Nonagricultural Civilian Employment
Belgium	+5.1	+3.7
Germany (F.R.)	+5.3	+1.8
Netherlands	+3.7	+1.9
Norway	+4.9	+2.0
Switzerland [a]	+0.4	−1.9
U.K.	+2.4	+1.8
France [b]	+3.4	+1.0

Source: Maurice Lengellé, *The Growing Importance of The Service Sector in Member Countries*. Organization for Economic Cooperation and Development, Paris, 1966, p. 43.
[a] 1950 to 1960.   [b] 1955 to 1962.

regression. They are shown on the chart by straight dashed lines, and are equal to 3 per cent, 57 per cent, and 40 per cent for Agriculture, Industry, and Service, respectively.[17]

Inspection of the chart reveals that the Agriculture sector in the United States has followed a pattern over time very similar to that revealed by the twenty OECD countries in cross section. Agriculture's share was somewhat larger in the United States especially in the nineteenth and early twentieth centuries when U.S. agricultural exports were important. The share of the Industry sector in the United States

[17] The adjusted coefficients of multiple determination ($\bar{R}^2$) are: Agriculture = .86, Industry = .73, and Service = .65. The regression coefficients, which are all highly significant, can be used to solve for the percentage point change in sector shares associated with a change of $100 in real per capita income. Because the relationship is curvilinear, the percentage change is different at different levels of per capita income. The following changes per increase of $100 were calculated at the first, second, and third quartiles of income for the twenty OECD countries.

	Income Per Capita		
	$344	*$839*	*$1,048*
Agriculture	−10.5%	−1.8%	−1.1%
Industry	6.3	1.1	0.7
Service	4.3	0.7	0.5

The Service Economy

TABLE 7

Sector Distribution of Employment: Twenty OECD Countries,
1960, and United States, 1870–1960

Per Capita National Income (1960 U.S. dollars)	Country (in descending order of income)	Sector Distribution of Employment (per cent)		
		Agriculture	Industry	Service
2,132	U.S. 1960	8	38	54
1,836	U.S. 1950	12	39	48
1,536	Canada	13	43	45
1,644	Sweden	14	53	33
1,364	U.S. 1940	19	35	46
1,361	Switzerland	11	56	33
1,242	Luxembourg	15	51	34
1,170	U.S. 1930	22	36	42
1,105	United Kingdom	4	56	40
1,050	U.S. 1920	24	41	35
1,048	Denmark	18	45	37
1,035	W. Germany	15	60	25
1,013	France	20	44	36
1,005	Belgium	6	52	42
977	Norway	20	49	32
927	U.S. 1910	28	38	34
839	Iceland	25	47	29
810	Netherlands	11	49	40
757	U.S. 1900	35	34	32
681	Austria	23	47	30
592	U.S. 1890	40	31	29
529	Ireland	36	30	34
504	Italy	27	46	28
499	U.S. 1880	47	27	26
344	Japan	33	35	32
340	U.S. 1870	47	27	26
324	Greece	56	24	20
290	Spain	42	37	21
238	Portugal	44	33	23
177	Turkey	79	12	9

has been below that observed in the OECD cross section and apparently reached a peak at a much lower level. This too can be explained, at least in part, by the role of exports; exports of manufactured goods in many OECD countries are relatively more important than in the United States. It should be noted that the observations for the United States in 1930 and 1940 tend to be relatively low in the Industry sector because the widespread unemployment of those years was highly concentrated in that sector.

The Service sector's share in the U.S. economy shows substantial divergence from the plotted curve in the four most recent decades. The most recent two, of course, involve levels of real per capita income not yet reached by any of the twenty OECD countries. In this panel of Chart 3 the U.S. observations for 1930 and 1940 tend to be raised because of the uneven incidence of unemployment. If they were adjusted to take account of this factor, we would see a pattern that followed the OECD curve for the first six or seven decades and then rose considerably above it in the most recent decades. There is no evident leveling off of the Service sector's share in the U.S. data, and Industry's share apparently reached a peak at a per capita income level of about $1,200 to $1,400 (in 1960 dollars).

Occupational Trends

The preceding discussion has been concerned with employment distribution by *industry*. Nearly all of the data come to us in that form and

Notes to Table 7

Note: The following countries include armed forces in the Service sector: Switzerland, Luxembourg (except males performing compulsory service), West Germany, France (plus alien armed forces not living in military camps and diplomatic personnel not living in embassies or consulates), Belgium, Norway, Netherlands, Ireland, Italy, Greece (excludes males performing compulsory service but includes alien forces stationed in area), Portugal, and Turkey. The following exclude all or some unemployed: Sweden, Switzerland, Luxembourg, United Kingdom, France, Iceland, Ireland and Japan.

Source: *Per capita income:* for United States, U.S. Bureau of the Census, *Historical Statistics of the United States*, Series F-4, 4a, 5, 5a; for OECD countries, United Nations, *Monthly Bulletin of Statistics*, November 1961 (for Greece, Ireland, and Luxembourg) and November 1965 (for all others). The data for the OECD countries were computed from Table 61 (national income), Table 64 (exchange rate), and Table 1 (population).

Industrial distribution of labor force: for United States, see Table 4, Variant 2; for OECD countries—Austria, Belgium and Italy—International Labor Office, *Yearbook of Labor Statistics*, 1964, Table 4A; Iceland and United Kingdom—OECD, *Manpower Statistics 1950–1962*, Table III; all others—United Nations, *Demographic Yearbook*, 1964, Table 9 (members of armed forces (Table 10) subtracted wherever possible).

CHART 3

Relation Between Sector Shares of Employment and Real Per Capita Income:
Twenty OECD Countries, 1960, and the United States, 1870–1960

● U. S., census years 1870–1960
○ 20 OECD countries, 1960

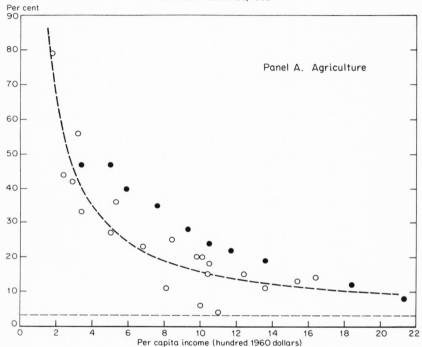

many of the most important policy questions, both private and public, are formulated in terms of industries. It is, however, of some interest to determine whether a classification of employment by *occupation* instead of industry would confirm the existence of a trend toward services.

In Table 8, the eleven major occupational groups have been classified as "service-type" or "goods-type" according to general information about them, including their distribution by sector in 1960. The "service-type" category is defined to include white collar and service occupations. These are typically found in the Service sector. The "goods-type" category is defined to include blue collar occupations, except service; these occupations are typically found in Agriculture and Industry.

We see that the service-type group has grown rapidly (2.1 per cent

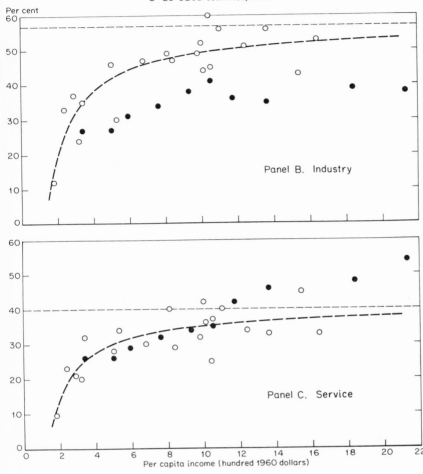

● U. S., census years 1870–1960
○ 20 OECD countries, 1960

Panel B. Industry

Panel C. Service

Per capita income (hundred 1960 dollars)

Note: The regression curves are fitted through the twenty OECD countries only.
Source: Table 7.

per annum between 1930 and 1960) while the "goods-type" occupations showed no net change over the period. Moderate gains in some goods-producing occupations were offset by absolute declines in others.

Table 9 supplies a more detailed look at occupational change within each of the major industry groups in the Agriculture and Industry sectors. It shows that between 1950 and 1960 there was an increase in the relative importance of the service-type occupations in each of the five groups.

TABLE 8

Occupational Distribution of Labor Force, 1930 and 1960

	Per Cent of Occupation Employed in Service Sector, 1960	Labor Force (millions)		Average Annual Rate of Change 1930–60 (per cent)
		1930	1960	
Service-type occupations				
Professional, technical, and kindred workers	74.5	3.3	7.3	2.7
Managers, officials, and proprietors excl. farm	69.0	3.6	5.9	1.4
Clerical and kindred workers	63.2	4.3	9.6	2.7
Sales workers	84.3	3.1	4.8	1.5
Private household workers	100.0	2.0	1.8	−0.3
Service workers excluding private household	91.8	2.8	5.8	2.5
Total service-type	76.0	19.1	35.2	2.1
Goods-type occupations				
Craftsmen, foremen, and kindred workers	24.3	6.2	9.2	1.3
Operatives and kindred workers	19.9	7.7	12.8	1.7
Laborers excluding farm and mine	27.4	5.3	3.5	−1.4
Farmers and farm managers	0.0	6.0	2.5	−2.9
Farm laborers and foremen	0.0	4.3	1.6	−3.5
Total goods-type	19.2	29.5	29.6	0.0
Total, all occupations	50.4	48.6	64.8	1.0

Source: 1930, U.S. Bureau of the Census, *Occupational Trends in the United States, 1900 to 1950,* Working Paper No. 5, 1958, Table 1; 1960, U.S. Bureau of the Census, 1960 Census of Population; Vol. I, *Characteristics of the Population,* Part 1, "U.S. Summary," Table 201, and "Occupation by Industry," Table 1.

As a share of each industry's total, the shifts were particularly large in mining and manufacturing.

Thus, the occupational data suggest that the industry shift in employment, far from exaggerating the growth of service employment, may actually understate it, because even within industries there has been a shift from the direct production of goods to service activities.

Trends in Output

The demand for labor is derived from the demand for output. One possible explanation, therefore, for the rapid growth of service employment would be a relatively rapid rate of growth of demand for service output. This demand is of two types: intermediate and final. Intermediate demand would grow if there were a shift in the production of intermediate services from manufacturing and other goods-producing industries to separately identifiable service industries. Relative growth of final demand might be the result of a high income elasticity of demand for services, a decline in the relative price of services, or a change in taste.[18]

The available evidence rejects the hypothesis that the shift to service employment can be attributed in any significant degree to a shift in the composition of output. To be sure, many questions arise concerning the measurement of real output in the Service sector (and in portions of the Industry sector also).[19] Table 10, therefore, presents sector distributions of output based on two alternative measures. The first takes the Office of Business Economics series gross product in constant (1958) dollars as the measure of real output. This is probably the best available measure but it has been criticized on the grounds that the implicit price deflators exaggerate the rise in the price of services. This bias is attributed in part to the fact that for government and certain other service industries prices are *assumed* to rise as rapidly as wages and no possibility of an increase in productivity is admitted. If this criticism is valid, then measures of real output based on gross product in constant dollars would tend to understate the growth of service output relative to that of the rest of the economy.

The second measure of real output presented is based on gross product in current dollars. This assumes that the prices of services changed at the same rate as did the over-all price deflator.[20] This measure probably overstates the growth of real output in services relative to the rest of the economy, since it seems unlikely that the over-all price index did in fact rise by as much or more than the price of services.

[18] Some empirical evidence concerning shifts in intermediate and final demand will be discussed later in the chapter.

[19] See especially discussions in Chapters 3, 4, and 5.

[20] Because industry differences in rates of change of gross product in current dollars provide a good measure of relative changes in factor inputs, this second version implies that real output per unit of total factor input changed at approximately the same rate in both sectors. See Edward F. Denison, *The Sources of Economic Growth in the United States and the Alternatives Before Us,* Supplementary Paper No. 13, Committee for Economic Development, New York, 1962, pp. 218, 219.

TABLE 9

Occupational Distribution of Labor Force, by Major Industry Group, 1950 and 1960

(per cent)

	Agriculture		Mining		Construction		Manufacturing		Transp., Comm. and Pub. Util.[a]		Total: Agriculture and Industry[a]	
	1950	1960	1950	1960	1950	1960	1950	1960	1950	1960	1950	1960
Service-type occupations												
Professional, technical & kindred workers	0.6	1.3	3.5	7.5	3.7	4.7	4.9	7.7	3.2	4.7	3.5	5.9
Managers, officials, propr's. excl. farm	0.3	0.6	4.0	5.9	8.4	9.9	4.8	5.2	7.2	7.8	4.5	5.5
Clerical & kindred workers	0.3	0.7	4.5	7.5	3.2	4.5	11.0	12.2	29.1	30.6	10.3	12.5
Sales workers	0.1	0.2	0.2	0.4	0.3	0.4	3.0	3.8	0.4	0.8	1.5	2.3
Service workers, excl. private h.'hold	0.1	0.3	0.7	1.0	0.5	0.5	1.9	1.7	3.3	2.8	1.5	1.5
Total service-type	1.4	3.0	13.0	22.4	16.1	20.0	25.6	30.5	43.2	46.7	21.3	27.7
Goods-type occupations												
Craftsmen, foremen & kindred workers	0.3	0.7	17.2	22.6	57.1	54.1	19.6	19.9	19.4	19.4	19.2	21.4
Operatives & kindred workers	0.8	2.4	69.7	55.1	7.6	8.9	46.0	43.5	25.4	25.3	28.8	30.8
Farm laborers & foremen	34.5	33.2	–	–	–	–	–	–	–	–	7.9	4.7
Laborers, except farm & mine	2.0	2.9	0.1	–	19.2	17.0	8.8	6.0	11.9	8.6	8.6	7.2
Farmers & farm managers	61.1	57.8	–	–	–	–	–	–	–	–	14.0	8.2
Total goods-type	98.6	97.0	87.0	77.6	83.9	80.0	74.4	69.5	56.7	53.3	78.5	72.3
Total (excluding occup. not reported)	100.0	100.0	100.0	100.0	100.0	100.0	100.0	100.0	100.0	100.0	100.0	100.0
Number employed (thousands)												
Service-type occupations	98	132	121	145	544	757	3,678	5,255	2,069	2,309	6,510	8,598
Goods-type occupations	6,915	4,210	805	502	2,841	3,032	10,708	11,960	2,717	2,639	23,986	22,343
Annual rate of change, 1950–60 (per cent)												
Service-type occupations	+3.0		+1.8		+3.3		+3.6		+1.0		+2.8	
Goods-type occupations	–5.0		–4.7		+0.6		+1.1		–0.3		–0.8	

Note: Due to rounding, some columns do not total 100.0.
Source: U.S. Bureau of the Census "Occupation by Industry," 1950 and 1960, Table 1.

TABLE 10

Sector Shares of Gross National Product in Constant and
Current Dollars, Selected Years, 1929–65
(per cent)

	1929	1947	1956	1965
Constant (1958) dollars				
Agriculture	8.4	5.7	4.9	4.1
Industry	43.2	47.2	48.1	47.6
Service	48.4	47.0	47.0	48.3
Service subsector	29.6	27.4	26.3	27.1
Current dollars				
Agriculture	9.2	9.1	4.7	3.7
Industry	43.9	46.0	48.4	45.7
Service	46.9	45.0	46.9	50.5
Service subsector	26.6	27.8	26.4	27.3
Service as share of nonagricultural output				
Constant (1958) dollars	52.9	49.9	49.5	50.4
Current dollars	51.7	49.4	49.2	52.5

Source: Appendix Table C–3.

Because the probable bias runs in one direction for one measure and in the other direction for the other, the two measures of relative changes in output may be regarded as outer boundaries within which the true measure probably falls.

The most striking aspect of Table 10 is that, according to either measure, the Service sector's share of output has changed very little since 1929. The share in constant dollars was almost exactly the same in 1965 as in 1929, and the share in current dollars rose from 46.9 per cent to 50.5 per cent, with all the increase occurring after 1956. This stability is in sharp contrast to the share of employment shown in Table 2, which rose from 40 to 55 per cent over the same period. Agriculture's share has fallen to less than half of its 1929 levels and Industry has shown a moderate increase. If the Service sector is compared with Industry alone, its share fell slightly in constant dollars and rose slightly in current dollars.

In this book we are primarily concerned with comparing goods-producing and service-producing industries, but it is also possible to distinguish

TABLE 11

Sector Shares of Gross Product, by Type of Final Output in
Constant and Current Dollars, 1929 and 1965
(per cent)

	1929	1965
Constant (1954) dollars		
Services	33.2	35.3
Goods and construction	66.8	64.7
Durables	16.9	21.8
Nondurables	35.6	32.6
Construction	14.4	10.2
Current dollars		
Services	35.4	38.5
Goods and construction	64.6	61.5
Durables	17.3	20.3
Nondurables	36.5	30.3
Construction	10.7	10.9

Source: 1929, Office of Business Economics, *U.S. Income and Output,* 1958, Tables
1–6 and 1–7; 1965, *Survey of Current Business,* April 1967, Table 2, p. 6, and July 1962,
Table 65 (for implicit price deflators to convert from 1958 to 1954 dollars).

between goods and services on the basis of final expenditure. Table 11 shows the distribution of gross product by type of final output for 1929 and 1965. We see that the share of "services" increased only slightly during this period, whether measured in constant or current dollars. There are important differences between services defined as final output and the Service sector,[21] but the data in Table 11 confirm the conclusions based on the industrial distribution of gross product.

What might explain the Service sector's relatively stable share of final output? From casual observation one would expect the growth of urbanization and education, and the relative increase in the number and purchasing power of elderly people, to favor the demand for services. Also, many observers have argued that the income elasticity of demand for services is much higher than for goods.

I think the principal explanation is that, for the period studied, the income elasticity of demand for services has been only moderately above

[21] The classification by final output treats government as a consumer rather than a producer. Also, the value of wholesale and retail trade services and of many business service industries is assigned to goods rather than services.

that for the rest of the economy. Moreover, to the extent that the growth of income and urbanization would have produced a shift of output to services, the income effect has probably been offset by a substitution effect induced by a relative rise in the price of services. Before examining the evidence on income elasticities, however, let us look at the growth of services as an intermediate input to Agriculture and Industry.

Some Evidence on Intermediate Demand

Many service industries produce intermediate output (sold to other firms) as well as final output.[22] Most observers believe that a portion of the growth of services is attributable to an increase in specialization and division of labor, i.e., a relative increase in intermediate demand for services.[23] Precise data concerning this shift are not available, but it is possible to form a rough judgment about its relative importance from a comparison of the input-output tables of 1947 and 1958.

Table 12 shows, for each of the principal service industries involved, the percentage of total output that was distributed as intermediate input to Agriculture and Industry in 1947 and 1958. In every case this percentage rose; the change was in the predicted direction. Columns 3 and 4 of Table 12 show the employment in each industry in 1947 and 1958. Column 5 presents an estimate of the absolute growth of employment in each industry attributable to the growth of intermediate demand, under the assumption that employment requirements were proportional to output. Column 6 presents an estimate (using the same assumption) of the growth of employment attributable to the more rapid growth of intermediate than final demand for the output of these industries.

The employment increase is far from negligible for each measure, but, as Table 13 shows, the increase is small relative to the total gains of these five industries, and is considerably less than one-tenth of the absolute or relative gains of the total Service sector. Thus, the analysis confirms the hypothesis that some of the growth of service employment is attributable to the growth of intermediate demand for services by goods-producing industries, but this source accounts for only a small part of the total shift we are trying to explain.

[22] See Bert Hickman's discussion of the demand for intermediate services in *Growth and Stability of the Postwar Economy,* Washington, D.C., 1960, p. 203.

[23] See, for instance, George Stigler, *Trends in Employment in the Service Industries,* p. 139. It should be noted, however, that there has also been some shifting from Service back to goods-producing industries, e.g., much of drug making has been shifted from the drug store to manufacturing; the selection and packaging of fruits and vegetables has been shifted from retailing to agriculture or manufacturing.

TABLE 12

Employment and Intermediate Demand, Five Service Industries, 1947 and 1958

Service Industries	Per Cent of Total Output Distributed as Intermediate Input to Agriculture and Industry		Employment (thousands of persons engaged)		Employment Increase 1947–58 (thous. persons engaged) Attributable to:	
	1947 (1)	1958 (2)	1947 (3)	1958 (4)	Absolute Growth of Intermediate Demand (5)	Relative Growth of Intermediate Demand (6)
Finance and insurance	11.25	16.28	1,290	1,951	172	98
Real estate and rental	11.78	13.18	576	695	24	10
Business services	42.22	50.65	455	678	151	57
Auto repair services	19.74	23.78	338 [a]	350	17	14
Medical, educational, and other nonprofit organizations	2.48	2.86	2,057	3,498	49	13

[a] Employment in auto repair services for 1947 was estimated from 1948 data on auto services as a per cent of retail trade.

Sources: U.S. Bureau of Labor Statistics, *Interindustry Relations Study, 1947;* U.S. Department of Commerce, Office of Business Economics, *Survey of Current Business,* September 1965, "Interindustry Transactions–1958," pp. 34–39, and *The National Income and Product Accounts of the United States, 1929–1965,* August 1966.

TABLE 13

Employment Growth, 1947–58, Five Service Industries and Service Sector
(thousands of persons engaged)

	Absolute Growth	Relative Growth
Intermediate demand of Agriculture and Industry, five service industries	413 [a]	192 [b]
Total, five service industries	2,456	1,963 [c]
Total, Service sector	6,784	4,023 [c]

Source: Tables 1 and 12.

[a] The sum of column 5, Table 12.

[b] The sum of column 6, Table 12.

[c] The difference between the absolute growth and the growth that should have resulted if the rate of growth had been equal to the national rate.

Some Evidence on Income Elasticity

It is difficult to measure the income elasticity of demand for service output relative to other output. To calculate elasticities we need measures of real output or consumption; for many service (and some other) industries, however, accurate measures of real output are not available. Moreover, demand depends upon many variables, including changes in relative prices, urbanization, and the distribution of income. Also, the adjustment of spending patterns to changes in income may require time; thus the pattern observed at any given moment may depend upon past levels of income as well as present levels. This might be particularly true of services financed by state and local government expenditures. Finally, elasticities change from time to time.

Despite these difficulties, it is possible to form some judgment concerning relative elasticities for goods and services. Two experiments were attempted. The first compares the relative elasticities for goods and services by regressing changes in receipts or expenditures per capita on changes in income per capita across the forty-eight states. The periods chosen were 1939–58 for retail sales and sales of personal services, and 1942–57 for selected expenditures of state and local governments. Comprehensive data were available by state for those years.

The form of the regression equation was

$$\log Q = a + b \log Y$$

where Q = expenditures or receipts per capita in the terminal year divided by expenditures or receipts per capita in the initial year, and $Y =$

income per capita in the terminal year divided by income per capita in the initial year.

Because the regressions were run in double log form, the regression coefficient *b* may be regarded as a measure of the elasticity between income and expenditures. Expenditures are measured in current dollars and are used as a proxy for real consumption. Price does not enter into the equation because it is assumed that the *change* in price was the same in all states. If this is true, then the change in expenditures in current dollars gives exactly the same regression coefficient as would the change in real consumption. To the extent that prices rose faster in some states than in others, the bias is likely to be in the direction of a positive correlation between changes in price and changes in income. The regression coefficients may be slightly biased upward for this reason.

The equations were fitted in both weighted (1958 state populations) and unweighted form. The results were similar. I regard the weighted form as the more appropriate because the underlying process (except in the case of government expenditures) has nothing to do with states as such. They are units used merely as a statistical convenience for grouping the behavior of individuals. Moreover, weighting reduces the chances that a random event or reporting error in a small state can significantly influence the coefficients.

The results of this preliminary inquiry into a very complex econometric problem are consistent with the conclusions based on sector trends in output. Income elasticities appear to be slightly higher for services than for goods, but the difference is not large. The estimated elasticity for total retail sales of goods is .97, for personal services 1.12, and for total state and local government expenditures, 1.07.[24]

Interpretation of the results is complicated by the fact that changes in income were so highly correlated with changes in urbanization ($r = .90$ weighted and .79 unweighted) that the latter may have affected expenditures for some goods and services independently of changes in income; because the correlation between the two variables was so high, it is difficult to distinguish one effect from the other. Each regression was also run in multiple variable form, with changes in both income per capita and per cent urbanization as the independent variables; in most cases there was no additional explanation of the dependent variable after allow-

---

[24] The standard errors of the regression coefficient are .06, .08, and .13, respectively. Solomon Fabricant reported an income elasticity for state and local government expenditures in 1942 of .90. See *The Trend of Government Activity in the United States Since 1900*, New York, National Bureau of Economic Research, 1952, p. 125.

ing for the loss of one more degree of freedom. In general, it may be said that part of what we here call income elasticity may reflect increased urbanization.

The second experiment consisted of regressing expenditures for services and expenditures for goods on total expenditures across 160 income-education-region groups (ten income classes, four education classes, and four regions). The data were obtained from the Bureau of Labor Statistics *Survey of Consumer Expenditures 1960–61.*[25]

The form of the regression equation was

$$\ln X = a + b_1 \ln C + b_2 \ln E + b_3 A + b_4 E + b_5 R$$

where X = expenditures for goods (or services)
      C = total current consumption expenditures
      E = education
      A = age of head of family
      F = family size
      R = region, a dummy variable in which 1 = South and 0 = non-South.

The regressions were weighted by the number of observations in each cell.

The results show services with a total expenditure elasticity of 1.12, compared with .93 for goods.[26] When food and tobacco are excluded from goods, however, the elasticity rises to 1.05. The standard errors of the regression coefficients, as well as the results for all the variables, are shown in Table 14.

In addition to providing information about total expenditure elasticities, the regression results reveal that education, age of family head, family size, and region all show significant differences in their relation to goods and services. The demand for services is positively related to education. The regression coefficient tells us that an increase in education of 10 per cent (approximately one year of schooling) would be associated with an increase of about 1.9 per cent in expenditures on services. The demand for goods (and especially for food at home and tobacco) shows a significant negative elasticity for education. The demand for services is positively related to age and negatively related to family size.

[25] I am grateful to Robert Michael, of the National Bureau of Economic Research, for making available to me his unpublished material on consumer expenditures.

[26] Services include: food away from home, recreation, travel, education, household operations, personal care, medical care. Goods include: clothing, automobiles, reading matter, alcohol, house furnishings, food at home, tobacco, utilities, and shelter.

TABLE 14

Demand Elasticities for Goods and Services

	Total Consumption Expenditures (log C)	Education (log E)	Age of Head of Family (A)	Family Size (F)	Region: South = 1, Nonsouth = 0 (R)
Services	1.12	.19	.01	−.05	.10
	(.03)	(.03)	(.001)	(.02)	(.013)
Goods	.93	−.07	−.003	.03	−.05
	(.01)	(.017)	(.001)	(.01)	(.007)
Goods minus food at home and tobacco	1.05	.000	−.005	−.01	−.02
	(.02)	(.024)	(.001)	(.014)	(.01)
Food at home and tobacco	.65	−.22	−.001	.13	−.12
	(.04)	(.05)	(.002)	(.03)	(.02)

Note: Standard errors of the regression coefficients shown in parentheses.
Source: Basic data from U.S. Department of Labor, Bureau of Labor Statistics, *Survey of Consumer Expenditures, 1960–61,* BLS Report 237-93, Supplement 2, June 1966, Table 20: Education of head by income. Regression analysis by Robert Michael, NBER.

Also, the demand for services is stronger in the South than in the non-South. All of these results assume that other things are held constant and that expenditures are a good proxy for quantity, i.e., that prices do not vary systematically with any of the variables.

Again, it should be noted that the service–goods dichotomy for final consumption examined in these regressions bears only a rough correspondence to the industry classification used in the sector comparisons of output and employment. That agriculture faces a much lower income elasticity of demand than does the rest of the economy is scarcely in doubt. The Service–Industry differential is more difficult to ascertain, but it is probably small, perhaps about 5 to 10 per cent.

If we assume an income elasticity differential of 10 per cent, *ceteris paribus,* we would have expected the Service sector's share of nonagricultural output to rise by about 2 percentage points between 1929 and 1965, and Industry's share to fall by that amount. This is because the rise in real per capita income was about 80 per cent, and the 1929 shares of real output were approximately equally divided between the Service and Industry sectors. (See Table 10.) [27]

[27] With initial shares at 50 per cent for each, a *doubling* of real per capita income would produce sector shares of approximately 52.5 and 47.5 per cent if

When real output is measured in constant dollars, we find that the Service sector's share fell from 52.8 to 50.4 per cent instead of rising to 54.8 per cent. This might be explained by the increase of about 14 per cent in the price of Service sector output relative to Industry output.[28] Assuming that only the income and price effects were operative, this implies an elasticity of substitution between the Service and Industry sectors of approximately −1.15.[29] If we assume no sector difference in income elasticities, the implied elasticity of substitution is about −.7.

When the alternative measure of real output (gross product in current dollars) is used, there is, by assumption, no price effect to be considered. The income elasticity differential implied by the shift of the Service sector share from 51.7 to 52.5 per cent is on the order of 5 per cent. Thus, the results of the income elasticity experiments are consistent with the elasticity differential implied by the trends in sector output.

If the relative growth of service employment cannot be explained by a shift of output to services, it follows as a matter of definition that there must have been a dramatic difference in sector rates of change of output per man.[30]

the sector differential in income elasticity is 10 per cent. An increase of only 80 per cent in real per capita income, therefore, implies an increase of 2 percentage points for the Service sector and a decrease of 2 percentage points for the Industry sector.

[28] The implicit price deflator for the Service sector was 233.5 in 1965 (1929 = 100) compared with 204.4 for the Industry sector.

[29] If the relative change in price was 14 per cent, and the shift in sector shares was approximately 4 percentage points each way (54.8 minus 50.4), the relative change in quantity was about 16 per cent suggesting an elasticity of substitution of −1.15.

[30] See Appendix A for a theoretical discussion of sector differentials in employment. This discussion attempts to specify all the information needed to provide a nontautalogical explanation of sector shifts in employment.

3

PRODUCTIVITY TRENDS
BY SECTOR AND
MAJOR INDUSTRY GROUP

This chapter compares sector trends in output, input, and productivity over the period 1929–65, the earliest and latest years for which comparable data are available. Annual rates of change are also calculated for subperiods 1929–47 and 1947–65, and the latter period is further subdivided into 1947–56 and 1956–65. The rates of change for the shorter periods are generally less reliable than for the longer ones as measures of trend, because cyclical and irregular factors as well as measurement errors in the initial and terminal years increase in importance as the span shortens.

In addition to the sector comparisons, rates of change for each major industry group are shown relative to the national rate and correlations are calculated across industry groups for various measures of output, input, and productivity. The productivity measures include output per man, output per unit of labor input, and output per unit of total factor input. Comparison of these measures suggests important sector differences in the growth of the quality of labor and of capital per worker. These differences are explored, and are used to help explain the relative growth of service employment.

Measures of Input and Output

The data used in this chapter are drawn primarily from material provided by the U.S. Office of Business Economics and from previous studies of the National Bureau of Economic Research. A discussion of the principal concepts and sources follows.

Output

Output is measured by estimates of gross product originating in each industry in 1958 dollars.[1] This is conceptually similar to the gross na-

[1] Gross product by industry for 1947–65 was taken from U.S. Department of

tional product, but the method of obtaining constant-dollar estimates differs from the total and from industry to industry. In principle, the effect of price change is eliminated by the method known as "double deflation"; that is, the output of an industry and its purchases are each deflated separately and the difference between the two deflated figures is taken as the gross product in constant dollars. With modifications, this method was used by the Commerce Department for farms, construction, manufacturing, the major portions of finance and insurance, electrical and gas utilities, and railroads. In other industries, real product was estimated by extrapolating the base-year product by an index of the quantity of total output. The estimates for the period 1929–47 are based on Kendrick's indexes of real output.[2]

Gross product in constant dollars is not a completely satisfactory measure of real output by industry, but it is probably the best available for industry productivity analysis. One advantage is that the industry totals (with the exception of a very small "statistical discrepancy") do equal the total GNP, and it is therefore possible to calculate industry productivity measures relative to the total economy. Probably the most important defect of the gross product measures is that output in some industries is estimated from employment data. This problem is most serious in government and some of the other industries in the Service sector. The possible effect of biases in the output measures on trends in productivity is discussed later in this chapter and in Chapter 5.

It should be noted that much of the analysis presented here is concerned with differential changes in various inputs and will be equally relevant if some different, and presumably superior, output measures become available.

Employment

The Department of Commerce series "Number of Persons Engaged in Production" is used to measure changes in employment. This series includes self-employed as well as employees reduced to full-time equivalents, and is probably reasonably accurate. The exclusion of unpaid

Commerce Office of Business Economics, "Revised Estimates of GNP by Major Industries," *Survey of Current Business,* April 1967. Data for 1929 were estimated from rates of change published in Martin L. Marimont, "GNP by Major Industries," *Survey of Current Business,* October 1962.

[2] John W. Kendrick, *Productivity Trends in the United States,* Princeton University Press for National Bureau of Economic Research, 1961. It may be noted that for the years after 1947, where comparison between Kendrick's output indexes and the Office of Business Economics estimates of real gross product is possible, the two methods yield almost identical results for the sector aggregates.

family workers may introduce some measurement errors in agriculture and trade, while the method of converting part-time employment into full-time equivalents may introduce some bias in industries, such as services, where part-time employment is significant.[3]

Total Labor Input

Employment data may not provide a completely satisfactory measure of total labor input for several reasons. First, there are possible defects in the employment series, as illustrated by the problem of converting part-time employment to full-time equivalents. Second, there is the problem of obtaining accurate information concerning the average number of hours actually worked each year by full-time employees. In a preliminary report on this problem,[4] estimates were made for changes in man-hours. However, recent investigations of changes in weekly hours for manufacturing and retailing have cast considerable doubt on the previously accepted estimates of changes in hours between 1929 and 1947.[5] Because of the uncertainty it was decided not to present measures of output per man-hour. Since 1947, there have been only small changes in weekly hours for full-time employees; therefore, measures of output per man-hour are substantially the same as output per full-time equivalent employed persons.

A third difficulty is in interpreting changes in man-hours even if accurate data were available. Decreases in weekly hours, when hours are long, may be offset in part by an increase in effective labor input per hour because of lessened fatigue.[6] Finally, man-hours data tell us nothing about the quality of labor attributable to differences in intelligence, strength, training, and so on. It would be useful to have a measure of labor input which took account of all these factors.

[3] In converting part-time employment into full-time equivalents, the Office of Business Economics divides the payroll of part-time employees by the average earnings of full-time employees. If, as seems likely, part-time employees earn less per hour than full-time employees, the OBE procedure will understate the true full-time equivalent employment and will overstate the average annual earnings obtained by dividing total payroll by full-time equivalent employment so estimated.

[4] Victor R. Fuchs, *Productivity Trends in the Goods and Service Sectors, 1929–61: A Preliminary Survey,* NBER, Occasional Paper 89, New York, 1964.

[5] Ethel B. Jones, "New Estimates of Hours of Work Per Week and Hourly Earnings, 1900–1957," *Review of Economics and Statistics,* November 1963; David Schwartzman, "Analysis of Productivity Change in Retail Trade 1929–63," NBER manuscript.

[6] See discussion of this point by Edward F. Denison, in *The Sources of Economic Growth in the United States and the Alternatives Before Us,* Committee for Economic Development, Supplementary Paper No. 13, New York, January 1962, p. 40. See also Irving F. Leveson, "Reductions in Hours of Work as a Source of Productivity Growth," *The Journal of Political Economy,* April 1967.

Provided we accept certain assumptions, we may be able to approach such a measure through the data on labor compensation. Total labor compensation includes wages and salaries, supplements to wages and salaries, and the labor income of the self-employed. If we assume that the price of labor (adjusted for quality, effort, etc.) changes at the same rate in all branches of the economy, then the change in total labor compensation in a particular industry relative to the change in the economy as a whole is equal to the change in labor input in that industry relative to the change in labor input for the economy as a whole.[7]

Note that this formulation does not require that a dollar's worth of compensation buy the same amount of labor input in all industries in either the initial or the terminal year. There may be variations based on nonpecuniary factors, monopoly or monopsony power, and so on. The relative change in compensation will still be equal to the relative change in labor input, provided these other factors do not change from industry to industry over time.

The estimates of total labor compensation by industry are based on the Office of Business Economics estimates of the compensation of employees (full-time equivalents) [8] plus estimates of the returns to labor for proprietors of unincorporated businesses. Proprietors' income is defined as the sum of income of unincorporated enterprises plus the inventory valuation adjustment of unincorporated enterprises. Labor's share of proprietors' income was assumed to be 60 per cent in agriculture, 80 per cent in finance, insurance, and real estate, 90 per cent in mining, manufacturing, transportation, communications, and public utilities, and wholesale and retail trades, and 95 per cent in construction and services. These percentages are based on information about the relative amounts of net worth in each industry.[9]

Total Factor Input

The foregoing suggests that relative changes in labor compensation may be used to estimate relative changes in labor input. Similarly, relative changes in total compensation (measured approximately by gross

[7] See equation 1, Appendix B. Possible biases in this measure are discussed later in this chaper in the section on the quality of labor.

[8] The Office of Business Economics data on compensation per man by industry were compared with industry wage and salary data collected by the Bureau of the Census in its *Current Population Survey* for 1948 through 1960, as reported in Herman P. Miller, *Trends in the Income of Families and Persons in the United States: 1947–1960*, Bureau of the Census Technical Paper No. 8, Washington, D.C., 1963, Table 17. The sector differentials were almost identical.

[9] See Irving Leveson, "Nonfarm Self-Employment in the United States," unpublished Ph.D. dissertation, Columbia University, 1967, Chapter 4.

product in current dollars) may be used to estimate relative changes in total factor input. In this case we assume that the price of a unit of composite factor inputs (land, labor, and capital) has changed at the same rate in all branches of the economy.[10] This assumption is less likely to be true than the same assumption for a single factor because relative factor prices have changed and industry factor proportions differ. Some independent verification is possible through direct estimation of capital input, to be discussed later.

Trends in Productivity

We are now ready to turn to productivity measures themselves. All changes are expressed as annual rates (continuously compounded) between the initial and terminal years. Productivity is always shown as a residual—the difference between the rate of change of real output and the rate of change of whatever input or combination of inputs we are concerned with at the moment.

Two of the variants of productivity—output per unit of labor input and output per unit of total factor input—are only shown in relative terms because of the great difficulties encountered in measuring the absolute change in these variables.[11] Many of the sources of errors affect most industries. It is possible, therefore, to have greater confidence in the sector differentials in the rates of change of these measures than in the absolute rates of change for any one sector or for the total economy.

Sector Comparisons of Productivity Change

Sector rates of change of output, employment, and output per man are presented in Table 15.[12] We see that gains in output per man have been much more rapid since 1947 than before, and that this is true for all sectors. In fact, the rate of growth of productivity in the Service sector, 1947–65, exceeded that of the Industry sector, 1929–47. Employment has grown at about the same rate over the entire span, except

[10] See equation 2, Appendix B. For a discussion of this method, see Denison, *Sources of Economic Growth,* pp. 218, 219.

[11] Edward F. Denison's study, *Sources of Economic Growth,* is one of the most ambitious attempts at such measurement for the total economy. According to Denison, total labor input (adjusted for hours, quality, etc.) grew at a rate of 2.2 per cent per annum between 1929 and 1957, and total factor input grew at a rate of 2.1 per cent per annum. There is some reason to believe that these rates are biased upward because the contribution of increased education to input was inferred from cross-sectional differences in *annual income* rather than from the smaller and more relevant cross-sectional differences in *hourly earnings.*

[12] The rates for the major industry groups will be discussed later in this chapter.

TABLE 15

Rates of Change of Output, Employment, and Output Per Man, by Sector and Major Industry Group, 1929–65 and Selected Subperiods
(per cent per annum)

	1929–65			1929–47			1947–65			1947–56			1956–65		
	Output	Employment	Output Per Man [a]	Output	Employment	Output Per Man [a]	Output	Employment	Output Per Man [a]	Output	Employment	Output Per Man [a]	Output	Employment	Output Per Man [a]
Total economy	3.1	1.2	1.9	2.5	1.2	1.3	3.7	1.2	2.6	3.9	1.4	2.6	3.5	1.0	2.6
Agriculture	1.1	-2.3	3.4	0.4	-1.5	1.9	1.9	-3.1	4.9	2.3	-2.8	5.1	1.5	-3.3	4.7
Industry	3.4	1.2	2.2	3.0	1.6	1.5	3.8	0.8	2.9	4.1	1.4	2.8	3.4	0.3	3.1
Service	3.1	2.0	1.1	2.4	1.9	0.5	3.9	2.2	1.7	3.9	2.3	1.6	3.8	2.0	1.8
Service subsector	2.9	1.6	1.2	2.1	1.7	0.4	3.7	1.6	2.1	3.4	1.3	2.1	3.9	1.8	2.1
Industry															
Mining	1.5	-1.2	2.7	1.0	-0.2	1.2	2.1	-2.1	4.1	3.2	-1.1	4.3	0.9	-3.1	4.0
Contract construction	2.2	1.5	0.7	1.2	1.5	-0.3	3.3	1.5	1.7	5.8	2.3	3.5	0.7	0.8	-0.1
Manufacturing	3.7	1.6	2.1	3.3	2.1	1.2	4.0	1.0	3.0	4.2	1.5	2.7	3.8	0.5	3.3
Transportation	2.8	-0.6	3.4	4.2	0.0	4.1	1.5	-1.1	2.7	0.9	-0.9	1.8	2.2	-1.3	3.5
Communications and public utilities	5.6	1.1	4.5	4.0	0.8	3.3	7.1	1.3	5.8	8.2	2.5	5.6	6.0	0.2	5.8
Government enterprise	3.3	2.8	0.5	2.7	2.8	0.0	3.8	2.8	1.1	3.0	3.0	-0.1	4.7	2.6	2.2
Service															
Wholesale and retail trade	3.1	1.5	1.6	2.4	1.8	0.6	3.9	1.2	2.7	3.7	1.2	2.5	4.0	1.1	2.9
Finance, insurance, real estate, and services	2.9	1.7	1.3	1.7	0.9	0.8	4.1	2.4	1.8	4.0	2.1	1.9	4.3	2.7	1.6
Finance, insurance, and services excl. households and institutions	2.5	1.9	0.6	1.7	1.6	0.1	3.3	2.2	1.2	3.0	1.5	1.5	3.7	2.9	0.8
General government	3.8	3.8	0.0	4.4	4.4	0.0	3.2	3.3	-0.1	4.1	4.3	-0.2	2.3	2.3	0.0

Source: See Appendix C.

[a] Output per man calculated from unrounded data.

for a slight acceleration in 1947–56 and a slight deceleration in 1956–65.

Of the three sectors, Agriculture has led in rate of change of output per man in every period. It is noteworthy that the sector that has been declining most rapidly in relative importance, as measured by either output or employment, should have achieved the greatest gains in output per man. Most studies of the relationship between growth and productivity, to be discussed, point to a positive correlation.

Some of the reasons for the rapid growth of output per man in agriculture include government supported research and education programs, substitution of capital (physical and human) for labor, and the movement out of agriculture of marginal producers who were attracted by the strong demand for labor in the nonagricultural sectors. U.S. agriculture, like that of most other countries, apparently harbored, and may still harbor, a considerable amount of "disguised unemployment."

Because many of the conditions in agriculture were fundamentally different from the rest of the economy, and because of the relatively small role of the Agricultural sector currently, the comparison that is emphasized in this book is the differential between the Industry and Service sectors. These differentials, for all measures in all periods, are presented in Table 16, the first portion of which shows each sector's rate of change relative to the national rate. The differential between any two sectors can be obtained by simple subtraction of the relative rates of change.[18]

The Industry-Service comparison reveals a differential of 1.1 per cent per annum in changes in output per man for the 1929–65 period. This differential was approximately the same in all the subperiods. It is this gap of 1.1 per cent that requires explanation. A look at the other measures of productivity provides some clues to portions of the answer.

The differential in output per unit of labor input was only .6 per cent per annum. This means that almost half the differential in output per man may be explained by the discrepancy between the rate of growth of employment and of labor input. The latter, it will be recalled, takes account of differential changes in hours per man and the quality of labor. It is clear from the figures on compensation per man that labor quality has been rising more rapidly in the Industry than in the Service sector. Possible biases in this measure of labor quality will be discussed, but such considerations do not alter this broad conclusion.

The Industry-Service productivity differential is further reduced—

[18] The Industry-Service differentials were calculated from unrounded data and may not, therefore, correspond exactly to those implied by the rounded figures shown in the upper portion of Table 16.

TABLE 16

Sector Rates of Change of Output and Other Variables Relative to the
Total Economy, 1929–65 and Selected Subperiods
(per cent per annum)

	1929–65	1929–47	1947–65	1947–56	1956–65
Agriculture					
Output	−2.1	−2.2	−1.8	−1.6	−2.1
Employment	−3.5	−2.8	−4.2	−4.2	−4.2
Output per man	1.5	0.6	2.4	2.6	2.2
Output per unit of labor input	0.8	−1.9	3.6	7.0	0.0
Output per unit of total factor input	0.5	−2.1	3.1	5.6	0.5
Compensation per man	0.6	2.5	−1.2	−4.4	2.0
Industry					
Output	0.3	0.5	0.0	0.2	−0.1
Employment	0.0	0.3	−0.3	0.0	−0.7
Output per man	0.3	0.2	0.4	0.2	0.6
Output per unit of labor input	0.3	0.5	0.1	−0.4	0.6
Output per unit of total factor input	0.2	0.2	0.1	−0.4	0.5
Compensation per man	0.0	−0.3	0.3	0.7	−0.1
Service					
Output	0.0	−0.2	0.1	0.0	0.3
Employment	0.8	0.7	1.0	0.9	1.1
Output per man	−0.9	−0.8	−0.9	−0.9	−0.8
Output per unit of labor input	−0.3	−0.2	−0.5	−0.4	−0.6
Output per unit of total factor input	−0.2	0.1	−0.5	−0.5	−0.6
Compensation per man	−0.5	−0.7	−0.4	−0.6	−0.2
Service Subsector					
Output	−0.2	−0.4	−0.1	−0.5	0.4
Employment	0.4	0.5	0.4	−0.1	0.8
Output per man	−0.7	−0.9	−0.5	−0.4	−0.5
Output per unit of labor input	0.0	−0.1	0.0	0.1	0.0
Output per unit of total factor input	−0.3	−0.7	0.0	0.1	0.0
Compensation per man	−0.7	−0.8	−0.5	−0.5	−0.4
Industry Minus Service					
Output	0.3	0.7	−0.1	0.2	−0.4
Employment	−0.9	−0.4	−1.3	−1.0	−1.7
Output per man	1.1	1.0	1.2	1.2	1.4
Output per unit of labor input	0.6	0.7	0.6	−0.1	1.2
Output per unit of total factor input	0.4	0.2	0.6	0.1	1.1
Compensation per man	0.5	0.3	0.7	1.2	0.1

Source: See notes to Table 15.

to .4 per cent per annum—when we look at output per unit of total factor input. This measure is based on the reciprocal of the rates of change of prices in the two sectors. That is, the implicit price deflator for the Service sector rose .4 per cent per annum faster than did the implicit price deflator for the Industry sector. This definition of productivity comes closest to what is often inferred from the term, namely, efficiency in the use of resources. It also comes closest to measuring the rate of technological advance. To the extent that output per man has been rising more rapidly in Industry than in the Service sector because the quality of labor or capital per man has been rising more rapidly, there is no basis for inferring that efficiency or technology have been lagging in the Service sector. To be sure, this method of measuring total factor productivity may be biased, and some of the possible biases will be discussed later in this chapter.

The sector differentials in output per man are remarkably similar in each of the subperiods. The other productivity measures show greater variability, but much of this may be spurious. It is probably the result of the method of measuring changes in labor input and total factor input, which is much less reliable for short than for long periods. In particular, 1947 was almost certainly not a year characterized by the long-run equilibrium conditions that this method requires.

Productivity by Major Industry Group

The discussion thus far has been entirely in terms of sector totals. It is important also to look at productivity change in the individual industry groups that make up the two sectors. At the end of his study of employment in the service industries, Stigler reached the conclusion that "No simple rule describes the trend of employment in the promiscuous ensemble of service industries. . . . Responsible predictions of trends in this large area will not be possible until we have pushed much further in the study of individual industries." [14]

Table 17 shows the relation of the change in output, employment, and output per man (shown in absolute terms in Table 15) to the total economy for 1929–65. The range of productivity gains across industries is very large, with communications and public utilities typically leading and general government typically showing the slowest growth. There is considerable variation within each sector as well as between sectors, but for output per man the between-sector variance is considerably larger than

[14] George J. Stigler, *Trends in Employment in the Service Industries,* Princeton University Press for National Bureau of Economic Research, 1956, p. 166.

TABLE 17

Rates of Change of Output, Input, and Productivity, Major Industry Groups Relative to Total Economy, 1929–65
(per cent per annum)

Major Industry Group	Output	Employ-ment	Output Per Man	Output Per Unit of Labor Input	Output Per Unit of Total Factor Input	Compen-sation Per Man
Agriculture, forestry, and fisheries	−2.0	−3.5	1.5	0.8	0.5	0.6
Mining	−1.6	−2.4	0.7	0.6	−0.3	0.2
Contract construction	−0.9	0.3	−1.2	−1.1	−1.3	−0.2
Manufacturing	0.5	0.4	0.2	0.2	0.0	0.0
Transportation	−0.3	−1.8	1.4	1.2	1.3	0.2
Communications and public utilities	2.4	−0.1	2.6	2.2	1.8	0.4
Government enterprise	0.2	1.6	−1.4	−0.8	−0.7	−0.6
Wholesale and retail trade	0.0	0.3	−0.3	0.3	−0.2	−0.6
Finance, insurance, real estate, and services	−0.2	0.5	−0.7	−0.1	0.1	−0.6
Finance, insurance, and services excluding households and institutions	−0.6	0.7	−1.3	−0.5	−0.6	−0.8
General government	0.6	2.6	−2.0	−1.6	−1.7	−0.4

Source: Appendix Table C–3.

The Service Economy

TABLE 18

Coefficients of Rank Correlation Between Rates of Change, 1929–47
and 1947–65, Across Ten Major Industry Groups

Measure	Coefficient of Rank Correlation
Output	.22
Employment	.81 [a]
Output per man	.72 [b]
Output per unit of labor input	−.09
Output per unit of total factor input	−.19
Compensation per man	−.34

Source: Appendix Table C–4.
[a] Statistically significant at .01 level of confidence.
[b] Statistically significant at .05 level of confidence.

the within-sector variance. Most of the industries in the Industry sector show high rates; contract construction is an outstanding exception, and government enterprise tends also to lag behind the rest of the sector. All of the service industries show below-average rates. It is interesting to note that every industry group that had a below-average rate of growth of compensation per man also was below average in growth of output per man, and a similar identity holds for industry groups with above-average rates.

*Correlations Between Time Periods and Between Different
Measures of Productivity*

A comparison of the two subperiods, 1929–47 and 1947–65, shows considerable stability in the rankings of the industry groups with respect to rates of change of output per man (see Table 18).[15] The rankings are also very stable with respect to employment growth, but none of the other variables has significant coefficients of rank correlation and in three cases the sign is negative. These last three measures are particularly sensitive to nonequilibrium conditions in either the initial or terminal years. It seems likely that relative wages and prices in 1947 were distorted by the surge of demand during the war, the uneven impact of wage and price controls, and the dislocations of the period immediately

[15] The rank correlations are across ten industry groups. The finance, insurance, service group excluding households and institutions is used.

TABLE 19

Coefficients of Rank Correlation Between Changes in Output, Input, and Productivity, 1929–65, Across Ten Major Industry Groups

	Output	Employment	Output Per Man	Output Per Unit of Labor Input	Output Per Unit of Total Factor Input
Employment	.56	—	−.88 [a]	−.82 [a]	−.70 [b]
Output per man	−.18	−.88 [a]	—	.94 [a]	.92 [a]
Output per unit of labor input	−.09	−.82 [a]	.94 [a]	—	.95 [a]
Output per unit of total factor input	.05	−.70 [b]	.92 [a]	.95 [a]	—
Compensation per man	−.16	−.79 [a]	.88 [a]	.73 [b]	.71 [b]

Source: Table 17.
[a] Statistically significant at .01 level of confidence.
[b] Statistically significant at .05 level of confidence.

after the war. For these reasons, it is probably wise to concentrate the analysis on the full 1929–65 period.

Table 19 shows that, for this period, there is a very high correlation among the three measures of productivity. In all cases the coefficient is above .90. If one is interested only in the rankings of the industry groups, it makes very little difference which measure is used. On the other hand, Table 17 shows that the actual differentials vary considerably from one measure to the other. In general, the intergroup variance is greatest for output per man and smallest for output per unit of total factor input. The median differential (without regard to sign) is 1.3 per cent per annum for output per man, 0.8 per cent for output per unit of labor input, and 0.6 per cent for output per unit of total factor input.

Several previous studies of industry productivity have found a high correlation between changes in output and changes in productivity, particularly over long periods.[16] Some of these studies have found even employment change to be positively correlated with productivity. Two

[16] See Solomon Fabricant, *Employment in Manufacturing, 1899–1939,* New York, National Bureau of Economic Research, 1942, pp. 88, 146; Kendrick, *Productivity Trends,* pp. 207–216; W. E. G. Salter, *Productivity and Technical Change,* Cambridge, England, 1960, p. 123; W. B. Reddaway and A. D. Smith, "Progress in British Manufacturing Industries in the Period 1948–54," *Economic Journal,* March 1960, p. 31.

CHART 4

Rates of Change of Output and Output Per Man, Ten Major Industry Groups
Relative to the Total Economy, 1929–65

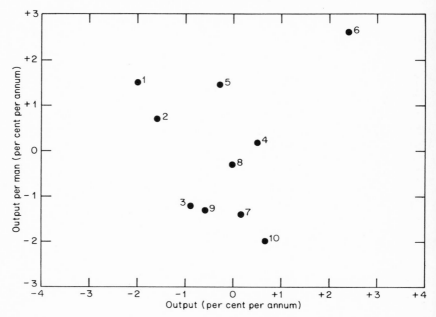

INDUSTRY LEGEND

1. Agriculture, forestry, and fisheries
2. Mining
3. Contract construction
4. Manufacturing
5. Transportation

6. Communications and public utilities
7. Government enterprise
8. Trade
9. Finance, insurance, and services ex-
    cluding households and institutions
10. General government

principal explanations have been offered for this relationship. First, it is
argued that increased output (determined by income change, changes in
taste, or variables exogenous to the industry) permits the realization of
increased economies of scale, thus causing increased productivity. On
the other hand, it is also claimed the industries with rapid gains in productivity show declines in relative prices which result in an increase in
the quantity demanded and therefore an increase in output.[17]

[17] Michael Grossman has pointed out to me that a positive correlation between
income elasticities and technological change would result in this relationship even
if there were no economies of scale and zero price elasticities. Such a correlation
might result if (1) the search for innovation was influenced by potential growth
prospects, and (2) these prospects could be forecast.

CHART 5

Rates of Change of Employment and Output Per Man, Ten Major Industry
Groups Relative to the Total Economy, 1929–65

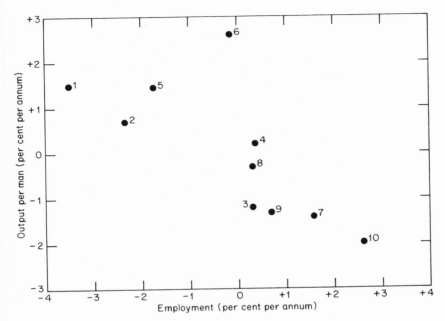

Note: For industry legend see Chart 4.

The pattern of productivity change by major industry group is not
consistent with these previous findings. There appears to be no significant relation between productivity change and change in output; the relation with change in employment is clearly negative (see Table 19 and
Charts 4 and 5).[18] There is some element of spurious correlation to be
sure, but in the case of output and productivity, the direction of the bias
is positive. A finding of low or zero correlation, therefore, is all the more
significant.

Most previous studies of this relationship were either limited to or
highly dominated by manufacturing industries. In Chapter 4 the results
for detailed industries within the Service sector are found to be similar

---

[18] Product-moment correlation coefficients are similar to the coefficients based
on rank correlation. Between changes in output per man and output, the coefficients
are +.13 (unweighted) and −.26 (weighted). Between changes in output per man
and employment, the coefficients are −.74 (unweighted) and −.83 (weighted).

to those for manufacturing. Therefore, we are left with the tentative conclusion that growth and productivity do seem to be related across industries *within* major industry groups, but that no correlation is evident *across* major industry groups.

The comparison of productivity and growth across groups does not confirm previous studies. When we compare changes in productivity and compensation per man, the results again differ from those obtained in studies of manufacturing and those reported for trade and services in Chapter 4. Whereas studies across industries within major groups have not found any significant correlation between rates of change of productivity and of compensation per man,[19] the correlation across the ten major industry groups for 1929–65 is high and statistically significant (see Table 19 and Chart 6).[20]

The small number of observations and their aggregative nature must be noted. Certainly no firm conclusion is warranted on the basis of such limited data, but the results are suggestive. Most economists believe that rapid productivity gains in particular industries do not lead to particularly rapid wage gains in those industries, but are diffused broadly over the entire economy, especially if one looks at a reasonably long period. Earlier studies limited to or dominated by manufacturing have substantially confirmed this belief. One possible inference, therefore, is that differential change in labor quality has not been a major determinant of productivity change within manufacturing. The high correlation between productivity and compensation per man across major groups, on the other hand, suggests that differential trends in productivity have been associated with differential trends in labor quality.[21]

Quality of Labor

Portions of the preceding analysis suggest that differential change in the quality of labor may have been an important factor accounting for sector differences in the rate of growth of output per man.

Although it is difficult to define "labor quality" with precision, a few words concerning the use of the term in this book may be helpful. We know from casual observation that man-hours of labor are not homogeneous with respect to productivity. The effect of a given number of

[19] See, for example, Kendrick, *Productivity Trends,* p. 198.
[20] The product-moment correlation between changes in output per man and compensation per man is .83 (unweighted) and .79 (weighted).
[21] An alternative inference—that the differential trends in compensation are a result of the weakness of competitive forces and are unrelated to labor quality—seems less plausible but cannot be rejected a priori.

CHART 6

Rates of Change of Compensation Per Man and Output Per Man, Ten Major
Industry Groups Relative to the Total Economy, 1929–65

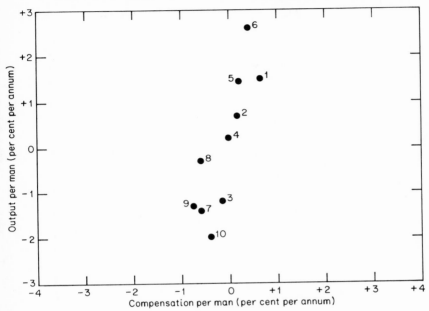

Note: For industry legend see Chart 4.

man-hours on output, holding technology and other inputs constant, is likely to vary depending upon such factors as the knowledge, intelligence, and strength of the persons supplying the hours of work. All of the factors that contribute to such variation are subsumed under the term "labor quality."

It is possible to measure some of the characteristics that we believe contribute to labor quality, such as age and number of school years completed. We can never specify all of the characteristics that might be related to quality, however, nor have we measures for many that we can name.

Table 16 indicates that the Industry-Service differential in the rate of change of compensation per man between 1929 and 1965 was .5 per cent per annum. As a first approximation, we may say that this more rapid rate of growth of compensation per man in the Industry sector is evidence of a more rapid rate of growth of the quality of labor in that sector. This is subject to modification to the extent that the compensation per man differential can be explained by other factors. We consider a few of these now.

1. AVERAGE HOURS PER MAN. Some of the differential change in compensation per man may be attributable to a more rapid decline of average hours in Service than in the Industry sector. Previously accepted figures indicated that this differential might explain .3 percentage points of the differential in earnings per man.[22] This now appears to be an overestimate for two reasons. First, some new hours figures for manufacturing, estimated by Ethel Jones, suggest that the decline in manufacturing hours since 1929 had been understated, and David Schwartzman's new estimates for retailing suggest that the decline in that industry may have been previously overestimated (see footnote 5 above). Second, to the extent that hours in services were very long in 1929, the decline was probably partially offset by increased output per man-hour attributable solely to the decline in hours (see footnote 24 below).

Average weekly hours in each sector have been calculated for 1929 and 1965, using Kendrick's estimates in all instances except manufacturing (1929) and trade (1929 and 1965).[23] The Industry sector shows a decline from 47.2 hours to 39.7 hours. The Service sector shows a slightly greater decline from 50.8 hours in 1929 to 40.1 hours in 1965. The sector differential in rate of decline is approximately .18 per cent per annum. However, if Denison's formula for calculating a productivity offset to shorter hours is applied, the sector differential practically disappears.[24]

The above calculations suggest that the sector differential in compensation per man of .5 per cent need not be modified at all to take account of hours if one follows the Denison formula, or should be modified by about .2 percentage points if no allowance is made for a productivity offset. An allowance for a .1 percentage point differential trend in hours provides a compromise between these two positions.

2. CHANGES IN UNIONIZATION. One of the factors that might account

[22] See Victor R. Fuchs, *Productivity Trends in the Goods and Service Sectors,* p. 12.

[23] The data for the individual industry groups are presented in Appendix Table C-5.

[24] Denison, *Sources of Economic Growth,* p. 40. The Denison formula posits that, because of the adverse effects of fatigue, a decrease in hours when the level is above 48.6 per week is fully offset by an increase in output per man-hour. It is possible that fatigue is not as important in trade and services as in industry and therefore the productivity offset is not as likely. On the other hand, a decrease in the number of hours that the store is open is likely to produce a productivity offset through more intensive utilization.

for the more rapid rise of compensation per man in the Industry sector is union power. We know that unionization has grown rapidly in Industry since 1929, and that it has grown very slowly in the Service sector. In order to estimate the possible effect on compensation per man, we need measures of the extent of unionization in each sector in 1929 and 1965, and a measure of the union-nonunion differential in wages. Neither requirement can be filled with precision, but it is possible to obtain some notion of the possible order of magnitude of this effect.

The union effect on wages has been evaluated by H. Gregg Lewis as follows: "Apart from periods of unusually rapid inflation or deflation, the average relative wage effect of unionism . . . was 0.10–0.20 per cent per percentage point difference in extent of unionism." [25] Lewis views the union effect as more or less equal and continuous over the entire range from zero to 100 per cent unionization. Thus, if one industry were 100 per cent unionized, and another one completely unorganized, Lewis would expect a wage differential (adjusted for quality) of approximately 10 to 20 per cent. If one industry were 60 per cent unionized, and another one 20 per cent unionized, the expected differential would be 4 to 8 per cent.

In an analysis of interindustry differentials in hourly earnings, to be discussed in Chapter 6, I find a somewhat greater union effect; I also find that the effect is not equally strong at all levels of unionization. No union effect on wages is evident below 20 per cent unionization. The strongest effect, about .35 per cent per percentage point difference in unionization, is evident in the range 20 to 60 per cent unionized, after which the union effect is appreciably smaller and approaches zero for changes at high levels of unionization.

My analysis was based on data for 1959, a year when the union effect was probably particularly strong. The generally weak demand in the economy in 1958 and 1959 [26] tended to keep wages from rising in un-

---

[25] "The Effects of Unions on Industrial Wage Differentials," in *Aspects of Labor Economics,* Universities—National Bureau Conference 14, Princeton University Press for National Bureau of Economic Research, 1962, p. 332. Note that neither Lewis nor I am concerned here with the effect of unions on the general wage level. To the extent that the presence of unions in the economy raises wages generally, union power cannot be the source of a sector differential. Note also that Lewis and I are concerned with wages for a given quality of labor. If unions (or efforts to avoid them) produce higher wages in an industry, this may result in higher-quality labor being attracted to it, and may permit employers to be more selective in hiring. If a higher wage is offset by higher quality, it is not greater compensation in the relevant sense.

[26] The unemployment rate was 6.8 per cent in 1958 (the highest rate since 1941) and 5.5 per cent in 1959.

organized industries; the high profits and rising prices of the preceding
capital goods boom provided the type of setting in which union demands
are likely to be strongest and the differential between union and nonunion
wages likely to be greatest. In applying the results of my estimate to
1965, a year of strong demand for labor, I would reduce the estimated
union effect to .25 per cent per percentage point difference in extent of
unionization over the range 20 to 60 per cent.

In order to apply the Lewis formula, it is only necessary to have the
percentage of each sector's employment that was unionized in the initial
and terminal years. In order to apply my formula, information is required about the distribution of industries by extent of unionization
within each sector. In particular, it is necessary to know the percentage
of the sector's employment in industries with unionization under 20 per
cent and over 60 per cent, and to know the percentage unionized in the
range 20 to 60 per cent. All the industries with unionization below 20
per cent or above 60 per cent are then set equal to 20 and 60, respectively.

Table 20 shows the change in the sector differentials in unionization
between 1929 and 1960 according to both approaches. Detailed estimates of unionization by industry are not available for 1965; the 1960

TABLE 20

Extent of Unionization, Industry and Service Sectors, 1929 and 1960
(per cent of total employment)

	1929	1960	1960 Minus 1929
Unadjusted			
Industry	16	50	34
Service	2	8	6
Industry minus Service	14	42	28
Adjusted [a]			
Industry	24	48	24
Service	20	20	0
Industry minus Service	4	28	24

Source: 1929 figures, H. G. Lewis, *Unionism and Relative Wages in the United States,* Chicago, 1963; 1960 figures, see Appendix H.

[a] All industries with unionization below 20 per cent are set equal to 20; all with unionization above 60 per cent are set equal to 60. See Chapter 6.

figures are applied under the assumption that the sector differential in unionization remained unchanged between 1960 and 1965.[27] If we apply the midpoint of the Lewis estimate of the union effect, .15 per cent per percentage point, to the unadjusted change in the sector differential, 28 per cent, we obtain an estimate of 4.2 per cent (.15 × 28) as the effect of the differential change in unionization on sector differences in earnings. This says that wages in the Industry sector relative to the Service sector in 1965 were 4.2 per cent higher than they would have been if the degree of unionization in each sector had remained the same as it was in 1929. Spread over thirty-six years, this represents an annual rate of change of .12 per cent.

Applying my estimate of .25 per cent per percentage point to the adjusted differential of 24 per cent changes the unionization effect to 6 per cent, or .16 per cent per annum. Taking both these results into account, and bearing in mind the crudeness of the estimates, one can draw the tentative conclusion that the effect of changes in unionization between 1929 and 1965 was to raise wages in the Industry sector relative to the Service sector at the rate of between .1 and .2 per cent per annum.

3. CHANGES IN NONPECUNIARY ADVANTAGES. A factor that may work in the opposite direction is nonpecuniary advantages not included in labor compensation. If these increased more rapidly in the Industry than in the Service sector, the compensation data understate the quality differentials; if they increased more rapidly in services the reverse is true. This assumes that industries that offer more nonpecuniary advantages, such as recreation programs, subsidized lunches, and in-plant health services, will be able to attract and hold better-quality workers. The data on changes in unionization imply that the change has been in favor of the Industry sector, given Lewis's judgment that "The relative gains won by unions probably consist partly of relative improvements in the nonpecuniary aspects of employment." [28]

One bit of evidence that points in this direction is the differential trend in supplements to wages and salaries. These supplements, per full-time equivalent employee, grew 1.6 per cent per annum faster in Industry

[27] It is possible that the differential narrowed as a result of unionization drives in hospitals, schools, and retail stores. If so, then the estimates presented here of the effect of unionization on differential earnings trends are biased upward.

[28] *Unionism and Relative Wages,* p. 46. Note also Melvin Reder's generalization that "As industries have shifted away from unskilled labor, they have also improved working conditions and reduced nonpecuniary disutilities." Melvin W. Reder, "Wage Differentials: Theory and Measurement," in *Aspects of Labor Economics,* p. 278.

than in the Service sector between 1929 and 1965.[29] It seems plausible that the industries that show relative improvement in their wage supplements were also experiencing relative improvement in nonpecuniary advantages.

4. CHANGES IN LOCATION OF INDUSTRY. Another factor tending to hold Industry wages down for given quality has been the shift of manufacturing away from the large industrial cities of the Northeast and North Central regions. Wages for workers of given color, age, sex, and education are considerably lower in small towns and in the South; indeed, this is one of the reasons why manufacturing has shifted.[30] This introduces a bias in the direction opposite to that introduced by changes in unionization.

To sum up, the growth of unions and differential changes in hours probably do bias the estimate of quality based on compensation, although there are possible offsets related to nonpecuniary advantages and changes in the location of manufacturing. If the assumptions and inferences described above are at all close to the mark, they suggest the sector differential trend in labor quality may have been approximately .3 per cent per annum, rather than the .5 per cent implied by the compensation data. There are undoubtedly other variables that might be considered, but it seems highly unlikely that these would alter the conclusion that there was a true differential trend in labor quality.

Additional Evidence on Labor Quality

The conclusion concerning differential trends in labor quality is supported by available evidence on changes in occupational and demographic characteristics of workers in the two sectors. A test of the significance of these factors must, unfortunately, be limited to the changes between 1950 and 1960 because comparable data are not available for earlier Census years.

We see in Table 21 that the relative importance of professional and managerial workers increased substantially in the Industry sector between 1950 and 1960, and declined slightly in the Service sector. The shift to these high-skill, high-earnings occupations is evident in every

[29] Calculated from Office of Business Economics data in Tables 6-1, 6-2, and 6-4 of *The National Income and Products Accounts of the United States, 1929–1965, Statistical Tables.*

[30] See Victor R. Fuchs, *Differentials in Hourly Earnings by Region and City Size, 1959,* New York, NBER, Occasional Paper 101, 1967; and *Changes in the Location of Manufacturing in the United States Since 1929,* New Haven and London, 1962.

TABLE 21

Professional and Managerial Workers as Percentage of All Occupations, by Sector and Major Industry Group, 1950 and 1960

	Professional, Technical, and Kindred Workers		Managers, Officials, Proprietors, Except Farm		Total Professional and Managerial	
	1950	1960	1950	1960	1950	1960
Industry, total	4.3	6.7	5.8	6.4	10.1	13.1
Service, total	15.6	17.7	14.4	12.1	30.0	29.8
Industry						
Mining	3.5	7.5	4.0	5.9	7.5	13.4
Construction	3.7	4.7	8.4	9.9	12.1	14.6
Manufacturing	4.9	7.7	4.8	5.2	9.7	12.9
Transportation, communications, and public utilities [a]	3.2	4.7	7.2	7.8	10.4	12.5
Service						
Wholesale trade	2.5	3.0	20.6	19.3	23.1	22.3
Retail trade	1.9	1.7	23.7	19.3	25.6	21.0
Finance, insurance, and real estate	3.3	3.4	16.9	17.6	20.2	21.0
Business and repair services	10.0	8.9	12.9	11.9	22.9	20.8
Personal services	5.0	4.5	10.9	9.9	15.9	14.4
Private households	0.7	0.3	0.0	0.0	0.7	0.3
Entertainment and recreation services	25.2	19.9	17.2	15.3	42.4	35.2
Professional and related services	61.3	57.1	2.5	2.8	63.8	59.9
Public administration	14.4	16.7	10.2	10.9	24.6	27.6

Source: U.S. Bureau of the Census, *Census of Population 1950*, "Occupation by Industry," and *Census of Population 1960*, "Occupation by Industry," Table 1.   [a] Includes postal service and other government enterprise.

group in the Industry sector, and was particularly pronounced in mining and manufacturing. In the Service sector there was a decline in the importance of professional and managerial workers relative to other occupations in every group except finance, insurance, and real estate, and public administration.

A quantitative estimate of the differential trend in labor quality can be obtained from data on demographic characteristics. We know that at any point in time there are substantial differences in hourly earnings across groups of workers classified by age and sex. These differences are thought to reflect, for the most part, differences in labor quality as perceived by employers, resulting from differences in experience, on-the-job training, labor force attachment, and so on. Table 22 shows average hourly earnings in 1959 for fourteen age-sex groups as estimated from the 1/1,000 sample of the *1960 Census of Population.*

Using Census of Population data for 1950 and 1960, it is possible to find the percentage distribution of employment in the Industry and Service sectors in each year by age and sex. These distributions, also shown in Table 22, are multiplied by the earnings rates to obtain weighted average earnings for each sector in each year. Changes in the weighted average reflect changes in the weights, i.e., they indicate the extent to which the age-sex distributions of workers in each sector moved in the direction of higher or lower earnings. By this criterion, the Industry sector improved by 1 per cent between 1950 and 1960, while the Service sector labor force worsened by 1 per cent. The differential change was 2 per cent, or approximately .2 per cent per annum.

The Industry sector has increasingly drawn its workers from males in the prime age groups, while the Service sector has become more dependent upon females, the very young, and the very old. In addition, there is some evidence that the education levels in the Industry sector have been rising more rapidly than in the Service sector.

The distribution of white males by years of schooling in each sector in 1950 and 1960, and average hourly earnings in 1959, are shown in Table 23. These distributions were estimated from distributions of major occupations by years of schooling and of sectors by major occupations.[31] Weighted averages are obtained in the same manner as in Table 22. They indicate that the average educational level showed 1 per cent more improvement in Industry than in Service between 1950 and 1960; that

[31] A check of this method against education-sector distributions obtained from the 1/1,000 sample of the *1960 Census of Population* indicated that it provides fairly reliable estimates.

TABLE 22

Average Hourly Earnings in 1959, by Age and Sex, and Percentage
Distribution in Industry and Service Sectors, 1950 and 1960

Sex and Age	Average Hourly Earnings, 1959 (dollars)	Industry 1950	1960 (per cent)	Service 1950	1960 (per cent)
Males					
14–19	1.41	2.8	2.6	2.8	3.6
20–24	1.84	8.2	6.8	5.4	4.8
25–34	2.56	21.3	19.2	14.3	12.3
35–44	3.04	20.0	22.1	13.6	13.2
45–54	3.09	15.4	17.4	10.9	11.2
55–64	2.96	10.2	10.0	7.3	7.5
65 and over	2.83	3.1	2.4	3.4	3.2
Females					
14–19	1.34	1.3	1.0	3.6	3.5
20–24	1.54	3.4	2.3	6.0	4.9
25–34	1.74	5.2	4.1	9.2	7.5
35–44	1.74	4.5	5.6	9.8	10.1
45–54	1.77	2.9	4.3	7.8	10.3
55–64	1.75	1.3	2.1	4.4	6.0
65 and over	1.49	.3	.3	1.5	1.9
Weighted average (dollars)		2.53	2.56	2.28	2.26

Source: 1959 average hourly earnings and 1960 distribution in Industry and Service
sectors calculated from 1/1,000 sample of *1960 U.S. Censuses of Population and Housing.* The 1950 distribution of employed persons in Industry and Service sectors from
1950 U.S. Census of Population, Table 3, "Industrial Characteristics."

is, a differential rate of change of the educational component of quality
of .1 per cent per annum.[32]

The differential changes in the age, sex, and educational distributions
total .3 per cent per annum. The distribution by color was virtually un-

[32] It is important to distinguish between the rate of change of educational attainment and the actual levels at any fixed point. The rate of change has almost certainly been more rapid in Industry than in Service since 1929, but the level of
educational attainment in Service has been higher than in Industry throughout the
period. See Chapter 8.

TABLE 23

Average Hourly Earnings of White Males in 1959, by Years of
Schooling, and Percentage Distribution in Industry and
Service Sectors, 1950 and 1960

Years of School Completed	Average Hourly Earnings 1959 (dollars)	Industry		Service	
		1950	1960	1950	1960
		(per cent)		(per cent)	
0–4	1.95	6.6	4.2	4.9	3.2
5–8	2.40	36.1	29.1	27.0	21.8
9–11	2.58	22.2	24.3	18.6	20.4
12	2.78	23.0	26.1	24.6	25.8
13–15	3.33	6.6	8.7	11.1	13.0
16 and over	4.31	5.4	7.6	13.7	15.7
Weighted average (dollars)		2.66	2.75	2.87	2.94

Source: 1959 average hourly earnings from 1/1,000 sample of *1960 Censuses of Population and Housing.* Distribution of white employed males in Industry and Service sectors estimated from *1950 and 1960 Censuses of Population,* "Occupation by Industry," and "Occupation by Earnings and Education."

changed in both sectors between 1950 and 1960; therefore, .3 per cent represents the best estimate of the differential change in labor quality as revealed by demographic characteristics. It is approximately the same rate as that implied by differential change in compensation per man, 1929–65, adjusted for changes in hours and unionization.

Why should labor quality have increased more rapidly in Industry than in the Service sector? Possible explanations include the following:

1. A factor bias in the type of technological change occurring in the two sectors which increased the demand for skilled labor in Industry relative to Service.

2. A complementarity between labor quality and physical capital. The latter, as we shall see, has tended to grow more rapidly in the Industry sector, and the skilled labor may be needed to handle the more complex plant and equipment.

3. Sector differences in the elasticity of substitution between skilled and unskilled labor or between capital and unskilled labor. The price of the latter has tended to rise relative to skilled labor and capital, and firms in the Industry sector may have found it easier to substitute for unskilled labor.

4. Sector differences in the rate of growth of the price of unskilled labor. This price may have risen particularly rapidly in the Industry sector because of unionism and minimum wage legislation.

Whatever the reason, there is little doubt that the amount of human capital embodied in each worker rose more rapidly in Industry than in the Service sector since 1929. Furthermore, this differential was an important source of the sector differential in the growth of output per man.

Physical Capital and the "Residual"

Physical Capital Per Worker

The calculation of sector trends in labor input is difficult, but the problems encountered are trivial compared with those surrounding measures of physical capital. With respect to the latter, economists are not yet agreed on the "ideal" method; but even if they were, the paucity of data for early years makes it impossible to offer anything but rough impressions.

In the following discussion, use is made of two alternative estimates of the sector differential in the rate of growth of capital input, 1929–65. These alternative estimates, in my judgment, provide outer boundaries within which the true differential probably falls.

The lower boundary of the Industry-Service differential is obtained by assuming that capital per worker grew at the same rate in the two sectors.[33] This probably underestimates the differential because it is generally assumed that capital per worker grew more rapidly in Industry than in the Service sector. If we assume no differential trend in capital per worker, the differential trend in capital input is equal to the differential trend in employment, which is −.9 per cent per annum for Industry minus Service.

The upper boundary is obtained by assuming that output per unit of capital input grew at the same rate in the two sectors.[34] This probably overstates the differential because it is likely that there was some differential in capital productivity.[35] If we assume no differential trend in out-

---

[33] Some rough support for the notion that there was not much differential in the rate of growth of capital per worker can be found in estimates based on data from the Internal Revenue Service for 1929 and 1960. See Appendix D.

[34] Some rough estimates that seem to support this assumption can be found in capital stock figures presented by Bert G. Hickman for the 1945–62 period, in *Investment Demand and U.S. Economic Growth*, Washington, D.C., 1965, pp. 230–231. See Appendix D.

[35] The "residual" is larger for Industry than for Service (see Table 24), suggesting that technological change has been more rapid in Industry.

The Service Economy

TABLE 24

Sector Differentials in Rates of Growth of Output Per Unit of Labor
and Capital, Under Alternative Assumptions, 1929–65
(per cent per annum)

	Out-put	Labor Input	Capital Input [a]	Input of Labor and Capital Combined [b]	Output Per Unit of Labor and Capital Combined
Industry minus Service					
First alternative	.3	−.3	−.9	−.4	.7
Second alternative	.3	−.3	.3	−.2	.5
Industry minus Service subsector					
First alternative	.5	.2	−.4	.0	.5
Second alternative	.5	.2	.5	.3	.2

Source: See text and Appendix D.

[a] Assuming capital per worker (first alternative) or capital productivity (second alternative) changed at the same rate in both sectors.

[b] A weighted average with labor = 3 and capital = 1.

put per unit of capital, the differential trend in capital input is equal to that in output, which is .3 per cent per annum for Industry minus Service.

These alternative approaches yield an uncomfortably large range. But even the extreme values yield estimates of the residual that are not too far apart, because the Cobb-Douglas production function weights capital and labor according to their shares in national income, and capital's share has typically been only about 25 per cent. Using weights of 1 to 3, the sector residual is calculated and shown in Table 24.[36]

These calculations reveal that the sector differential in output per unit of labor and capital combined was probably about .6, with a margin of error of .15 in either direction. Similar estimates were made for Industry minus Service subsector, and they indicate a differential rate of change

[36] For more precise estimates, different weights should be used for each sector, but some experimentation with differences as large as 1 to 2 for Industry and 1 to 4 for Service, reveals that the assumption of equal weights for both sectors does not affect the results in the first decimal place. However, none of the estimates can be regarded as being accurate beyond one decimal place.

of output per unit of capital and labor combined of approximately .35, with a margin of possible error of about .15 in either direction.

These estimates of the differential trend in total factor productivity should be compared with the differential trends in output per man of 1.1 per cent and 1.0 per cent per annum for Industry minus Service and Industry minus Service subsector, respectively.

The results of Table 24 may also be compared with the estimates of output per unit of total factor input inferred from the rates of change of the implicit price deflators. This approach yields differentials of .4 per cent per annum and .5 per cent per annum, respectively.

The differential trend in output per unit of labor and capital combined, or per unit of total factor input, corresponds to the well-known "residual." It indicates the approximate importance of differential trends in technology and economies of scale. It may also reflect biases in the measures of output or factor input. Putting the question of bias aside for a moment, our best estimate of the Industry minus Service residual is .5 per cent per annum.

Possible Biases in Measurement of Residual

The residual can be biased by errors in measurement of the differential trends in output or input. We have already seen that there is probably a bias of .1 per cent per annum in the labor input differential as inferred from labor compensation. Industry sector wages, relative to the Service sector, have been raised by at least that amount because of the differential trend in unionization. Inasmuch as labor input constitutes about three-fourths of total factor input, the latter differential is also biased by about .1 per cent per annum.

Considerable critical attention has been given to the downward bias in the measurement of service output resulting from the arbitrary assumption of no productivity advance in government and some related non-profit activities. This criticism seems to be justified. Detailed studies of selected activities of the federal government have revealed significant advances in output per man-hour.[37] Years ago, Solomon Fabricant spelled out in detail many reasons why some upward trend in government productivity should be expected.[38]

The rapid rate of expansion of government activity (especially that

[37] See *Measuring Productivity of Federal Government Organizations,* Bureau of the Budget, Washington, D.C., 1964.
[38] Solomon Fabricant, *The Trend of Economic Activity in the United States Since 1900,* New York, National Bureau of Economic Research, 1952, especially Chapter 5.

of local and state governments) in itself sets up a presumption in favor of some productivity advance. As we shall see in the next chapter, there is a positive correlation between rates of growth of productivity and rates of growth of employment for seventeen service industries where an independent measure of output is available. The striking point is that the rates of growth of employment in government and other service industries for which we do not have an independent measure of output were much more rapid than for the seventeen industries. Thus, if a similar relationship held for all service industries between productivity and employment, the true rates of growth of output for the industries where zero productivity change is assumed are being seriously underestimated.

Those industries account for about one-third of the total Service sector employment. If their rate of growth of output is being underestimated by, say, 1.0 per cent per annum,[39] then the Industry-Service differential trend is biased by about .3 per cent per annum.

It is unwise, however, to conclude that this is the only bias in the measurement of the sector differential in output. Two other important matters must be considered. First, there is the possibility of a strong upward bias in the measurement of real output in retail trade. Second, there is the likelihood of some important downward biases in the measurement of output in the Industry sector, notably in construction and government enterprise.

The probable bias in retail trade is discussed in Chapter 5. David Schwartzman has argued that there has been a significant decline in the quantity and quality of service *supplied by retailers* per unit of goods sold. Part of this decline represents no diminution in service as perceived by consumers because it has been offset by services supplied by manufacturers. These include product information, guarantees, return and repair services, better control of quality and size, etc. Part of the decline has been offset by consumer-supplied services, such as selection of purchases, delivery, and storage. Schwartzman argues that the price of retail service has risen relative to other prices, and that consumers have therefore tended to substitute goods for retail service. The supermarket and other low-margin retail operations cannot be regarded as technological advances since they were part of the "state of the art" in 1929. They came into wide use as a result of the rise in the price of retail service and the growth of automobile ownership.

Over the period under study, retail trade accounted for as large a share of employment as did government. Thus, an upward bias of, say,

---

[39] This is the approximate rate of growth of output per man for the Service subsector where some independent measures of output are available.

1 per cent per annum in retailing (Schwartzman estimates the bias as above that level) would tend to offset a similar downward bias in government.

Another offsetting bias is the probable underestimation of the growth of output in construction.[40] This industry accounts for one-eighth of the Industry sector. A bias of even 1 per cent per annum could affect the sector rate of growth of output by more than .1 per cent per annum.

There are undoubtedly other biases present in the measurement of output in both sectors.[41] Most output indexes fail to capture changes in quality; this would be true for medical care as well as for nonstandardized manufacturing output. However, to the extent that quality improvement takes the form of *new* services or products, e.g., open-heart surgery or television sets, there is no satisfactory way of entering such changes into the analysis and, indeed, such changes are not accounted for in studies of output and productivity in the economy as a whole.

The problem of measuring service output relative to industry output is far from solved, but the above consideration of various biases leads to the tentative conclusion that the differential trend implied by the Office of Business Economics figures on deflated gross product may not be far from the truth. If there is some understatement of the trend in Service output relative to Industry, it probably is not large, perhaps on the order of .1 or .2 per cent per annum. It almost certainly is small relative to the observed differential trend in output per man of 1.1 per cent per annum, and can be dismissed as the major explanation of this differential.

Reexamination of the Shift to Service Employment

This chapter has concentrated on differential trends in productivity in the Industry and Service sectors between 1929 and 1965. The results can be applied to the original question posed at the end of Chapter 2: Why has employment grown so much more rapidly in Service than in Industry? The reader is again reminded that many of the measures used are imperfect; the following conclusions must, therefore, be regarded as indicating orders of magnitude rather than precise results.

1. Over the period studied, employment grew .9 per cent per annum

---

[40] See, for example, Douglas Dacy, "Productivity and Price Trends in Construction Since 1947," *Review of Economics and Statistics,* November 1965.

[41] The growth of real output in commercial banking is almost surely understated. See John A. Gorman, "Alternative Measures of Real Output and Productivity in Commercial Banks," in *Production and Productivity in the Service Industries,* V. R. Fuchs, ed., NBER, in press.

faster in Service than in Industry. *None* of this increase can be explained by a shift of final output to services. In fact, the OBE figures on deflated gross product originating show a differential trend in output in favor of Industry of about .3 per cent per annum. Correction for possible biases might reduce this by .1 or .2 per cent per annum.

2. About .1 percentage point per annum of the differential can be accounted for by a faster decline of hours in Service than in Industry. The actual differential trend in hours was somewhat greater than this, but was probably offset in part by an inverse correlation between changes in productivity and average weekly hours when weekly hours are very long.

3. About .3 percentage points per annum can be accounted for by a more rapid rise in the quality of labor in Industry than in Service. This is the differential implied by changes in demographic characteristics between 1950 and 1960. The sector differential in compensation per man, 1929–65, was .5 per cent per annum, but .2 percentage points of this is probably explained by changes in hours and unionization, and .3 percentage points by labor quality. Of all the variables identified, labor quality is probably the most important one in explaining the differential trend in employment.

4. About .1 or .2 percentage points per annum can be accounted for by the more rapid rise of capital per worker in Industry than in Service.

5. The unexplained portion of the differential trend in employment (the "residual") is about .4 or .5 per cent per annum. This differential is probably attributable to a faster rate of technological change in Industry, or to the realization of greater economies of scale in that sector.

Although the analysis presented in the chapter does support the hypothesis that productivity (however measured) has increased more rapidly in Industry than in Service, it refutes the notion that productivity does not grow at all in the service industries. A more detailed look at the extent and variability of gains in service productivity is presented in the next chapter.

4

PRODUCTIVITY DIFFERENCES
WITHIN THE SERVICE SECTOR:
A STATISTICAL ANALYSIS

This chapter and the following one are concerned primarily with differential trends in productivity within the Service sector. Whereas the previous chapter was focused at a highly aggregative level, the present one attempts to study productivity at a much finer level of industry detail. Such an approach has some clear limitations. It will not be possible to include all the service industries. Moreover, the danger of errors in the data may be greater than when we work with sector aggregates or broad industry groups; generalizations can be made only with the greatest caution. Nevertheless, we know from preliminary study that substantial differences in rates of growth of productivity exist within the Service sector. It may be that an analysis of such differences will provide some insight as to why services as a group tend to improve their output per man less rapidly than do other industries. Also, the analysis of interindustry differences in productivity within the Service sector can serve as a check on conclusions that have been reached from the study of interindustry differences within goods-producing industries. There are a number of important conceptual problems concerning the measurement of output and input in service industries which are likely to be brought out more clearly by a consideration of detailed industries. Finally, the analysis of changes in productivity over time in selected service industries may provide some guidance for the study of intercountry differences in productivity at a given point in time.

In this chapter, differential trends in productivity are examined across eighteen service industries from 1939 to 1963. The analysis is largely statistical in nature, relying heavily on correlation and regression techniques. No attempt is made to explore any particular industry in depth; Chapter 5 does precisely that: it contains a more detailed examination of productivity in personal services, retailing, and medical care.

Scope, Definitions, and Sources

The service industries discussed in this chapter are shown in Table 25. They include all of retailing, divided into ten retail trades, and eight services, mostly of the "personal service" category. Together, they account for 17 per cent of total U.S. employment in 1963, 30 per cent of Service sector employment, and 51 per cent of Service sector employment excluding government, households, and institutions.

The industries chosen were those for which there was sufficient data to obtain reasonably comparable measures of output and input for selected years during the period 1939–63.[1] Also, they are industries for which it is possible to calculate a measure of real output that is not based on labor input. It is widely recognized that where real output is estimated from labor input, as in government and much of the households and institutions categories, analysis of productivity change is scarcely possible. The selected industries' rates of growth of employment were considerably below the rate for the rest of the Service sector.[2]

A summary of the definitions, methods, and sources follows. Detailed information, as well as the raw data, are provided in Appendix G.

Real Output

For the eight services, real output was defined as receipts in constant (1954) dollars. These were estimated from receipts in current dollars, as reported in the *Census of Business,* deflated by components of the Consumer Price Index published by the Bureau of Labor Statistics (BLS).[3] To the extent that the price indexes take account of changes in the quality of services rendered, the real output measures do also.

For the ten retail trades, real output was assumed to change at the same rate as the volume of sales of goods in real terms. This was estimated from receipts by type of store, in current dollars (as reported in the *Census of Business*), deflated by price indexes prepared by David Schwartzman at the National Bureau. Because of differences in the combination of price indexes used to calculate the average price index by store type, in a few instances the deflators differ from those used by the

---

[1] The most recent *Census of Business* was conducted in 1963. The earliest Census year with comparable data for both trade and services was 1939.

[2] For 1939–63, aggregate employment in the selected industries grew at a rate of 1.9 per cent per annum compared with 3.2 per cent for the rest of the Service sector. For the period 1948–63, the rates were 1.1 and 3.0 per cent, respectively.

[3] Prices for hotels and motels were obtained from Horwath and Horwath, *Hotel Operations in 1963.*

TABLE 25

Level of Employment and Percentage of Total U.S. Employment
in Eighteen Selected Service Industries, 1963

Industry	Level of Employment (thousands)	Percentage of U.S. Total
Services		
Auto repair	414	.61
Barber shops	180	.27
Beauty shops	345	.51
Dry cleaning	268	.40
Hotels and motels	544	.80
Laundries	346	.51
Motion picture theaters	106	.16
Shoe repair	34	.05
Total	2,238	3.30
Retail trades		
Apparel stores	659	.97
Automobile dealers	860	1.27
Drug stores	365	.54
Eating and drinking places	1,933	2.85
Food stores	1,490	2.20
Furniture and appliances	459	.68
Gasoline stations	682	1.01
General merchandise	1,434	2.12
Lumber dealers	466	.69
Other	870	1.28
Total	9,217	13.60
Total, 18 selected service industries	11,455	16.90

Source: U.S. Bureau of the Census, *1963 Census of Business.* Coverage details are in Appendix G. U.S. employment is the number of persons engaged in production from U.S. Department of Commerce, *The National Income and Product Accounts of the United States, 1929–65, Statistical Tables.*

Office of Business Economics. Schwartzman's indexes were based on detailed commodity components of the BLS Consumer Price Index weighted by the importance of each commodity in each store type as reported in the *1948 Census of Business*. The BLS price indexes for retail sales of commodities do not allow for changes in quality of service rendered by retailers.[4]

The real output measures for the eighteen industries should be considered only as approximations; they are not exactly equivalent either to the gross measures of physical output that are possible for some goods industries or to the estimates of real gross product originating that would be obtained through separate deflation of outputs and inputs.

Employment

The basic employment concept used is "persons engaged" as defined by the Office of Business Economics of the U.S. Department of Commerce. This is estimated from *Census of Business* data on employment and payrolls, with part-time wage and salary employees converted to full-time equivalents by assuming that their share of total wage and salary employment is equal to their share of total payroll. In addition to wage and salary workers, persons engaged includes self-employed proprietors, as reported in the *Census of Business,* all of whom are counted as employed full-time.

The estimates of the number of self-employed may be subject to considerable error because it is difficult to obtain complete coverage of numerous small firms and because the Bureau of the Census definitions of the minimum-sized firm to be included have varied from one census to another. It is some comfort to note that the number of self-employed reported in the *Census of Business* for 1948 corresponds closely to the number reported in the *Census of Population* for 1950 for the eighteen industries.

The importance of obtaining an accurate count of the self-employed is considerable; they account for a significant fraction of total employment in many of the service industries, as may be seen in Table 26. The employment estimates for these industries are probably not as reliable as those that can be obtained for manufacturing or for other industries in which the self-employed play a much less important role.

Doubts may arise concerning the accuracy of the figures on self-employment, but the situation with respect to unpaid family workers is far worse. The *Census of Business* does not regularly report the number

---

[4] For a discussion of possible biases in the measurement of real output in retail trade, see Chapter 5.

TABLE 26

Number of Self-Employed as a Percentage of Total Employment
in Eighteen Service Industries, Selected Years, 1939–63

Industry	1939	1948	1954	1958	1963
Services					
Auto repair	48.6	41.3	40.4	34.9	33.1
Barber shops	66.9	61.8	62.3	60.7	61.4
Beauty shops	47.4	47.8	46.6	46.7	44.8
Dry cleaning	37.9	24.4	24.4	23.6	22.1
Hotels and motels	10.4	12.2	12.3	14.1	11.6
Laundries	8.2	10.2	9.2	10.0	12.8
Motion picture theaters	5.8	5.0	6.1	7.7	7.0
Shoe repair	71.9	69.1	68.4	64.8	65.2
Retail trades					
Apparel stores	19.5	15.9	15.8	15.0	13.8
Automobile dealers	11.7	11.2	10.0	10.5	9.0
Drug stores	22.1	17.2	17.0	14.7	12.4
Eating and drinking places	29.3	23.7	23.1	21.0	16.9
Food stores	44.8	38.1	31.6	26.7	21.6
Furniture and appliances	17.7	18.4	21.6	21.5	20.8
Gasoline stations	52.0	44.0	38.9	35.8	31.2
General merchandise	8.8	5.4	5.9	6.2	3.2
Lumber dealers	21.8	16.8	17.4	19.9	16.5
Other	34.8	28.9	34.0	30.5	28.5

Source: U.S. Bureau of the Census, *Census of Business.* Coverage details are in
Appendix G.

of such workers, and no attempt has been made in this study to include
them in the measure of total employment. Some data for the eighteen
service industries reported in the 1948 *Census of Business* indicate that
unpaid family workers amounted to about 8 per cent of total employment. The *Census of Population* for 1950, on the other hand, presents
figures showing that unpaid family workers accounted for less than 2
per cent of employment in these industries.[5]

[5] The exclusion of unpaid family workers probably exerts a downward bias on
the estimates of the growth of output per man because paid employment probably rose more rapidly than unpaid employment over the period studied. David
Schwartzman, in the study of productivity growth in distribution that he is preparing for the National Bureau, estimates that the annual rate of growth of output
per man in retailing, 1929–58, would be raised .06 per cent if unpaid family
workers were included.

Labor Input

Differentials in rates of change of labor input are estimated from rates of change in labor compensation. The rationale for this approach was described in Chapter 3. Labor compensation for wage and salary workers was calculated from payroll data in the *Census of Business.* Compensation per man for self-employed was estimated using a method similar to that described in Chapter 3.[6]

Output Per Man and Per Unit of Labor Input

Output per man is real output divided by employment; output per unit of labor input is real output divided by labor input. Absolute percentage rates of change for this measure have not been calculated because of the way in which the relative percentage rates of change of labor input are estimated.[7] Relative values were obtained and used to rank the industries.

Output Per Unit of Total Input

If one is interested only in ranking the industries according to their relative rates of change of output per unit of total input, an estimate can be obtained for the eight services by using the reciprocal of the rates of change of price. The rationale is that, under competitive conditions, rates of change of price of service industries that have very little material input will tend to be inversely correlated with the rates of change

[6] It is assumed that the same percentage of proprietors' income represents returns to labor for total trade and for total services as in Chapter 3. Within a major industry, it is assumed that the same relative annual earnings of proprietors in each detailed industry prevailed as that shown by the 1/1,000 sample for 1959. Specifically: Compute the 1959 ratio of annual earnings per proprietor of each of the ten retail trades relative to wholesale trade (R). Then multiply the ratios (R) by the number of proprietors (P) in each industry. Obtain a percentage distribution of these products. For the ith year, the share of trade proprietors' labor income going to the jth industry is

$$S_{ij} = \frac{R_j P_{ij}}{\sum_{j=1}^{11} R_j P_{ij}}$$

where $\sum_{j=1}^{11} S_{ij}$ is equal to 90 per cent of the sum of (1) income of unincorporated enterprises and (2) inventory valuation adjustment of unincorporated enterprises from the OBE. For the eight selected services, the ratio is computed relative to "all other services." For those, labor's share of entrepreneurial income is 95 per cent.

[7] See pp. 49 and 50, Chapter 3.

of productivity. The implicit assumption is that the price of a composite unit of total input changes at the same rate in all industries.

Annual Percentage Rates of Change

The average annual percentage rate of change between 1939 and 1963 and between 1948 and 1963 [8] for each variable was calculated using continuous compounding between the initial and terminal years. The percentage rate of change of a variable, formed by dividing one variable by another (e.g., real output per man), is equal to the percentage rate of change of the numerator minus the percentage rate of change of the denominator.

It should be noted that such trend measures are influenced by the cyclical position of the initial or terminal year. They may also be influenced by random events or errors in the data for one of those years. The question of cyclical effect as opposed to trend is most important for comparisons based on 1939 because the economy had not yet fully recovered from the Depression, and the unemployment rate in that year was 17.2 per cent. The years 1948 and 1963 were characterized by a much higher level of activity than 1939. The unemployment rates for those years were 3.8 and 5.7 per cent, respectively. In an attempt to modify the cyclical effects, rates of change were also derived by fitting regressions across *Census of Business* years including 1954 and 1958, but the rates of change obtained in this way differed very little from those between terminal years.

Empirical Results

Rates of Change, 1939–63

Table 27 presents average percentage rates of change for each of the eighteen service industries. Table 28 gives comparable figures for the aggregates, the total of the eighteen service industries, the manufacturing industry total, the Industry and Service sector totals, and the total economy. These tables are more or less self-explanatory and only a few brief comments need be made.

Perhaps the first and the most important point is that sixteen of the eighteen service industries show positive rates of change of output per man. There may be some upward bias in the rates of change of real output in retail trade (see Chapter 5) but these results suggest caution in

---

[8] Analysis over a longer time span is preferable, but the 1948–63 period is included because comparisons between these years are free of the major cyclical element present in the 1939–63 comparison.

TABLE 27

Average Annual Percentage Rates of Changes of Output Per Man and Related Variables, Eighteen Selected Service Industries, 1939–63 and 1948–63

Industry	1939–63				1948–63			
	Real Output Per Man	Real Output	Employment	Compensation Per Man	Real Output Per Man	Real Output	Employment	Compensation Per Man
Services								
Auto repair	3.5	7.3	3.8	5.8	2.0	5.5	3.5	3.6
Barber shops	.6	.5	-.1	6.2	.3	1.3	1.0	3.9
Beauty shops	1.5	4.0	2.5	5.9	1.7	6.7	5.0	3.8
Dry cleaning	2.6	4.5	1.9	5.1	1.7	.9	-.8	3.2
Hotels and motels	.9	2.6	1.7	5.6	-.5	.8	1.4	3.4
Laundries	1.8	2.6	.9	5.4	.0	.8	.8	2.5
Motion picture theaters	-2.7	-3.1	-.4	3.3	-3.2	-6.3	-3.2	2.1
Shoe repair	1.1	-2.2	-3.2	6.1	1.3	-3.0	-4.3	2.9
Retail trades								
Apparel stores	1.0	2.8	1.9	4.4	1.7	2.0	.4	2.4
Automobile dealers	2.2	5.1	2.8	5.7	2.2	3.6	1.4	3.3
Drug stores	2.8	4.8	2.0	5.0	2.3	3.6	1.3	2.9
Eating and drinking places	-.2	2.3	2.6	4.9	.2	1.6	1.4	2.2
Food stores	2.4	3.5	1.1	5.7	2.8	3.6	.8	2.8
Furniture and appliances	2.9	5.4	2.4	5.1	3.5	3.4	-.1	3.1
Gasoline stations	3.4	5.2	1.8	5.1	2.1	4.9	2.8	2.2
General merchandise	1.5	3.7	2.2	4.6	2.3	3.8	1.4	2.5
Lumber dealers	1.4	3.2	1.8	5.1	1.2	.2	-1.0	3.2
Other	2.2	4.2	1.9	4.9	1.1	2.8	1.6	2.7

Source: Appendix Table G-1.

TABLE 28

Average Annual Percentage Rates of Change of Output Per Man and Related Variables, Industry Groups and Total Economy, 1939–63 and 1948–63

	1939–63				1948–63			
	Real Output Per Man	Real Output	Employment	Compensation Per Man	Real Output Per Man	Real Output	Employment	Compensation Per Man
8 Services, total	1.4	2.9	1.6	5.5	.3	1.6	1.3	3.3
10 Retail trades, total	1.7	3.7	2.0	5.1	1.8	2.9	1.1	2.6
18 Selected service industries, total	1.6	3.6	1.9	5.2	1.5	2.6	1.1	2.8
Manufacturing, total	2.3	4.6	2.3	6.3	2.9	3.5	.6	4.8
Service sector, total	1.8	3.9	2.1	5.8	.6	3.8	2.2	4.1
Industry sector, total	2.5	4.5	2.0	6.2	3.0	3.3	.4	4.8
Total economy	2.5	4.0	1.6	6.3	2.5	3.4	1.0	4.4

Note: The real output measures used in this table correspond to gross product originating, except for the eight services and their portion of the eighteen selected services; the output measure for these is based on deflated gross sales.

Source: Appendix Table G-1.

assuming that productivity cannot or does not increase in service industries. However, Table 28 does show that the rate of increase for the services and the retail trades as a group was not as rapid as for manufacturing, the total Industry sector, or the total economy.

If service industries generally tend to show positive rates of change of output per man, a serious question arises concerning the practice of assuming a zero rate of change for government and other service industries—those for which no convenient method of estimating output, independently of employment, has yet been found. Why not instead assume some constant positive rate of increase, e.g., 1 per cent per annum? It could be argued that such a procedure would be no more arbitrary and perhaps more accurate. Alternatively, one could assume for such industries the same average rate of increase as is found for those service industries for which an independent measure of output is available.[9]

The practice of assuming no differences in output per man for service industries across countries at a given point in time must also be questioned. Is it not likely that some of the same factors that have contributed to increases in output per man in U.S. service industries over time such as increased size of transactions might also be contributing to international differences in output per man at a given time?

Another point to be noted is the tremendous diversity of experience among the eighteen service industries. In five cases, output per man actually grew more rapidly than in the total economy. The range of variation for output and employment was also very great; only compensation per man tended to change at similar rates in the various industries.

Rates of Change, 1948–63

In Tables 27 and 28, output per man in manufacturing shows a higher rate of increase for the 1948–63 period, as do half of the retail trades, but the services all show higher rates for 1939–63. A tentative explanation is that *cyclical* fluctuations in output per man are more important in services, where employment is relatively insensitive to changes in demand and output. (This hypothesis is explored in Chapter 7.) We again observe tremendous diversity among the eighteen industries in rates of growth of all the variables except compensation per man.

Tables 29 and 30 present data for seventeen service industries,[10]

---

[9] This is the practice followed implicitly in the construction and use of price indexes. If, for instance, we can measure the price change for certain components of medical care but not for others, we do not assume that the unmeasured components had zero price change; we assume that they changed at the same rate as the measured components.

[10] "Other retail trade" is omitted from the rankings because it is a miscellaneous category of questionable significance for economic analyses across industries.

Rankings of Seventeen Selected Service Industries, Average Annual Percentage Rates of Change of Output Per Man and Related Variables, 1939–63

Industry	Real Output Per Man	Real Output Per Unit of Labor Input	Real Output	Employment	Compensation Per Man	Real Output Per Unit of Total Input [a] (8 services only)
Auto repair	17	14	17	17	15	7
Gasoline stations	16	17	15	7	9	—
Furniture and appliances	15	15 [b]	16	15	7	—
Drug stores	14	15 [b]	13	11	5	—
Dry cleaning	13	13	12	10	6	8
Food stores	12	11	9	5	14	—
Automobile dealers	11	9 [b]	14	16	13	—
Laundries	10	8	6	4	10	5
General merchandise	9	12	10	12	3	—
Beauty shops	8	6	11	14	11	6
Lumber dealers	7	7	8	8	8	—
Shoe repair	6	4	2	1	16	2
Apparel stores	5	9 [b]	7	9	2	—
Hotels and motels	4	5	5	6	12	3 [b]
Barber shops	3	2	3	3	17	1
Eating and drinking places	2	3	4	15	4	—
Motion picture theaters	1	1	1	2	1	3 [b]

Note: Highest value of each variable is given the highest rank.
Rankings were computed from the more detailed data underlying Table 27.

Source: Table 27 and Appendix Table G–1.

[a] Based on the reciprocal of the price index.
[b] Rankings of these industries are halfway between the figures shown and the next highest figure.

TABLE 30

Rankings of Seventeen Selected Service Industries, Average Annual Percentage Rates of Change of Output Per Man and Related Variables, 1948–63

Industry	Real Output Per Man	Real Output Per Unit of Labor Input	Real Output	Employment	Compensation Per Man	Real Output Per Unit of Total Input [a] (8 services only)
Furniture and appliances	17	14	10	5	10	—
Food stores	16	17	14	7	7	—
General merchandise	15	15	12	14	5	—
Drug stores	14	13	11	10	9	—
Automobile dealers	13	11	13	13	13	—
Gasoline stations	12	16	15	15	3	5
Auto repair	11	8	16	16	15	8
Dry cleaning	10	10	6	4	12	7
Beauty shops	9	5	17	17	16	—
Apparel stores	8	12	9	6	4	6
Shoe repair	7	9	2	1	8	—
Lumber dealers	6	6	3	3	11	1
Barber shops	5	3	7	9	17	—
Eating and drinking places	4	7	8	12	2	—
Laundries	3	4	4 [b]	8	6	4
Hotels and motels	2	2	4 [b]	11	14	2
Motion picture theaters	1	1	1	2	1	3

Note: Rankings were computed from the more detailed data underlying Table 29.

Source: Table 28 and Appendix Table G–1.

[a] Based on the reciprocal of the price index.
[b] Rankings of these industries are halfway between the figures shown and the next highest figure.

ranked according to the various measures of output, input, and productivity. Table 31 shows the correlations between the rankings for 1939–63 and 1948–63. Most of these correlations are significantly different from zero; this is not surprising since there is a great deal of overlap between these two periods. The correlations are sufficiently below 1.00, however, to indicate that the inclusion or exclusion of 1939 can make a substantial difference, especially for the retail trades.

Relation Between Changes in Output Per Man and Other Variables

Given the substantial variation among service industries in rates of change of output per man, it is of interest to see whether the same pattern of variation can be found in some of the other variables, i.e., whether rates of change are correlated across industries.

The relation between industry rates of growth and output per man is of particular interest. Many previous studies have found a significant positive correlation between these two variables. However, these studies were mostly confined to or dominated by manufacturing industries. When

TABLE 31

Coefficients of Rank Correlation Between Average Annual Percentage
Rates of Change of Output Per Man and Related Variables,
Selected Service Industries, 1939–63 and 1948–63

	Seventeen Selected Service Industries	Eight Services	Nine Retail Trades
Real output per man	.76	.81	.65
Real output per unit of labor input	.78	.64	.76
Real output	.75	.75	.62
Employment	.62	.81	.17
Compensation per man	.66	.64	.45
Real output per unit of total input	n.a.	.71	n.a.

Note: Minimum values of rank correlation coefficients for various levels of statistical significance (two-tailed test):

α	$N = 8$	$N = 9$	$N = 10$	$N = 25$
.10	.64	.58	.56	.34
.05	.73	.68	.65	.40
.01	.86	.82	.79	.53

Source: Tables 29 and 30.

TABLE 32

Coefficients of Rank Correlation, Average Annual Percentage Rates of Change of Output Per Man and Related Variables, Across Selected Service Industries, 1939–63

	Real Output Per Unit of Labor Input	Real Output	Employment	Compensation Per Man	Real Output Per Unit of Total Input
Real output per man					
17 service industries	.93	.91	.42	.17	n.a.
8 services	.98	.90	.71	−.05	.81
9 retail trades	.91	.90	−.27	.52	n.a.
Real output per unit of labor input					
17 service industries		.89	.44	−.11	n.a.
8 services		.95	.81	−.10	.85
9 retail trades		.81	−.28	.15	n.a.
Real output					
17 service industries			.70	.05	n.a.
8 services			.93	−.05	.85
9 retail trades			.10	.42	n.a.
Employment					
17 service industries				−.15	n.a.
8 services				−.10	.80
9 retail trades				−.28	n.a.
Compensation per man					
17 service industries					n.a.
8 services					−.53
9 retail trades					n.a.

Source: Table 29.

TABLE 33

Coefficients of Rank Correlation, Average Annual Percentage Rates of Change of Output Per Man and Related Variables, Across Selected Service Industries, 1948–63

	Real Output Per Unit of Labor Input	Real Output	Employment	Compensation Per Man	Real Output Per Unit of Total Input
Real output per man					
17 service industries	.89	.69	.25	.08	n.a.
8 services	.86	.71	.33	.48	.69
9 retail trades	.72	.48	−.02	.35	n.a.
Real output per unit of labor input					
17 service industries		.55	.13	−.27	n.a.
8 services		.34	−.10	.12	.83
9 retail trades		.73	.37	−.25	n.a.
Real output					
17 service industries			.83	.21	n.a.
8 services			.84	.85	.26
9 retail trades			.80	−.08	n.a.
Employment					
17 service industries				.25	n.a.
8 services				.74	−.05
9 retail trades				−.42	n.a.
Compensation per man					
17 service industries					n.a.
8 services					−.10
9 retail trades					n.a.

Source: Table 30.

TABLE 34

Summary of Coefficients of Rank Correlation Between Rates of Change
of Output Per Man and Output and Employment, Across Industries

	Output Per Man and	
	Output	Employment
1. U.S., 1939–63 – 17 service industries	.91	.42
2. U.S., 1948–63 – 17 service industries	.69	.25
3. U.S., 1899–1937 – 56 manufacturing industries	.73	.31
4. U.S., 1899–1953 – 33 industry groups	.64 [a]	.33 [a]
5. U.S., 1899–1954 – 80 manufacturing industries	.67 [b]	.33 [c]
6. U.K., 1924–50 – 28 manufacturing industries	.83	.57
7. U.K., 1954–63 – 28 manufacturing industries	.69	.04
8. U.S., 1929–65 – 10 major industry groups	−.18	−.88

Source: 1, Table 32; 2, Table 33; 3, Fabricant, *Employment in Manufacturing;* 4
and 5, Kendrick, *Productivity Trends in the U.S.;* 6, Salter, *Productivity and Technical
Change;* 7, *ibid.,* second edition; 8, Fuchs, *Productivity Trends.*
[a] Based on output per unit of total factor input.
[b] Based on output per adjusted man-hour.
[c] Based on output per man-hour.

this relationship was tested across ten major industry groups in the United
States, no correlation between growth and productivity could be observed.[11] In this chapter the hypothesis is tested across the seventeen
service industries.

Tables 32 and 33 show the coefficients of rank correlation for every
combination of variables. Correlations between rates of change of output
per man ($\dot{O}$–$\dot{E}$) and output ($\dot{O}$) and employment ($\dot{E}$) are considered
first. Either output or employment can be used to measure industry rates
of growth; therefore, we must look at both sets of correlations. The correlation with output tends to be biased upward, and the reverse is true
of employment.[12]

The coefficients shown in Tables 32 and 33 tend to support the hypothesis of a positive correlation between growth and productivity. Table
34 indicates that the relationship found among the seventeen service

[11] See Chapter 3.
[12] Whenever a correlation coefficient is calculated between one variable and
another which is based in part on the first, the danger of spurious correlation arises.
For the correlations described above, to the extent that there are errors in the
observations, these errors alone would tend to produce a positive correlation for
($\dot{O}$–$\dot{E}$): $\dot{O}$, and a negative correlation for ($\dot{O}$–$\dot{E}$): $\dot{E}$.

industries is of the same order of magnitude as that found by other investigators for manufacturing industries.

One way of circumventing the problem of spurious correlation between output per man and output, or between output per man and employment, is to fit by least-squares two equations relating changes in output and changes in employment (see Charts 7 and 8). In one equation, output is the dependent variable; in the other equation, the relationship is reversed. If there is no correlation between industry rates of growth (measured by output or employment) and industry rates of change of output per man, the slope of the regression line between output and employment should equal unity. Regression lines with slopes greater than unity indicate a positive correlation. Slopes smaller than unity indicate a negative relationship.[13]

The regression lines for Charts 7 and 8 are as follows:

1939–63

$$\dot{O} = \quad .914 + 1.433\dot{E}$$
$$\qquad\qquad (.217)$$

$$\overline{R}^2 = .727$$

$$\dot{E} = -.088 + \quad .519\dot{O}$$
$$\qquad\qquad (.079)$$

1948–63

$$\dot{O} = 1.095 + 1.253\dot{E}$$
$$\qquad\qquad (.167)$$

$$\overline{R}^2 = .776$$

$$\dot{E} = -.546 + \quad .631\dot{O}$$
$$\qquad\qquad (.084)$$

The slopes of the lines on the charts when employment is dependent are the reciprocals of the regression coefficients. In all cases the slope of the regression line is considerably above unity. These results, however, depend primarily on the relationship among the services; the retail trades alone yield an ambiguous result.

Both the rank correlations and the regression slopes indicate that the relation between growth and productivity was stronger for 1939–63 than for 1948–63. This probably reflects a cyclical relation between growth and productivity in addition to the secular one.

The finding of a positive relation between industry rates of growth and changes in productivity raises an interesting question about productivity trends in those service industries not included in this chapter.[14]

---

[13] See Fabricant, *Employment in Manufacturing*, p. 87.
[14] I am grateful to Edward F. Denison for calling this question to my attention.

CHART 7

Relation Between Average Annual Percentage Rates of Change of Real Output and Employment, Seventeen Selected Service Industries, 1939–63

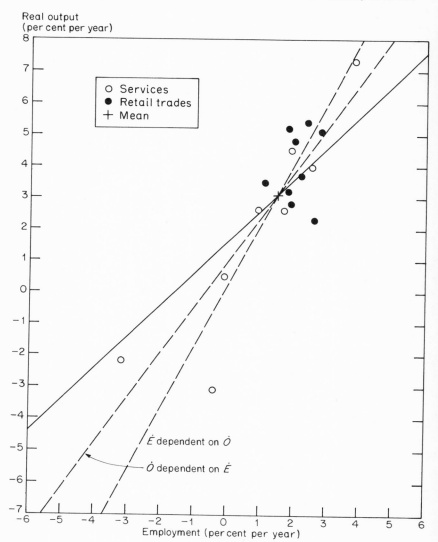

CHART 8

Relation Between Average Annual Percentage Rates of Change of Real Output and Employment, Seventeen Selected Service Industries, 1948–63

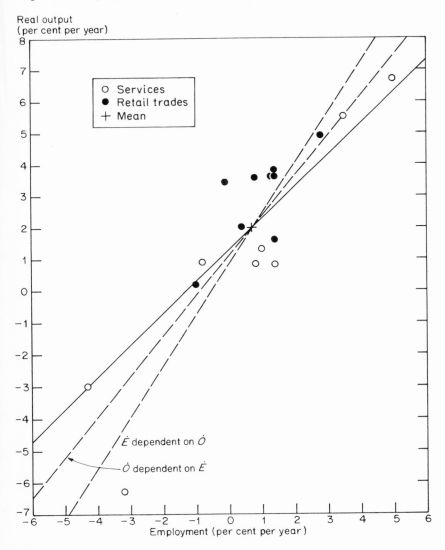

As can be seen in Table 35, the excluded industries had, on average, much faster rates of growth of employment than did the seventeen included industries. If we were to assume that the relationships shown in Charts 7 and 8 between growth of output and growth of employment extended to the excluded industries, we would have to conclude that output per man in those industries grew much more rapidly than in the seventeen industries covered in the present study. Present measures of real gross product originating do not yield that conclusion, but the assumptions underlying those measures are the subject of considerable

TABLE 35

Annual Rates of Change of Employment: Comparison of Twenty Excluded Service Industries with Seventeen Selected Service Industries, 1939–63
(per cent per annum)

Industry	1939–63	1948–63
Federal general government, military	8.64	4.12
Miscellaneous professional services	7.84	4.80
Miscellaneous business services	5.08	6.24
Nonprofit membership organizations	5.05	3.54
Federal general government, civilian	4.92	1.62
Educational services	4.29	4.50
Medical and other health services	4.22	4.55
Credit agencies, holding and other investment companies	4.10	5.96
Banking	3.80	3.79
State and local, public education	3.57	4.73
Insurance carriers	2.84	2.72
State and local general government, nonschool except work relief	2.80	3.29
Amusement and recreation services except motion pictures	2.58	2.19
Miscellaneous repair services	2.23	.84
Wholesale trade	2.05	1.18
Security and commodity brokers	1.95	4.46
Real estate	1.66	.89
Insurance agents, brokers and services	1.59	3.49
Legal services	1.25	2.73
Private households	−1.26	−.18
Median of 20 excluded industries	3.20	3.52
Median of 17 selected services	1.86	1.00

Source: U.S. Office of Business Economics, *The National Income and Product Accounts of the United States, 1929–1965,* Table 6–6.

TABLE 36

Coefficients of Rank Correlation Between Change in Self-Employment as
Percentage of Total Employment and Rate of Change of Output Per Man,
Output, and Employment, 1939–63

		1939–63	1948–63
ΔS: $\dot{O}$–$\dot{E}$	17 service industries	−.44	−.41
	8 services	−.48	−.79
	9 retail trades	−.10	.03
ΔS: $\dot{O}$	17 service industries	−.33	−.56
	8 services	−.44	−.44
	9 retail trades	.30	−.46
ΔS: $\dot{E}$	17 service industries	−.15	−.44
	8 services	−.30	−.26
	9 retail trades	−.63	−.59

Note: ΔS = Percentage self-employed in terminal year minus percentage self-employed
in initial year. $\dot{Q}$, $\dot{E}$, $\dot{O}$–$\dot{E}$ = Average annual percentage rate of change of real output,
employment, and real output per man, respectively.
Source: Tables 26, 29, and 30.

debate. However, no widely acceptable alternative measures of real output for the excluded industries are available.

The results shown in Tables 32 and 33 parallel those reported for manufacturing in one other respect, namely, the absence of any correlation between changes in output per man and changes in compensation per man. This result would appear to refute the hypothesis that differential changes in the quality of labor can make a significant contribution to the explanation of differential changes in output per man in these industries. On the other hand, there have been very large differences in rates of change of compensation per man between the service industries and manufacturing.

One other set of correlations was run to test the relation between changes in output per man and changes in the percentage of employment accounted for by self-employed. It has been argued that large numbers of the self-employed are not very active and have very low productivity.[15]

[15] Edward F. Denison, "Improved Allocation of Labor as a Source of Higher European Growth Rates," in Michael J. Brennan, ed., *Patterns of Market Behavior*, Providence, 1965.

Their alternative to self-employment may be unemployment. One would expect, therefore, that industries which showed a large absolute decline in the percentage of employment accounted for by self-employed might show large increases in output per man. The coefficients of rank correlation shown in Table 36 provide some slight support for this hypothesis, particularly with respect to the eight services. The same table also shows the correlations between changes in the self-employment percentage and the percentage rates of change of output and employment. There is apparently some intercorrelation among all these variables, and much more work needs to be done before any conclusions concerning causality would be warranted.[16]

This brief statistical analysis of changes in productivity and other variables within the Service sector tends to support conclusions based on studies of manufacturing industries. In appraising these results, it is well to recall that the measures of real output and productivity can be considered only as approximations. Additional insights into some of the conceptual and statistical problems require more intensive scrutiny of particular industries.

The three case studies to be discussed in the next chapter are intended to probe more deeply into the relation between growth, technological change, labor quality, etc., in order to increase our understanding of the process of productivity change.

[16] See Irving F. Leveson, "Nonfarm Self-employment in the U.S.," unpublished Ph.D. dissertation, Columbia University, January, 1968.

5

PRODUCTIVITY IN SERVICES:
THREE CASE STUDIES

Retail trade, barber and beauty shops, and medical care are important and diverse areas of the Service sector. These industries are large; they account for more than one-third of total Service sector employment— and for almost one-half if government is excluded. They are also representative in several respects. Many of the problems to be discussed in connection with retailing are also found in wholesaling and banking; the discussion of medical care has important analogues in education, religious and welfare services, and other professional services; and the lessons to be drawn from the case study of barber and beauty shops could be applied profitably to the study of laundry and dry cleaning and other personal services.

In two of the case studies, medical care and retailing, the problem of measuring real output is particularly great and receives major attention. Other issues that are given careful scrutiny in one or more of the studies are the quality of labor, the role of demand, and technological change.

Retail Trade

Retail trade is one of the largest industry groups in the economy. In 1967 there were 10 million persons engaged in retailing, as many as in mining, construction, transportation, communications, and public utilities combined. The course of productivity in retail trade has a significant impact on the trend for the economy as a whole, and the problem of measuring productivity correctly in this industry group is probably second only in importance and difficulty to that encountered for government. Because the problems with respect to government are well-known many investigators confine their analysis to productivity trends in the private economy. Such analyses are heavily influenced by trends in retailing, and more explicit attention to the conceptual and statistical problems encountered in measuring retail output is therefore desirable.

Problems of Measuring Output

The Office of Business Economics and most other investigators measure the real output of retail trade by attempting to measure the real quantity of goods sold by retailers. The usual method is to deflate current dollar sales by an index of retail prices. The deflation is done separately for each retail store "type" where type is defined primarily in terms of the kinds of goods sold, e.g., food, apparel, lumber. The output of each type, weighted by the average gross margin [1] of that type, is summed in order to obtain the output for total retail trade. This assumes that differences in gross margin among store types reflect differences in the output produced by the retail store for each dollar's worth of goods sold.

The basic underlying assumption of this method is that the quantity and quality of service supplied by retailers per constant dollar's worth of goods sold remains constant over time within each store type.[2] This assumption is open to a number of objections; there are many aspects of retailing that may vary over time or cross sectionally.

1. Terms of sale: credit, delivery, guarantees, replacement of parts, repairs and services, return privileges.

2. Amenities provided to the customer: heating, air-conditioning, lighting, music, rest rooms.

3. Convenience: location with respect to homes, places of work, and other stores; availability of parking facilities; store hours.

4. Aids to customer choice: variety of merchandise, displays, "test drives," "home demonstrations," "try-on" privileges.

5. Sales personnel: intelligence, information, courtesy, attention.

6. Demands on customer: time and effort required to accomplish purchase.

The period since 1929 has witnessed many changes in retailing, most notably in food, furniture and appliances, and general merchandise stores. The advent of supermarkets, "discount" houses, and "promotional" department stores is too well-known to need recounting here. The major difference between the newer type retail operations and the older ones is that the new ones typically operate with lower gross margins. Some observers interpret the lower margin as evidence of greater efficiency;

---

[1] Sales minus cost of goods sold, all divided by sales.

[2] However, the method of calculating the retail price indexes does partially reflect shifts within store types. See p. 101.

others believe it indicates that the store is providing less service (and hence less output) per dollar of goods sold.

The method used by the Bureau of Labor Statistics to calculate the price indexes that are used to deflate current dollar retail sales actually results in a compromise between the two positions described above. This is because the BLS specifications for a commodity typically include the "kind" of store as well as the characteristics of the commodity itself.[3] Thus, if bread sells for thirty cents per loaf in a small grocery store, and twenty-five cents per loaf in a supermarket, the BLS price index for bread would show no change, even if there was a marked shift of purchases from one kind of store to another, as long as the price in each store remained unchanged.

The following numerical example may help to clarify this point:

Kind of Store	Wholesale Price	Margin	Retail Price	Quantity	Sales
		Period 1			
Small grocery	$.20	$.10	$.30	80	$2.40
Supermarket	.20	.05	.25	20	.50
				100	$2.90
		Period 2			
Small grocery	$.20	$.10	$.30	20	$ .60
Supermarket	.20	.05	.25	80	2.00
				100	$2.60

According to present methods of measuring real output in retailing in the United States, the index of real output would be 89.7 (i.e., 2.60 ÷ 2.90) because the price index used to deflate sales would be unchanged from period 1 to period 2. Those economists who regard the supermarket as simply a more efficient way of providing the same retail output per loaf of bread sold would say that this output index is biased downward. They would argue that the index should be 100, on the grounds that the same quantity of real goods was sold by retailers in both periods.

Others might argue that the index is biased upward. They would say that the difference in gross margin reflects differences in the quantity and quality of service supplied per loaf of bread sold. From this point of view,

[3] The term "kind" of store is used here to denote the form of operation, e.g., high margin or low margin within a particular store type. Food stores are a "type"; supermarkets are one "kind" within that type.

the real output index should be 66.7, the result obtained if deflated sales in each kind of store is weighted by its own margin and then summed.[4]

Where does the truth lie? No precise answer is possible. The fact that there has been a dramatic shift of business to the low-margin kinds of stores lends some support to the view that they are offering the same or similar service more efficiently. On the other hand, some high-margin stores continue to flourish, and it is apparent that the credit, delivery, and other services that they offer (and the low-margin store does not) are valued by some consumers.

If, in the example given above, we were to assume that one-half of the difference in margin represents greater efficiency, and one-half represents more output per loaf of bread sold in the high-margin store, we would conclude that the index of real output should be 84.2.[5]

An additional problem arises because, although the BLS commodity specifications identify the kind of store, they do not specify the quantity or quality of retail service supplied in that store. Thus, if a particular store altered its service over time, this would not be reflected in either the price index or the index of real output.

Casual observation suggests that many of the high-margin retailers, faced with the competition of the low-margin stores, have tended to reduce service in order to hold down prices and keep business. This is evident in the trend toward self-selection in department stores and self-service in small grocery stores.

Casual observation also suggests a number of reasons why a diminution in retail service per constant dollar of sales is not always perceived as such by the consumer. Many of the services that were formerly provided by the retailer, such as product information, guarantees, return privileges, and so on, are now supplied by the manufacturer. From the point of view of the consumer, and in terms of measuring real output in the economy as a whole, there has been no change. But in terms of allocating real output between retail trade and manufacturing, this trend has probably resulted in overstating the growth of output and productivity in retailing, and understating it in manufacturing.

To be sure, there may be some respects in which retailers have generally upgraded their service over time. Most stores are now air-conditioned; they probably have better lighting; and the display fixtures are probably more attractive and more functional. On the other hand, one cannot help being impressed with the extent to which prepackaging, pre-

[4] $\dfrac{20\ (.10) + 80\ (.05)}{80\ (.10) + 20\ (.05)}$ [5] $\dfrac{20\ (.10) + 80\ (.075)}{80\ (.10) + 20\ (.075)}$

labeling, and preselling by manufacturers have relieved the retailer of many of his former chores.

In addition, it is reasonably clear that some services that were formerly supplied by the retailer are now supplied by the consumer himself. This is most apparent in the case of food supermarkets, where the consumer typically waits on himself, provides his own delivery service, and, to the extent that he shops less frequently, provides storage service as well.

Because of other changes that have occurred—in automobile ownership, in the trend toward suburban living, in the increase in the value of the consumer's time—it may suit the consumer to do these things. When interviewed, he may respond that he "prefers shopping in the supermarket," but this does not negate the fact that the supermarket is providing less service.

David Schwartzman's point that the discount house and the supermarket are *not* post-'29 technological innovations has considerable force. Long before that time, retailers knew that it was possible to reduce margins by cutting out delivery and credit service and making other cuts in overhead. The growth of low-margin retailing must be regarded, at least in part, as a movement within a known production-function frontier, resulting from many exogenous changes in the economy rather than from a breakthrough in technology and productivity.[6] To choose an analogy, if consumers should decide that they prefer compact cars to large ones (because the price of gasoline has risen, or insurance is cheaper, or parking spaces are hard to find), and there is a shift of production to the easier-to-make compacts, the output of the automobile industry should not be considered unchanged if it produces the same number of cars as it did when most of the demand was for large ones.

Another conceptual problem, which is particularly important in retail trade (but is found to some degree in every industry), is the treatment of changes in the size of transactions. Let us suppose that the number of transactions and all other aspects of retail sales remain unchanged, except that each consumer buys twice as much in each transaction as before. Should we say that real output in retailing has doubled? Some economists have argued that because an increase in the size of the transaction nor-

---

[6] Schwartzman also emphasizes a substitution effect. He argues that consumers have substituted goods for retail service because the price of services has risen relative to the price of goods. Some evidence to support this view is found in cross-sectional studies of differences in sales per person among standard metropolitan statistical areas. See David Schwartzman, "The Growth of Sales Per Man-hour in Retail Trade, 1929–1963," *Production and Productivity in the Service Industries*, V. R. Fuchs, ed., NBER, in press.

mally does not require a proportionate increase in inputs, the volume of real goods should not be used as the measure of real output in retailing. It has been suggested that the number of transactions be used, or at least considered, in determining real output in retailing.[7]

One difficulty with this line of reasoning is that it is not applied in measuring real output in other industries, such as manufacturing. Businessmen and economists have known for a long time that productivity is often positively related to the "length of the run," but rarely, if ever, does anyone adjust a manufacturing output index based on volume of goods produced in order to allow for changes in the "length of the run," i.e., in the number of transactions, holding sales constant.

In retailing, the size of the transaction corresponds to the "length of the run," and there would seem to be little reason for treating this industry differently from others. Unless output is redefined in all industries, it seems more reasonable to try to identify what portion of the observed change in productivity in retailing can be attributed to change in the size of transactions.

Some Empirical Estimates

Having reviewed some of the pitfalls that beset attempts to measure output and productivity in retail trade, let us look at the available figures and see what they imply about trends in this industry, in absolute terms and relative to manufacturing. Table 37 is based on OBE figures for trade and manufacturing. Trade is a reasonably good proxy for retail trade because employment in retailing is three times as large as in wholesaling, and the trends for the two trade components have not been markedly dissimilar.[8]

It should be noted that the measures of labor input and total factor input are subject to the biases discussed in Chapter 3. The differential in the rates of growth of unionization in manufacturing and retailing was particularly marked, and probably accounted for .2 percentage points per annum of the differential in compensation per man. If an adjustment is made for this bias, the differentials in output per unit of labor input, and per unit of total factor input would be $-.1$ and $-.35$ respectively.

All three measures of productivity show relatively small differentials

[7] See Margaret Hall and Don Knapp, "Productivity and Distribution with Particular Reference to the Measurement of Output," *Productivity Measurement Review,* February 1957.

[8] The Office of Business Economics provides a breakdown of persons engaged in trade back to 1929, but a similar breakdown for real gross product is not available. The rate of growth of employment in retail trade alone, 1929–65, was 1.4 per cent per annum compared with 1.5 per cent for total trade.

TABLE 37

Trends in Output and Productivity in Trade and Manufacturing, 1929–65
(per cent per annum)

	Trade	Manufacturing	Trade Minus Manufacturing
Gross product in current dollars	5.5	5.8	−0.3
Real output	3.1	3.7	−0.6
Employment	1.5	1.6	−0.1
Real output per man	1.6	2.1	−0.5
Real output per unit of labor input	n.a.	n.a.	0.1
Real output per unit of total factor input	n.a.	n.a.	−0.2
Compensation per man	3.6	4.2	−0.6

Note: Rates have been calculated from unrounded data.
Source: Appendix Table C–4.

between trade and manufacturing. This is surprising. Manufacturing is commonly regarded as having enjoyed significant technological change, and as being in the forefront of productivity advance. Notice has often been taken of the huge expenditures for research and development in manufacturing. Trade, on the other hand, is often regarded as a relatively static industry. Table 37 can be interpreted as saying that these casual impressions are incorrect. It may be that, despite the expenditures for research and development and the upgrading of physical and human capital in manufacturing, the true productivity differentials are small. An alternative interpretation, first advanced by David Schwartzman in his NBER study, is that the real output measure for trade is biased upward relative to manufacturing.

Table 38 presents some other results that are more speculative in character. Included are estimates derived from David Schwartzman's attempt to measure output and input independently. Use is also made of Edward Denison's estimates of labor input, capital input, and total factor input for the total economy.[9]

[9] Denison's *The Sources of Economic Growth in the United States and the Alternatives Before Us,* New York, 1962, p. 265. Denison estimated the rates of change for 1929–57 as 2.16 per cent, 1.88 per cent, and 2.10 per cent for labor input, capital input, and total factor input, respectively. The rate of growth of labor input slowed down between 1957 and 1963, and capital input was somewhat faster. An estimate of 2.0 for both variables for the entire period seems warranted. This would result in a figure of 2.0 for total factor input also, regardless of the weights assigned to each factor.

TABLE 38

Some Alternative Estimates of Rates of Change of Output, Input, and
Productivity in Retail Trade, 1929–63
(per cent per annum)

	(1)	(2)
Real output [a]	2.8	1.3
Employment [b]	1.6	1.6
Labor input [c]	1.5	0.5
Total factor input [d]	2.0	0.8
Output per unit of total factor input	0.8	0.5
Attributable to:		
Capacity and scale economies [b]	0.2	0.2
Transaction size [b]	0.8	0.8
Unexplained residual	−0.2	−0.5

Source: David Schwartzman, "Retail Trade in the United States, 1929–63," NBER manuscript: Denison, *Sources of Economic Growth.*

[a] Col. 1, Schwartzman's estimate of margin-weighted-constant dollar sales; col. 2, first figure adjusted for Schwartzman's estimate of a change in service per transaction of −1.5 per cent per annum.

[b] Schwartzman.

[c] Col. 1, derived from Denison's estimate of change in labor input for total economy and the difference between the change in total labor compensation in retail trade and in the total economy (−0.5 per cent per annum); col. 2, Schwartzman's estimate based on independent estimates of change in hours per man (−.5 per cent per annum) and change in labor quality (−.6 per cent per annum) in retail trade.

[d] Col. 1, equal to Denison's estimate for total economy inasmuch as rate of change of current dollar output in retail trade is equal to that for the total economy; col. 2, Schwartzman's estimate based on weighted average of capital input (1.8 per cent per annum) and labor input.

Schwartzman estimates the rate of change of deflated retail sales as 2.8 per cent per annum in 1929–63. Since the gross product in current dollars grew at the same rate in retail trade as in the total economy, we can assume that total factor input also grew at about the national rate, which Denison estimates at about 2.0 per cent per annum. This implies a rate of growth of total factor productivity of .8 per cent per annum. Schwartzman estimates that fuller use of capacity and realization of scale economies explains about .2 percentage points of the growth of retail trade output, and that increases in the average size of transactions explains about .8 percentage points.

The second column in Table 38 shows a much lower rate of change of real output which, in Schwartzman's view, takes account of the decline in the quantity and quality of service provided by retailers. The estimate of total factor input is also very much lower, first because Schwartzman finds a decrease in the quality of labor in retail trade since 1929 and second because Schwartzman takes the decrease in hours at full value rather than allowing for an offsetting increase in output per man-hour as Denison does. Since the rates for both output and input are sharply reduced, the implied change in productivity is similar to that shown in the first column.

My own view is that the true measures of changes in real output and labor and total factor input probably fall somewhere between those shown in the columns of Table 38. I believe that there probably has been some decline in service per constant-dollar's worth of goods sold, and I believe there is some upward bias in Denison's measures of factor input. There is no reason why the residual should be negative.

Barber and Beauty Shops *

The measurement of real output in barber and beauty shops appears to be relatively straightforward. Current dollar receipts in the *Censuses of Business* are deflated by price indexes compiled by the Bureau of Labor Statistics. Trends in current dollar receipts are believed to be fairly accurate; the principal source of uncertainty is the differential coverage of very small establishments in different Census years.[10] The price indexes are based on reported prices for reasonably standard services such as haircuts and permanent waves. The growth in importance of many new services in beauty shops in the past two decades may introduce some bias into the price index for that industry.

The principal interest in this case study concerns the sources of growth of output per man, and particularly the differential trends in two apparently similar industries. Both barber and beauty shops are typically small: fewer than half of the shops in each industry have as many as one paid employee. They are also highly labor intensive; the capital investment per

* Most of this section is drawn from the work of Jean Wilburn at the National Bureau of Economic Research. Her work is reported in greater detail in Victor R. Fuchs and Jean Alexander Wilburn, *Productivity Differences Within the Service Sector,* New York, NBER, OP 102, 1967.

[10] Two issues are involved. First, the Bureau of the Census periodically changes the definition of firms considered too small to be included in the Census. Second, the "enumerator misses" of firms that should be covered probably varies from one Census to another.

worker is probably under $2,000. Together, the two industries employ over half a million persons and have receipts of over $250 million.[11]

Despite the many similarities between barber and beauty shops with respect to function and market structure, they have experienced divergent trends in output, employment, productivity, and prices, as indicated in Table 39. Productivity has risen much more rapidly in beauty shops than in barber shops, especially since 1948. Prices in beauty shops have risen much more slowly than in barber shops. The reasons for the disparate trends can be discussed under three related categories: labor, technology, and demand.

Labor

The labor force in both industries has shown a significant shift in age distribution over the last several decades. (See Table 40.) In the case of barber shops, the shift probably tended to lower productivity; in beauty shops, it had the opposite effect. Barber shops now rely heavily on older men; more than one-third of the barbers are over 55. The work is physically demanding, and some decrease in speed is to be expected with age. This is not likely to be offset by any increase in quality because maximum proficiency is reached long before the age of 55. In beauty shops, the shift in age distribution has been away from very young, inexperienced workers to persons of middle age. This is advantageous because the greater complexity of work in beauty shops provides greater opportunity for additional years of experience to be reflected in increased productivity.

The other major change in labor input that has implications for productivity is the rapid growth of part-time employment in beauty shops, but not in barber shops (see Table 41). Given the uneven flow of demand (to be discussed), the employment of part-time labor raises productivity because it is only used when demand is heavy. Most of the workers in beauty shops are female, and many of them prefer part-time employment. Barbers are almost exclusively male, and nearly all work full time.

Technology

The technological changes that have had the greatest effect on barber shops are the development of the safety razor and the electric razor. Both innovations resulted in a sharp decrease in the demand for shaves in barber shops. In the late 1920's, shaves accounted for a substantial frac-

[11] *Census of Business,* 1963.

TABLE 39

Rates of Growth of Barber and Beauty Shops, Selected Variables, 1939–63

(per cent per annum)

	1939–63			1939–48			1948–63		
	Barber Shops	Beauty Shops	Barber Minus Beauty	Barber Shops	Beauty Shops	Barber Minus Beauty	Barber Shops	Beauty Shops	Barber Minus Beauty
Current dollar output	5.7	7.8	−2.1	6.2	6.1	0.1	5.4	8.8	−3.4
Price	5.2	3.8	1.4	7.1	6.7	0.4	4.1	2.1	2.0
Real output	0.5	4.0	−3.5	−0.9	−0.6	−0.3	1.3	6.7	−5.4
Employment	−0.1	2.5	−2.6	−2.0	−1.7	−0.3	1.0	5.0	−4.0
Real output per man	0.6	1.5	−0.9	1.1	1.1	0.0	0.3	1.7	−1.4

Source: Appendix Table G–1.

TABLE 40

Percentage Distribution of Barbers and Beauticians, by Age, 1930–60

Years [a]	16–24	25–34	35–44	45–54	55–64	65+	55 Years and Over	Median Age
Barbers								
1930	11.6 [b]	26.6	29.0	19.4	9.3	2.9	12.2	37.8
1940	4.9	20.4	28.2	26.4	14.8	5.4	20.2	43.4
1950	4.8	15.1	21.9	26.6	21.6	10.1	31.7	47.6
1960	6.9	17.2	17.6	23.5	21.7	13.3	35.0	48.1
Beauticians								
1930	26.6 [b]	37.1	23.9	8.0	1.8	0.4	2.2	29.3
1940	34.5	34.2	20.6	8.3	2.0	0.4	2.4	28.5
1950	16.3	34.2	29.7	13.9	4.7	1.0	5.7	34.3
1960	15.6	20.3	33.2	20.7	7.9	2.3	10.2	38.7

Source: *Census of Population,* 1930, 1940, 1950, 1960.

[a] For 1930, the concept is "gainful workers"; for the remaining years, it is "employed persons." For 1930, 1940, and 1950, males are assumed to be barbers and females, beauticians; for 1960, the two occupations are listed separately: barbers are the sum of male and female barbers; the same is true of beauticians.

[b] 18–24 years. This row will not total 100 per cent since years 16–17 have been omitted.

TABLE 41

Percentage of Barbers and Beauticians Working Part-Time,[a]
1940, 1950, 1960

	1940	1950	1960
Barbers			
Wage and salary workers	5.1	7.6	n.a.
Employed persons	n.a.	6.4	10.7
Beauticians			
Wage and salary workers	11.1	20.2	n.a.
Employed persons	n.a.	23.4	30.1

Note: Since "barbers and beauticians" were classified as a single occupation in 1940 and 1950, a division of the occupation has been arbitrarily made here on the assumption that barbers are males and beauticians are females. In 1960 the occupations were listed separately. If the same assumption had been made in 1960 as in the previous years, the figures would have been 9.9 for barbers (instead of 10.7) and 32.8 for beauticians (instead of 30.1).

Source: *Census of Population,* 1940, pp. 171–172; 1950, pp. 18–139, 145, 151, 157; 1960, pp. 191–201.

[a] Less than 35 hours per week.

tion of the industry's output; by the 1960's, shaves were of negligible importance in most shops.

The effect of these new razors on productivity of shaving in the home was very great, but this, of course, is not reflected in the data for the barber shop industry. The effect on measured productivity was probably adverse because it cut down the flow of customers to barber shops and tended to limit the typical transaction to one service—a haircut.[12]

Two technological changes in barber shops—the electric clipper and the electric lather-making machine—apparently had only a minor impact on productivity, though no measure of it is available. A barber can cut hair more rapidly with clippers than with scissors, but there may be some decline in the quality of the service. The time required for lather making is small regardless of method.

The principal technological changes in beauty shops, in contrast, have had a significant impact on productivity through reductions in the costs of providing services, improvements in quality, and stimulation of demand.

The first big stimulus was provided by the permanent-wave machine.

[12] Specialization normally increases productivity, but this assumes no decrease in demand.

This was introduced in the beginning of this century, but did not become commercially important until the 1920's when women began to wear short hair. Given the increase in demand for permanent waves resulting from the change in fashion, research was stimulated and a number of improvements in the original heat process were introduced throughout the 1930's. In the early 1940's, the cold-wave permanent was discovered. The new process was originally much more expensive than the heat process, and the effectiveness of its results was controversial. In the past two decades, however, numerous minor technological improvements have resulted in making an improved service available at a much lower price. The reduction in price has in turn reinforced the fashion trend. The cold-wave process, which cuts labor requirements in half and reduces discomfort and risk, has completely replaced the heat process.

A similar interaction between technology, fashion, and productivity can be observed with respect to hair coloring. Tinting agents have been available since 1920. Demand was small, however, because the quality of the product was imperfect and fashion trends were not favorable. Several technological improvements introduced during the past two decades have reduced the time required for hair tinting, improved the quality of the product, and increased the range of colors available. At the same time, fashion trends have favored artificially colored hair. This service now represents a substantial fraction of total beauty shop output.

The innovations in waving and coloring hair have been the most important ones for this industry in recent decades, but there have been several other technological innovations that have contributed to increased productivity in beauty shops. Some, such as reductions in the time required to dry hair, increased productivity in much the same way that a reduction in processing time improved productivity in manufacturing, or any other industry. Other innovations, however, do not affect processing time directly, but take the form of new products and processes, or improvement in old ones, that stimulate demand. Examples include: nail enamel, facial packs, and rinses. These developments have made a favorable contribution to productivity through increased demand.

Demand

It is a well-established proposition that productivity tends to vary with the "length of the run." In retailing and personal services, such as barber and beauty shops, the "run" is the total purchase of a customer at one time. The effort required to sell a customer X dollars' worth of merchandise, or to provide X dollars' worth of service is normally less than twice that required to sell or provide one-half X dollars' worth.

The shift of shaving from barber shops to the home has adversely affected demand and productivity in barber shops in several ways. First, it has reduced the total demand for barbering services because of the almost complete elimination of shaves. Second, it has probably reduced the demand for haircuts and other barber shop services, because part of the cost of these services is the time spent going to and from the barber shop.[13] When men visited the barber shop frequently for shaves, the cost (including time) of haircuts and other services was relatively lower. Finally, the size of the average transaction was reduced.

In beauty shops the trend has been in the other direction. A single transaction now may include a haircut, a wave or set, hair coloring, manicure, facial, etc. Large transactions tend to enhance productivity because the fixed cost of the set-up time is spread over a larger number of services. Also, frequently more than one service can be performed at the same time. Finally, there is greater latitude and flexibility in planning and timing the work load.

The implications for productivity of the relatively weak demand for barbering services is reflected in the hourly earnings of barbers. According to figures derived from the 1/1,000 sample of the *1960 Census of Population,* the average hourly earnings of barbers in 1959 was $1.68 including tips.[14] A good way of determining whether this is a high or low figure is to compare it with the earnings of other workers having similar demographic characteristics. By classifying workers in all nonagricultural occupations by color, age, sex, and education, and calculating hourly earning rates for each category, it is possible to estimate what barbers would have earned if their earnings had equaled those of other workers having similar characteristics.[15] This figure, known as "expected" earnings, was $2.51 for barbers in 1951. The ratio of actual to "expected" earnings was .67, or only two-thirds of what was expected given the demographic characteristics of barbers. The low hourly earnings of barbers relative to "expected" earnings applies to wage and salary workers as well as to the self-employed, and is true regardless of nativity status, as may be seen in Table 42. This comparison is limited to white males to eliminate effects of sex and color.

Comparable figures for beauticians suggest that their time is spent much more productively. Average hourly earnings of $1.64 in 1959 were

[13] It should be noted that real output per capita of barber shops declined at the rate of 1 per cent per annum between 1939 and 1963.

[14] The accuracy of the hourly earnings figure has been investigated and substantially confirmed by earnings data from the 1958 *Census of Business.* See Fuchs and Wilburn, *Productivity Differences Within the Service Sector,* pp. 91–94.

[15] See Chapter 6 for a fuller discussion of this approach.

TABLE 42

Hourly Earnings of White Male Barbers, by Class of Worker and
Nativity, Actual and Expected, 1959

	Number in Sample	Actual Hourly Earnings (dollars)	Expected Hourly Earnings (dollars)	Actual ÷ Expected
Class of Worker				
Self-employed	84	1.85·	2.63	.70
		(.03)		
Wage and salary workers	60	1.61	2.55	.63
		(.10)		
Nativity				
Native, native parents	95	1.71	2.61	.65
		(.09)		
Native, one or both parents foreign-born	28	1.93	2.67	.72
		(.16)		
Foreign-born	21	1.73	2.46	.70
		(.23)		

Note: Numbers in parentheses indicate standard deviation. Expected earnings based
on earnings in all nonagricultural occupations for comparable color, age, sex, and education.
Source: *U.S. Census of Population and Housing: 1960. 1/1,000, 1/10,000 Sample.*

close to "expected" earnings of $1.80. The ratio of actual to "expected"
was .91, indicating that beauticians earned almost as much as did workers
with similar demographic characteristics in other industries.

The low earnings of barbers, compared with the price of haircuts, suggests that barbers, on average, are idle more than half the time. The average price of a haircut in 1959 can conservatively be estimated at $1.50.
A barber working steadily could give three haircuts in an hour, and thus
gross $4.50 plus an estimated $.50 in tips. The return to labor in this industry is not less than 75 per cent (the rate paid to barbers working on a
straight commission basis) and is probably over 80 per cent. Thus, a
fully occupied barber would earn about $4.00 per hour. The difference
between this figure and the actual earnings of only $1.68 per hour reflects
the time spent in waiting for customers.

Both barber and beauty shops are subject to an uneven flow of demand. Business is likely to be brisk toward the end of each week and

before holidays. As was indicated in Table 41, beauty shops cope with this uneven flow through extensive use of part-time labor. There are very few part-time barbers. One possible explanation is that most males are looking for full-time work, and barbering has been traditionally a male occupation. The legal requirements for obtaining a license as a barber are considerable.[16] Also, the skill requirements, though not great, are sharply different from those of other occupations, Thus, barbering is not an attractive occupation for students, moonlighters, and other males who do seek part-time jobs.

The high value placed by our society on at least nominal employment also should be considered. As has been indicated, a substantial fraction of the labor force in barber shops consists of older men. These men, many of whom are paid on a commission basis, prefer to be nominally employed, even when demand is very light, than to be unemployed. Given their age, and their specialized skill, there are few good alternatives available to them. The industry appears to have low productivity, but as Jean Wilburn has pointed out, forced retirement or part-time unemployment would raise measured productivity without necessarily being socially advantageous.[17]

Medical Care

The medical care industry, defined to include the services of physicians and other health professionals plus the capital, labor, and intermediate goods used at their direction, is one of the largest and fastest growing in the entire economy. In round numbers, expenditures for medical care have risen from under $4 billion in 1929 to over $40 billion in 1965 and close to $50 billion in 1967. Even as recently as 1947, expenditures were only $10 billion.[18] The share of total spending allocated to medical care has also been rising, from under 4 per cent in 1929 to about 6 per cent

[16] Every state, except one, requires some barber school attendance; the number of hours required ranges from 900 to 2,000. Examination after graduation, before the period of apprenticeship begins, is customary; the fee for examination is as high as $50 in some states and as low as none or $5 in others. The period of apprenticeship, during which earnings are restricted by law, ranges from 6 to 36 months. Following the apprenticeship there is another examination costing from $5 to $50. A further barrier to entry is created by the refusal of some states to give credit for out-of-state experience. Formal educational requirements exist in most states and range from 8 through 12 years. Many of the requirements appear to be excessive.

[17] *Ibid.*, p. 108.

[18] Part of this increase was due to the sharp rise in medical care prices. In terms of 1967 medical care prices, the increase has been from $10 billion in 1929 to $21 billion in 1947 to $46 billion in 1965.

in recent years. Nearly all of this relative increase has occurred since 1947. The rise in spending has been accompanied by a rapid rise in employment. The average annual increase in medical care employment in the postwar period has been about 5 per cent.

Despite its size, the medical care industry has not received a great deal of attention from economists.[19] The measurement and analysis of productivity in this industry have been particularly neglected, largely because of conceptual and statistical difficulties. Undoubtedly the greatest difficulty is that of measuring the output of the industry. Traditionally, output has been measured in terms of the number of physician visits, or number of patient-days in a hospital. This approach is roughly comparable to measuring the output of the automobile industry in terms of the number of cars produced without regard to size, durability, performance characteristics, and so on. For an industry that has experienced rapid technological change, as medical care has, such an approach cannot be regarded as satisfactory and provides only a crude approximation to the desired measure.

The official data on expenditures, price, and employment yield the rates of change shown in Table 43. They imply an average rate of growth of real output per man of about 1 per cent per annum between 1929 and 1965.[20] It is of some interest to note that this rate is midway between the rate for the total economy (1.9 per cent) and zero. If medical care were provided by the government, a zero rate would be assumed just as it is for other governmental services. This points up the probable bias in this assumption.

To the extent that the price indexes for medical care fail to take account of changes in the quality and quantity of service associated with a visit to a physician, or a day spent in a hospital, the existing measures of real output may be biased upward or downward. Many observers believe the latter to be more likely because of significant advances that have been made in medical science, as evidenced by declines in mortality, and so on. Yoram Barzel has attempted to develop a price index for medical care based on changes in the price of health insurance plans.[21] He concludes

[19] For a review of the relevant literature see Herbert E. Klarman, *The Economics of Health,* New York, 1965. See also, Selma J. Mushkin, "Health as an Investment," *Journal of Political Economy,* Supplement 70, October 1962, pp. 129–157, and Martin Feldstein, *Economic Analysis for Health Service Efficiency,* Amsterdam, 1967.

[20] The dramatic differences between subperiods probably reflect offsetting biases in the price index more than real phenomena.

[21] Yoram Barzel, "Productivity and the Price of Medical Service," University of Washington, Mimeograph.

TABLE 43

Rates of Growth of Medical Care Industry, Selected Variables,
1929–65 and Subperiods
(per cent per annum)

Variables	1929–65	1929–47	1947–65	1947–56	1956–65
Current dollar output	7.0	5.8	8.1	7.7	8.5
Price	2.5	1.6	3.5	3.8	3.2
Real output	4.5	4.2	4.6	3.9	5.3
Employment	3.6	2.3	4.9	5.2	4.7
Real output per man	0.9	1.9	−0.3	−1.3	0.6

Sources

Current dollar output: **1929,** Ida C. Merriam, "Social Welfare Expenditures, 1965–66," *Social Security Bulletin,* 29, No. 12 (December, 1966); **1965,** Ruth S. Hanft, "National Health Expenditures, 1950–65," *Social Security Bulletin,* 30, No. 2 (February, 1967); **1947** estimated by assuming that the proportion of the 1945 to 1950 change which took place between 1945 and 1947 was the same for the Merriam series as for the OBE series on personal consumption expenditures for medical care published in *The National Income and Product Accounts of the United States, 1929–1965;* **1956,** Hanft series benchmarked to OBE.

Price: Medical care component of Consumer Price Index with no change assumed between 1929 and 1935.

Employment: *Census of Population, 1940, 1950, and 1960* with extrapolation and interpolation based on number of persons engaged. The rates of change of persons engaged were used for 1929–40 and 1960–65. Employment in 1947 was estimated assuming that the proportion of the 1940 to 1950 change which took place from 1940 to 1947 was the same for census employment as for persons engaged. A similar procedure was used for 1956.

that the BLS price index has a strong upward bias. On the other hand, it should be noted that the cost of treating specific episodes of illness for five fairly common conditions appears to have risen more rapidly than the BLS medical care price index between 1951 and 1965.[22] This suggests a possible downward bias in the index. Much work will have to be done before the question is resolved.

The problem of measuring changes in the real output of the medical care industry consists of three parts. First the various types of output must be defined; second, the changes in each type must be quantified; and third, the various types must be made commensurate, that is the changes must be translated into dollar equivalents.

At least three types of output are readily apparent. Probably the most

[22] See Anne A. Scitovsky, "Changes in the Cost of Treatment of Selected Illnesses, 1951–65," *American Economic Review,* December 1967, pp. 1182–1195.

important one is the contribution that medical care makes to health. This surely is uppermost in the minds of consumers when they purchase medical care. In addition, physicians frequently provide a "validation service," i.e., an evaluation of an individual's health status, that may be required by third parties. Such an evaluation represents output independent of its effect on health, as in the case of a life insurance examination. Finally, there are a number of other consumer services provided in connection with medical care, e.g., the room-and-board aspects of hospitalization.

The following discussion concentrates on the problem of putting a dollar value on the health-affecting aspects of medical care.

First we must be able to define and measure health levels, or at least changes in levels. Second, we must say what these changes are worth; and third, we must estimate what portion of the changes can be attributed to the medical care industry as distinct from genetic and environmental factors that also affect health.[23]

Measures of Health

Definitions of health abound, but agreement is hard to find.[24] A few points seem clear. First, health has many aspects—anatomical, physiological, mental, and so on. Second, the relative importance of different disabilities varies considerably, depending upon the particular culture and the role of the particular individual in that culture. Third, most attempts at measurement take the negative approach; that is, they make inferences about health by measuring the degree of ill health as indicated by mortality, morbidity, disability, etc. Finally, as in so many other cases, detecting changes in health is easier than defining or measuring absolute levels.

The most widely used indicators of health levels are those based on mortality rates, either age-specific or age-adjusted. The great virtue of death rates is that they are determined objectively, are readily available in considerable detail for most countries, and are reasonably comparable for intertemporal and interspatial comparisons.

Table 44 shows the trends in death rates and infant mortality rates in the United States since 1929. Substantial reductions have been achieved

[23] A discussion of these three questions, summarized here, can be found in V. R. Fuchs, "The Contribution of Health Services to the American Economy," *Milbank Memorial Fund Quarterly*, October 1966.

[24] Compare, for example, the World Health Organization's definition: "A state of complete physical and mental and social well being" (World Health Organization Constitution Annex 1, Geneva, 1958), with Ffrangcon Roberts' emphasis on the absence of, or the ability to resist, disease and death in *The Cost of Health*, London, 1952.

TABLE 44

U.S. Death Rates, Selected Years, 1929–65

	Crude Death Rates (per 1,000 persons)	Age-Adjusted Death Rates [a]	Infant Death Rates (per 1,000 live births)
1929	11.9	13.2	67.6
1935	10.9	11.6	55.7
1940	10.8	10.8	47.0
1945	10.6	9.5	38.3
1950	9.6	8.4	29.2
1955	9.3	7.7	26.4
1960	9.5	7.6	26.0
1965	9.4	7.4	24.7

Sources

Crude and infant death rates: **1929–40**, U.S. Bureau of the Census, *Vital Statistics Rates in the United States, 1900–1940* (16th Census of the U.S.: 1940), 1943, pp. 124, 573; **1945–65**, U.S. Bureau of the Census, *Statistical Abstract of the United States,* 1965, p. 47; 1967, *ibid.,* p. 56.

Age-adjusted death rates: **1929–40** and **1950–55**, U.S. Bureau of the Census, *Historical Statistics of the United States, Colonial Times to 1957* (A *Statistical Abstract* Supplement), 1961, p. 27; **1945**, U.S. Department of Health, Education and Welfare, *Vital Health Statistics,* "Mortality Trends in the United States 1954–1963," National Center for Health Statistics, Series 20, Number 2, 1966, p. 7; **1960–65**, U.S. Bureau of the Census, *Statistical Abstract of the United States,* 1967, p. 56.

[a] Age-adjusted death rates are computed by the direct method, i.e., age-specific death rates for each year have been applied to the age distribution of the total population of the United States as enumerated in 1940.

since 1929, but the relative stability of these rates since 1955 also deserves notice. Some have argued that we are approaching a biological minimum, but many European countries enjoy much lower rates, and large interstate differences within the United States indicate that further declines are biologically feasible.

During this period of relative stability in death rates, the inputs into the medical care industry have increased considerably, and medical science has certainly made some progress. This has suggested to some people that there *must* have been improvement in health levels not reflected in the mortality indexes. This type of reasoning begs the question. An alternative explanation is that changes in environmental factors over the same period have had, on balance, a negative effect on health, thus offsetting the favorable effects of increases in medical care and medical knowledge. Such changes might include increases in smoking and drinking, air pollution, lack of exercise, and the tensions of urban life.

Some suggestions have been made for indexes of health that would combine mortality and morbidity information.[25] One possibility, suggested by Sanders, would be to calculate years of "effective life expectancy," using mortality and morbidity rates to measure the number of years that a person could expect to live and be well enough to fulfill the role appropriate to his sex and age. This approach could be modified to take account of the fact that illness or disability is a matter of degree. The years deducted from life expectancy because of disability should be adjusted by some percentage factor that represents the degree of disability. The determination of these percentage weights is one of the most challenging research problems to be faced in calculating an index of health.

The Value of Changes in Health

An increase in health has two potential values for individuals—consumption and production. Good health is clearly something consumers desire for itself. In addition, better health may contribute to an individual's productive capacity. It may do this, first, by increasing the supply of potential man-hours through a reduction in mortality or in time lost because of illness and disability. Second, better health may increase production by improving productivity, i.e., increasing output per man-hour.

No measures of the value of health in consumption are available. Surprisingly, there is also a dearth of information on the relation between health and output per man-hour. The available measures of the value of changes in health deal primarily with the effect of these changes on potential man-hours of work.

One frequently used approach is to ask how many more people are available for work as a result of a decrease in death rates, and what potential or actual production can be attributed to this increased supply of manpower. The capitalized value of the increase, at a given point in time, can be obtained by summing the value of future potential earnings discounted at some appropriate rate of interest.

[25] See D. F. Sullivan, "Conceptual Problems in Developing an Index of Health," in *Vital and Health Statistics, Data Evaluation and Methods of Research,* Public Health Service Publication No. 1,000, Series 2, No. 17, Washington, D.C., May 1966, and B. S. Sanders, "Measuring Community Health Levels," *American Journal of Public Health,* July 1964, pp. 1063–1070.

The details of such calculations vary greatly from one investigator to another, but one result is common to all: the value of a man (in terms of discounted future earnings) is very different at different ages. It rises steadily from birth and reaches a peak at about age 30 or 35. Peak values may vary from two to ten times the values at birth depending upon the rate at which future earnings are discounted. After the peak, values decline steadily and approach zero at very old ages.

The principal implication of the age-value profile is that the economic return from saving a life is not the same at all ages. Different kinds of health programs, and different kinds of medical research, affect various age groups differently; in estimating the output of the medical care industry, therefore, some consideration must be given to these matters. For example, accidents accounted for only 6.6 per cent of all male deaths in the United States in 1960, but accounted for 12.8 per cent of the economic cost of these deaths as measured by 1960 earnings discounted at the rate of 7.2 per cent per annum. On the other hand, vascular lesions accounted for 9.5 per cent of all male deaths but only 5.7 per cent of the value of discounted future earnings.[26]

To obtain some notion of the economic value (in terms of discounted future earnings) of the decline in death rates between 1929 and 1960, the 1929 rates were applied to the 1960 U.S. male population and compared with the actual deaths in 1960. There would have been approximately 475,000 more male deaths at the 1929 rate, and the discounted value (at 7.2 per cent per annum) of these lives amounted to $14 billion. A similar comparison between the U.S. male deaths in 1960 and the substantially lower Swedish male death rate in 1960 shows a potential saving of 220,000 lives annually, with a discounted future earnings value of $7.5 billion if the U.S. age-specific rates could be reduced to Swedish levels. These are large sums, but the connection between death rates and medical care is not obvious and requires considerable investigation.

The Contribution of Medical Care to Health

The impact of medical care on health depends upon the answers to two questions: (1) How effective are the best known techniques of diagnosis, therapy, etc.? (2) How wide is the gap between the best known techniques ("treatment of choice") and those actually used across the country? The second question has been reviewed extensively

[26] See Victor R. Fuchs, "The Contribution of Health Services to the American Economy," *Milbank Memorial Fund Quarterly*, October 1966.

in medical literature under the heading "quality of care." [27] A useful introduction to the first question is provided by Terris.[28]

Infectious disease is an area where medical services are demonstrably effective. Although the decline of some infectious diseases (e.g., tuberculosis) can be credited in part to environmental changes, such as improved sanitation, the important role played by improvements in medical science should not be downgraded. For many infectious diseases the health service is preventive rather than curative and "one-shot" rather than continuous. Such preventive services do not occupy a large portion of total physician time, but the results should nevertheless be included in the output of the health industry.

Examples of infectious diseases controlled through immunization are diphtheria, tetanus, and poliomyelitis; chemotherapy is effective in tuberculosis and pneumonia.[29] The decline in mortality from these causes has been dramatic, and some correlation can be observed between changes in the rate of decline and the adoption of specific medical advances. For example, during the fifteen-year period, 1935 to 1950, which spanned the introduction and wide use of sulfonamides and penicillin, the United States death rate from influenza and pneumonia fell at a rate of more than 8 per cent per annum; the rate of decline was 2 per cent per annum from 1900 to 1935. In the case of tuberculosis, considerable progress was made throughout this century, but the relative rate of decline in the death rate accelerated appreciably after the adoption of penicillin, streptomycin and PAS (para-aminosalicylic acid) in the late 1940's, and of isoniazid in the early 1950's.

The situation with respect to the noninfectious diseases is more mixed. Some examples of demonstrable effectiveness are the following: replace-

[27] See Alice L. Anderson and Isidore Altman, *Methodology in Evaluating the Quality of Medical Care, An Annotated Selected Bibliography, 1955–61,* Pittsburgh, 1962.

[28] Milton Terris, "The Relevance of Medical Care to the Public Health," paper delivered before the American Public Health Association, November 13, 1963.

[29] For further information on the control of these diseases, see George Rosen, "The Bacteriological, Immunologic and Chemotherapeutic Period 1875–1960," *Bulletin of the New York Academy of Medicine,* 40, 1964, pp. 483–494; A. P. Long and P. E. Sartwell, "Tetanus in the U.S. Army in World War II," *Bulletin of the U.S. Army Medical Department,* April 1947, pp. 371–385; A. P. Long, "Immunization to Tetanus," in Army Medical Services Graduate School, *Recent Advances in Medicine and Surgery,* Walter Reed Army Institute of Research, Washington, 1955, pp. 311–313; American Medical Association, *Commission on the Cost of Medical Care Report,* Chicago, 1963–64, Volume III, Chapters 4 and 7; and Monroe Lerner and Odin W. Anderson, *Health Progress in the United States, 1900–1960: A Report of the Health Information Foundation,* Chicago, 1963, p. 43.

ment therapy has lessened the impact of diabetes, dental caries in children are reduced by fluoridation, and medical care has become increasingly successful in treating trauma.[30] The diagnostic value of the Papanicolaou test for cervical cancer is established, and the incidence of invasive cancer of this site has been reduced, in the 1960's, presumably due to medical treatment during the preinvasive stage disclosed by the test. Also effective is the treatment of skin cancer.[31]

Less heartening are the reports on other cancer sites. The five-year survival rate for breast cancer (the most common single organ site of malignancy in either sex) is typically about 50 per cent.[32] Some writers stress the importance of prompt treatment for cancer; others question whether elimination of delay would dramatically alter survival rates. The problem of delay itself is complex, and not simply attributable to ignorance or lack of access to health services: "Physicians with cancer are just as likely to delay as are laymen." [33]

Heart disease is another major cause of death where the contribution of health services to health leaves much to be desired. Despite the contributions of surgery in correcting congenital and rheumatic cardiac defects and the decline in recurrence rates of rheumatic fever, apparently no curative treatment has been found for this disease.[34] The treatment

[30] Herbert H. Marks, "Longevity and Mortality of Diabetics," *American Journal of Public Health,* March 1965, pp. 416–423; World Health Organization, *Expert Committee on Water Fluoridation, First Report,* Technical Report Series, No. 146, Geneva, 1958; and A. W. Farmer and B. S. Shandling, "Review of Burn Admissions, 1956–1960—The Hospital for Sick Children," *Journal of Trauma,* September 1963, pp. 425–432.

[31] R. F. Kaiser *et al.,* "Uterine Cytology," *Public Health Reports* 75, 1960, pp. 423–427; John E. Dunn, Jr., "Cancer of the Cervix—End Results Report," in National Cancer Institute and American Cancer Society, *Fifth National Cancer Conference Proceedings,* Philadelphia, 1956, pp. 253–257; and Edward T. Krementz, "End Results in Skin Cancer," in National Cancer Institute and American Cancer Society, *Fourth National Cancer Conference Proceedings,* Philadelphia, 1961, pp. 629–637.

[32] Edwin F. Lewison, "An Appraisal of Longterm Results in Surgical Treatment of Breast Cancer," *Journal of the American Medical Association,* December 14, 1963, pp. 975–978.

[33] Robert Sutherland, *Cancer: The Significance of Delay,* London, 1960, pp. 196–202.

[34] John Stout *et al.,* "Status of Congenital Heart Disease Patients Ten to Fifteen Years After Surgery," *Public Health Reports,* 79, May 1964, pp. 377–382; May G. Wilson *et al.,* "The Decline of Rheumatic Fever—Recurrence Rates of Rheumatic Fever Among 782 Children for 21 Consecutive Calendar Years," *Journal of Chronic Diseases,* March 1958, pp. 183–197; The Rheumatic Fever Working Party of the Medical Research Council of Great Britain and The Subcommittee of Principal Investigators of the American Council on Rheumatic Fever and Congenital Heart Disease, American Heart Association, "Treatment of Acute Rheumatic

of coronary heart disease is only partially effective.[35] Definitive therapy is still not available for widespread afflictions such as cerebral vascular disease, and no cure is known for schizophrenia.[36]

Innovations in medical care are not limited to improvements in drugs, surgical techniques, or other technological changes. Research concerning the effects on health of group practice, intensive care units, and special arrangements for neonatal surgery has yielded encouraging results.[37] In other cases, results have been disappointing, e.g., multiple screening, periodic medical examination of school children, and cancer control programs differing in duration, intensity, and cost.[38]

This very brief review indicates that no simple generalization is possible about the effect of medical care on health. Although many health services definitely improve health, in other cases even the best-known techniques may have no effect. This problem of relating input to output is one of the most difficult ones facing economists who try to do research on the medical care industry. They must gain the support and advice of doctors and public health specialists if they are to make progress in this area.

Fever in Children: A Cooperative Clinical Trial of ACTH, Cortisone, and Aspirin," *British Medical Journal,* 1, 1955, pp. 555–574; and Ann G. Kutner, "Current Status of Steroid Therapy in Rheumatic Fever," *American Heart Journal,* 70, August 1965, pp. 147–149.

[35] Albert N. Brest, "Treatment of Coronary Occlusive Disease: Critical Review," *Diseases of the Chest,* 45, January 1964, pp. 40–45.

[36] Harvey D. Cain *et al.,* "Current Therapy of Cardiovascular Disease," *Geriatrics,* 18, July 1963, pp. 507–518; Milton Lowenthal *et al.,* "An Analysis of the Rehabilitation Needs and Prognoses of 232 Cases of Cerebral Vascular Accident," *Archives of Physical Medicine,* 40, 1959, pp. 183–186; and Philip R. A. May and A. Hussain Tuma, "Schizophrenia—An Experimental Study of Five Treatment Methods," *British Journal of Psychiatry,* June 1965, pp. 503–510.

[37] For a discussion of group practice, see Sam Shapiro *et al.,* "Comparisons of Prematurity and Prenatal Mortality in a General Population and in a Population of a Prepaid Group Practice," *American Journal of Public Health,* February 1958, pp. 170–187, and "Further Observations on Prematurity and Prenatal Mortality in a General Population and in the Population of a Prepaid Group Practice Medical Plan," *American Journal of Public Health,* September 1960, pp. 1304–1317. For intensive care units, see Lockwood *et al., op. cit.;* and United States Public Health Service, Coronary Care Units: *Specialized Intensive Care Units for Acute Myocardial Infarction Patients,* Washington, October 1964. For neonatal surgery, see Isabella Forshall and P. P. Rickham, "Experience of a Neonatal Surgery Unit—The First Six Years," *The Lancet,* October 1960, pp. 751–754.

[38] See C. M. Wylie, "Participation in a Multiple Screening Clinic with Five-Year Follow-Up," *Public Health Reports,* July 1961, pp. 596–602; Alfred Yankauer and Ruth A. Lawrence, "A Study of Periodic School Medical Examinations," *American Journal of Public Health,* January 1955, pp. 71–78; and N. E. McKinnon, "The Effects of Control Programs on Cancer Mortality," *Canadian Medical Association Journal,* June 25, 1960, pp. 1308–1312.

Some researchers at the National Bureau have attempted to gain insights into the contributions of medical care and environmental factors to health by examining interstate differentials in age-adjusted death rates.[39]

Two models are estimated. In the first, the quantity of medical services is measured by expenditures on medical care. In the second, expenditures are replaced by a Cobb-Douglas production function combining the factors of production: physicians, paramedical personnel, physical capital, and drugs. In this formulation a demand equation for medical services and supply curves of factors are introduced. Estimates are alternatively made by ordinary least squares and instrumental variables.[40]

Both medical services and environmental factors contribute to variations in age-adjusted death rates. The elasticity of the death rate with respect to medical services is about $-.1$. The most important environmental factors are income and education. States with above average education tend to have below average death rates; states with high income tend to have *high* death rates when the quantity of medical services and other factors are held constant.

This is an exploratory study and these tentative findings should be subjected to additional testing. They are, however, very suggestive. The authors note that the cost of an increase in medical service is several times the benefits of increased national output from reduced mortality. The interstate analysis indicates that almost as large a reduction in mortality is associated with an additional dollar spent on education as an additional dollar spent on medical care.

The estimates imply that the stability of the death rate in recent years should not be interpreted as a complete failure of medical care to improve health. Rather, declines in death rates that would have resulted from increases in the quantity and quality of medical care may have been offset by adverse changes in environmental factors, most notably those associated with the rise in real income. Whether the net positive relation between mortality and income is attributable to the adverse effects of earning a higher income or to the consumption effects, or to other changes in the environment that are beyond the range of individual choice remains to be explored.

[39] Richard Auster, Irving Leveson, Deborah Sarachek, "The Production of Health, an Exploratory Study," NBER manuscript. The analysis in this study is limited to whites because of sharp differences in death rates by color and the high correlation between percentage nonwhite and other variables across states.

[40] This technique involves regressing the independent variables on a set of exogenous variables and then using the predicted values (from the regressions) in the final regression instead of the observed values.

Summary

This brief and incomplete survey of productivity in three service industries serves to illustrate the heterogeneity of the sector and the complexity of problems encountered in measurement and analysis.

In the case of medical care, the very definition of output is unclear; there is as yet no agreement as to what, in principle, should be measured. The conventional measures of medical care output such as a physician-visit, or a hospital-day, are patently unacceptable to economists because they come close to measuring input instead of output. However, those economists who stress the "cure" dimension of medical care output overlook the fact that much of the service rendered by physicians is supportive or palliative and has very little connection with "cures." [41] The other major analytical problem is relating "cures" or "health" to medical care. Just as most disease is the result of a combination of causes, so are most "cures" the result of the efforts of the health industry combined with the efforts of the individual patient. As some new work on demand theory stresses, it is the individual (if anyone) who produces health, using medical care as an input.[42] A reconciliation between this realistic view of medical care and the conventional approaches to measuring output and productivity has not yet been achieved.

The problem with respect to retail trade is somewhat less severe than in health, at least at the conceptual level. There is wide agreement that the output of a retail firm should be measured by the services provided by the firm to the consumer in the distribution of goods. Most of these services can be specified: storage, information, credit, delivery, and the like. Many of them can, in principle, be quantified. In practice, no great effort has been made to do so and the conventional approach has assumed that the bundle of services associated with the sale of a given real volume of goods remains unchanged over time. For reasons mentioned in this chapter, and described more fully by David Schwartzman, this assumption probably leads to overestimating the growth of retail output and productivity between 1929 and the present.

The case of retail trade also brings to the fore the problem of inter-

---

[41] See Eli Ginzberg, "Medical Economics—More Than Curves and Computers," in *The Economics of Health and Medical Care,* Proceedings of the Conference on the Economics of Health and Medical Care, May 10–12, 1962, Ann Arbor, Michigan, 1964, p. 14.

[42] Kelvin J. Lancaster, "A New Approach to Consumer Theory," *The Journal of Political Economy,* April 1966, pp. 132–157, and Gary S. Becker, "A Reformulation of Consumption Theory," NBER, Mimeograph.

preting changes in the size of transactions, a problem also noted in the case of barber and beauty shops. Productivity, as conventionally measured, tends to increase with transaction size. This formulation is acceptable provided the increase from this source is sharply distinguished from productivity increases attributable to technological advance or to changes in the quality of factor inputs.

The complex interrelationship between demand, technological change, and productivity is well illustrated by the case study of beauty shops. Two of the major technological innovations in that industry, the permanent wave process and the hair coloring agents, were long available in imperfect form but were not important because the demand situation was not favorable. Changes in demand stimulated further technological improvements; these in turn stimulated demand, and the continuous interaction sparked sustained advances in productivity. In barbering, technology, demand, and productivity have all tended to be stagnant over the period studied.

Even barber shops, however, show some increase in output per man as do all the industries examined in this chapter. This result should serve as a warning that the simple assumption of no productivity increase in services [43] is unsatisfactory. At the same time, the case studies show how difficult it is to measure accurately and to determine the sources of the increases that have undoubtedly occurred.

[43] See William J. Baumol, "Macroeconomics of Unbalanced Growth: The Anatomy of Urban Crises," *American Economic Review,* June 1967.

6

INTERINDUSTRY AND INTERSECTOR DIFFERENCES IN HOURLY EARNINGS

In Chapter 3 we saw that earnings in most service industries have not grown as rapidly as in the Industry sector since 1929. The differential rate of growth of earnings was interpreted as implying a differential rate of growth of the quality of labor, although it was indicated that a portion of the gap in earnings could be attributed to the growth of unions in Industry. Some limited evidence on changes in demographic characteristics supported the inferences based on earnings trends.

In Chapter 5, questions concerning earnings, demographic characteristics, and labor quality were again raised. David Schwartzman's hypothesis of a decline in the service provided by retail trade per constant dollar of sales is closely tied to the hypothesis of a decline in the quality of labor in retailing. In the case study of barber and beauty shops, inferences concerning labor quality and idle time are dependent upon the interpretation of earnings data.

This chapter presents a much more systematic look at interindustry and intersector differences in earnings, particularly in relation to demographic characteristics and other variables, such as unionization. Use of the 1/1,000 sample of the *1960 Census of Population* permits systematic analysis of the *level* of earnings, and provides the basis for the estimates concerning unionization, labor quality, and demographic characteristics that were used in Chapters 3 and 5.

The richness of the data makes possible more comprehensive comparisons than those based on economic censuses or sample surveys. All service and nonservice industries can be included, and in considerable detail. Also, it is possible to include salaried employees and self-employed workers as well as production workers. This is particularly important in the Service sector where more than half of all employed persons are either salaried or self-employed.

Average hourly earnings are estimated for 1959 for every detailed industry, major industry group, and the Service and Industry sectors. Intersector differences in earnings are also examined by color, age, sex, and education. We find that hourly earnings in the Industry sector are, on average, 17 per cent higher than in the Service sector; much of the chapter is devoted to exploring and explaining this difference.

Differentials in Earnings

The Estimation of Actual and "Expected" Hourly Earnings

The basic data source for this chapter is the 1/1,000 sample of the *1960 Census of Population and Housing*. A detailed description of the 1/1,000 sample and of the statistical procedures followed in preparing the earnings estimates is given in Appendix E. The principal points to be made here are:

1. The population studied includes all persons who were employed in nonagricultural industries during the Census "reference" week (varying weeks in April) in 1960, and who had some earnings in 1959. The total number of persons covered in the sample was 56,247. Persons employed in agriculture were excluded because average hourly earnings for such persons present special problems of reliability and interpretation.[1]

2. Average hourly earnings for each industry are estimated in the following manner. Average annual hours are obtained by multiplying the number of weeks worked in 1959 by the number of hours worked in the Census reference week in April 1960, for each worker, and then summing for all workers in an industry. This method provides a more accurate estimate of total man-hours than would be obtained by multiplying average weekly hours by the average number of weeks worked because there is a positive correlation between number of weeks and hours per week across individuals. Although the use of hours for a single week in 1960 and inaccuracy in reporting of hours may produce considerable error in the estimate of annual hours (and hourly earnings) for any single worker, much of this error is random in nature and tends to cancel out for large groups.[2] Sampling errors are greatest when there are few observations; all measures that are based on fewer than fifty observations are identified. Aggregate annual earnings for 1959 for each

---

[1] Hours worked and earnings are both less likely to be reliably reported by agricultural workers. Moreover, some labor income may be earned in kind (unreported), or reported earnings may include substantial returns to land and capital as well as labor income.

[2] The reliability of the hours data is examined in Appendix F.

The Service Economy

TABLE 45

Average Hourly Earnings of Nonagricultural Employed Persons,
by Demographic Characteristics, United States, 1959

Characteristics	Dollar Earnings Per Hour	Characteristics	Dollar Earnings Per Hour
Color		Sex	
Whites	2.58	Males	2.79
Nonwhites	1.61	Females	1.70
Age		Years of schooling	
14–19	1.38	0–4	1.66
20–24	1.73	5–8	2.09
25–34	2.38	9–11	2.26
35–44	2.72	12	2.40
45–54	2.71	13–15	2.92
55–64	2.62		
65 and over	2.50	16 and over	3.96
		All	2.50

Source: *U.S. Censuses of Population and Housing: 1960. 1/1,000 Sample;* calculations by the author.

industry are divided by the aggregate annual hours for that industry to obtain the average hourly earnings.[3]

3. Past studies of industry differences in earnings have often tried to take account of industry differences in labor quality. One customary approach is to standardize for industry differences in occupation. This is a useful method, but deficient to the extent that there are labor quality differences within the same occupation across industries. Also, there are many occupations that are specific to only a few industries. An alternative, and possibly more direct, approach to the problem is to look at such labor quality proxies as color, age, sex, and education, since it is well-known that there are significant wage differentials at the national level associated with each of these variables. Table 45 summarizes these differentials in gross form; detailed tables are presented in Appendix E. It is readily apparent that industry differences in the composition of the

[3] This is equivalent to calculating average hourly earnings for each worker and then calculating a weighted average for all workers in an industry where the weights are the annual hours of each worker.

labor force with respect to these variables could be an important source of industry differentials in hourly earnings.

All nonagricultural employed persons who had some earnings in 1959 were grouped into 168 cells by color (two classes), sex (two classes), age (seven classes), and years of schooling (six classes). National hourly earnings rates for each cell were calculated by the method described in the preceding section. "Expected" hourly earnings for each industry were then calculated by assuming that each worker in the industry had an hourly earnings rate equal to the national rate for workers with his color, age, sex, and education. To the extent that labor quality is associated with these characteristics, differences in average "expected" earnings across industries measure differences in labor quality; differences between actual and "expected" earnings measure differences in wages holding labor quality constant.[4]

This quality adjustment is necessarily imperfect. Two shortcomings worth noting are: (1) the failure to take account of differences in ability within educational classes, and (2) the open-ended class, "16 years and over," includes workers with very varied degrees of schooling. Despite these and other shortcomings, however, this approach to standardization yields reasonable and useful results. Moreover, it has the advantage of allowing for important interactions between the various quality proxies, such as those between education and color and education and age.

Sector Differences in Earnings

Table 46 presents average hourly earnings in 1959 for each sector and major industry group. Also presented are the "expected" hourly earnings based on the color, age, sex, and education composition of the labor force. The last column in each category shows the ratio of actual to expected earnings.

We see that actual earnings in the Industry sector are 39 cents, or 17 per cent, higher than in the Service sector, and that this difference is not explained by the composition of the labor force since the expected earnings are almost identical in the two sectors.

With one exception, every major industry group in the Industry sector has a ratio of actual to expected of over 1.0, whereas in the Service sec-

---

[4] Systematic differences in national hourly earnings rates by color, age, sex, and education suggest that these variables do, to some extent at least, measure labor quality. The white-nonwhite differences are probably due in part to market discrimination, but color is relevant to quality because of the likelihood that, at given levels of education, nonwhites have received poorer quality schooling and less on-the-job training than have whites.

TABLE 46

Actual and Expected [a] Hourly Earnings, by Sector and Major Industry Group, 1959

	Total			Males			Females		
	Actual	Expected	Ratio of Actual to Expected	Actual	Expected	Ratio of Actual to Expected	Actual	Expected	Ratio of Actual to Expected
All Industries [b]	$2.50	$2.50	1.00	$2.79	$2.79	1.00	$1.70	$1.70	1.00
Industry sector	2.70	2.50	1.08	2.88	2.69	1.07	1.84	1.63	1.12
Service sector	2.31	2.51	.92	2.69	2.94	.91	1.63	1.74	.94
Mining	2.89	2.62	1.10	2.94	2.66	1.10	1.91 [c]	1.83 [c]	1.05 [c]
Construction	2.87	2.58	1.11	2.90	2.61	1.11	2.02	1.78	1.13
Manufacturing	2.67	2.47	1.08	2.91	2.70	1.08	1.80	1.61	1.12
Durable	2.79	2.54	1.10	2.94	2.69	1.09	1.96	1.65	1.19
Nondurable	2.51	2.38	1.05	2.86	2.72	1.05	1.69	1.58	1.07
Transportation	2.70	2.57	1.05	2.75	2.63	1.04	2.01	1.73	1.16
Communications and public utilities	2.63	2.45	1.07	2.90	2.75	1.06	1.96	1.71	1.15
Communications	2.69	2.28	1.18	3.40	2.87	1.18	2.00	1.70	1.18
Public utilities	2.58	2.59	1.00	2.68	2.70	.99	1.84	1.77	1.04
Postal service	2.58	2.78	.93	2.61	2.87	.91	2.24	1.77	1.27

Wholesale trade	2.88	2.71	1.06	3.04	2.89	1.05	1.95	1.73	1.13
Retail trade	1.96	2.37	.83	2.22	2.68	.83	1.34	1.63	.82
Finance, insurance, and real estate	2.92	2.63	1.11	3.58	3.17	1.13	1.82	1.72	1.06
Business and repair services	2.43	2.56	.95	2.50	2.70	.92	2.04	1.79	1.14
Personal services	1.36	1.82	.74	1.93	2.57	.75	1.00	1.35	.74
Entertainment and recreation	2.28	2.40	.95	2.39	2.62	.91	1.94	1.71	1.13
Professional and related services	2.63	2.77	.95	3.31	3.58	.92	1.97	1.99	.99
Public admin.	2.49	2.71	.92	2.64	3.02	.88	2.06	1.86	1.11
Industry not reported	2.35	2.29	1.03	2.61	2.58	1.02	1.72	1.61	1.07

Notes to Table 46

Note: The ratios of Actual to Expected Earnings in this and succeeding tables were computed from more detailed data than are shown in the tables.

Source: 1/1,000 Sample.

a Expected earnings are obtained by assuming that each worker in each industry had hourly earnings equal to the national average for his color, age, sex, and education.

b Excludes agriculture, forestry, and fisheries, as do all the tables in this chapter.

c Based on fewer than fifty observations.

tor every group except two has a ratio of below 1.0. Service sector earnings are particularly depressed by personal services and retail trade; communications, construction, mining, and durable manufacturing show the highest ratios in the Industry sector.

The sector differences in the ratios of actual to expected are similar for males and females, 17 per cent and 19 per cent, respectively. Within the Service sector, however, we find that females have relatively high earnings in several industry groups in which male earnings are low.

Table 47 explores the intersector differences in earnings for specific demographic groups. The difference for each group is summarized in the last column where the ratio of actual to expected in the Industry sector is shown relative to the actual/expected ratio in the Service sector. We find that the intersector difference is appreciably greater for nonwhites than for whites, and is greater the lower the level of education. Moreover, these results are confirmed for educational groups within each color and for white-nonwhite comparisons at each level of education.

It should be noted that the same data can be used to analyze absolute differentials, as shown in Table 48. In these terms, the Industry-Service differential is larger for males than for females, and is the same for whites as for nonwhites. The absolute differential first decreases with additional schooling, then rises, and increases steadily with age. In the regression analyses presented in the next section of this chapter, both relative and absolute differentials are studied.

Examination of the measures for the detailed industries reveals that industries differ much more with respect to actual than to expected earnings.[5] This is true within each sector as well as for the total. Charts 9 and 10 show that there is a very marked central tendency for expected earnings, around $2.50 per hour, whereas actual hourly earnings tend to be highly dispersed. Chart 9 is based on simple frequency distributions of industries, whereas Chart 10 is based on distributions in which each industry is weighted by its number of employees. The midpoints for the open-ended classes are based on the median and weighted median industries in those classes, respectively.

Comparison of the distributions for the two sectors shows that the service industries tend to be much more heterogeneous with respect to both actual and expected earnings. At the lower extreme are the personal services, while at the upper end are such high-wage, high-skill services as medical and legal.

[5] Appendix Table I-1 presents actual and expected hourly earnings for each of 139 industries. This represents the entire *Census of Population* industry list with the exception of a few "not specified" industries.

When we look at the ratios of actual to expected earnings, we find that most industries (73 per cent) in the Industry sector are greater than 1.0 and most service industries (66 per cent) are below 1.0. The cumulative frequency distributions, weighted and unweighted, are shown in Chart 11. A chi square test shows that the two sectors differ significantly from each other at the .001 level of confidence.

Regression Analysis

This section reports the results of regression analyses of interindustry differences in earnings. The primary purpose is to test certain hypotheses concerning industry characteristics that are believed to affect earnings. The use of expected earnings as one of the independent variables permits a rigorous test of these hypotheses after allowing for industry differences in demographic characteristics, i.e., it tests the influence of industry characteristics on standardized wages. The identification of wage-related industry characteristics helps to explain the sector differentials in earnings described in the previous section.

Demographic Characteristics (X_1)

Table 49 shows the results when actual earnings are regressed on expected earnings. We see that well over half the interindustry differences in hourly earnings can be explained by differences in demographic characteristics alone.[6] In the weighted logarithmic run, as much as 70 per cent of interindustry variation is explained by this one variable. In both the linear and logarithmic runs, weighting the industries by their total man-hours tends to improve the correlation because those industries with the greatest residuals are typically small industries. In the multiple regressions that follow, weighting by industry man-hours is applied throughout. This tends to minimize the disturbances introduced by the inclusion of industries whose estimated earnings are based on few observations.

The regression coefficient in the linear equation shows the number of cents change in actual earnings per hour that is associated with a one cent change in expected earnings. The logarithmic form, which gives a slightly better fit, shows the percentage change in actual earnings asso-

---

[6] By comparison, it may be noted that when actual earnings were regressed on expected earnings across twenty-eight region-city size cells, the $\bar{R}^2$ (adjusted coefficient of determination) was only .36. Demographic characteristics explain twice as much of interindustry variation in earnings as they do of geographical variation in earnings.

TABLE 47

Actual and Expected Hourly Earnings in Industry and Service Sectors, by Sex, Color, Education, and Age, 1959

	Industry Sector			Service Sector			Industry A/E Service A/E
	Actual Hourly Earnings (A)	Expected Hourly Earnings (E)	A/E	Actual Hourly Earnings (A)	Expected Hourly Earnings (E)	A/E	
All nonagricultural employed persons	$2.70	$2.50	1.078	$2.31	$2.51	.921	1.17
Males	2.88	2.69	1.072	2.69	2.94	.914	1.17
Females	1.84	1.63	1.124	1.63	1.74	.941	1.19
Whites	2.75	2.56	1.075	2.41	2.62	.923	1.16
Nonwhites	1.97	1.73	1.137	1.36	1.53	.888	1.28
Years of schooling							
0–4	1.95	1.76	1.109	1.26	1.54	.817	1.36
5–8	2.38	2.19	1.090	1.69	1.97	.857	1.27
9–11	2.56	2.38	1.078	1.91	2.14	.892	1.21
12	2.67	2.50	1.070	2.15	2.31	.928	1.15
13–15	3.30	3.08	1.072	2.68	2.82	.951	1.13
16 and over	4.42	4.14	1.068	3.75	3.90	.961	1.11

Whites							
0–4	2.05	1.88	1.093	1.47	1.80	.820	1.33
5–8	2.43	2.24	1.086	1.80	2.10	.858	1.27
9–11	2.60	2.41	1.077	1.99	2.22	.893	1.21
12	2.69	2.52	1.068	2.19	2.36	.930	1.12
13–15	3.33	3.12	1.071	2.74	2.88	.951	1.12
16 and over	4.45	4.16	1.070	3.79	3.95	.960	1.11
Nonwhites							
0–4	1.68	1.44	1.166	.95	1.17	.811	1.44
5–8	1.91	1.66	1.148	1.12	1.32	.847	1.36
9–11	2.02	1.80	1.121	1.29	1.47	.876	1.28
12	2.19	1.91	1.145	1.49	1.65	.899	1.27
13–15	2.27	1.96	1.159	1.74	1.82	.953	1.22
16 and over	2.47[a]	2.85[a]	.864[a]	2.71	2.71	.999	.86[a]
Age							
14–19	1.45	1.39	1.045	1.29	1.38	.934	1.12
20–24	1.91	1.75	1.092	1.59	1.72	.923	1.18
25–34	2.56	2.38	1.076	2.19	2.40	.911	1.18
35–44	2.89	2.71	1.065	2.54	2.73	.928	1.15
45–54	2.89	2.69	1.076	2.52	2.73	.925	1.16
55–64	2.88	2.63	1.096	2.41	2.62	.918	1.19
65 and over	2.94	2.50	1.177	2.28	2.52	.906	1.30

[a] Based on fewer than fifty observations.

Note: See note to Table 46.

TABLE 48

Absolute Differentials in Hourly Earnings in Industry and Service Sectors,
by Sex, Color, Education, and Age, 1959

	Actual Minus Expected Earnings		Column 1 Minus Column 2
	Industry (1)	Service (2)	
All	$.20	$−.20	$.40
Males	.19	−.25	.44
Females	.21	−.11	.32
Whites	.19	−.21	.40
Nonwhites	.24	−.17	.41
Years of schooling			
0–4	.19	−.28	.47
5–8	.19	−.28	.47
9–11	.18	−.23	.41
12	.17	−.16	.33
13–15	.22	−.14	.36
16 and over	.28	−.15	.43
Whites			
0–4	.17	−.33	.50
5–8	.19	−.30	.49
9–11	.19	−.23	.42
12	.17	−.17	.34
13–15	.21	−.14	.35
16 and over	.29	−.16	.45
Nonwhites			
0–4	.24	−.22	.46
5–8	.25	−.20	.45
9–11	.22	−.18	.40
12	.28	−.16	.44
13–15	.31	−.08	.39
16 and over	−.38 [a]	.00	−.38 [a]
Age			
14–19	.06	−.09	.15
20–24	.16	−.13	.29
25–34	.18	−.21	.39
35–44	.18	−.19	.37
45–54	.20	−.21	.41
55–64	.25	−.21	.46
65 and over	.44	−.24	.68

[a] Based on fewer than fifty observations.

CHART 9

Distribution of Industries, by Actual and Expected Hourly Earnings

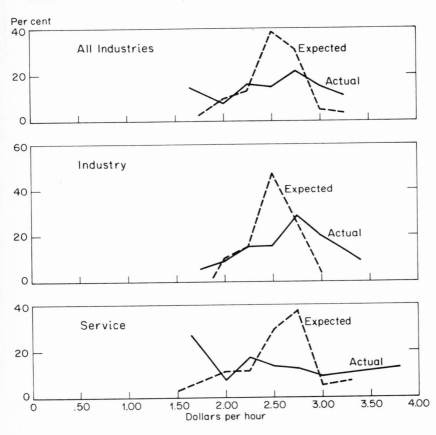

ciated with a 1 per cent change in expected earnings. A priori, this coefficient might be expected to be equal to 1.0, but we observe that it is
significantly above unity in all four runs. In regressions described later
in this chapter, inclusion of additional variables brings the demographic
characteristics regression coefficient closer to 1.0 and, for runs limited to
the Industry sector, it falls to slightly below 1.0. In the Service sector,
however, there are several industries at either end of the skill scale that
account for the coefficient exceeding unity. At the upper end, security
and commodity brokers, medical except hospital, and legal all have high
expected earnings, but actual earnings far exceed expected. At the
lower end, several of the personal services and retail trades have low

CHART 10

Weighted Distribution of Industries, by Actual and Expected
Hourly Earnings

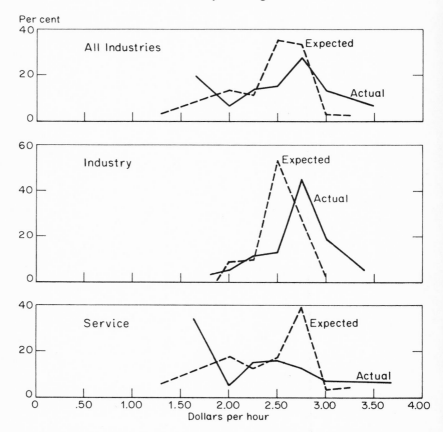

expected earnings but even lower actual earnings. These deviations suggest the possibility that the six education classes do not provide an adequate measure of skill at the extreme ends; it is also possible that there are errors in the reporting of earnings.[7]

The demographic characteristics variable goes a long way toward explaining interindustry differences in earnings generally but it is of no help in explaining the differential between the Industry and Service sectors. When the residuals are examined for the log-weighted run, we find

---

[7] For instance, reported earnings for food stores, eating and drinking places, and private households might omit income in kind.

CHART 11

Cumulative Frequency Distribution of Industries, by Ratio
of Actual to Expected Earnings

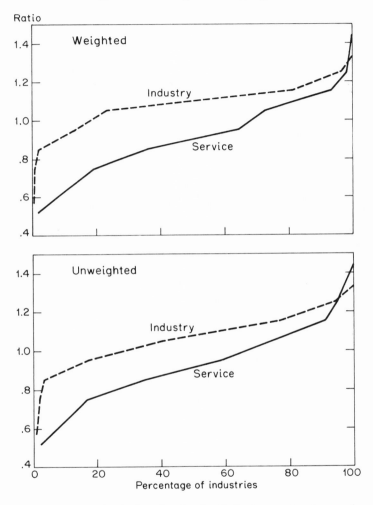

that 74 per cent of the industries in the Industry sector have observed
earnings that exceed predicted values, while only 30 per cent of the
Service sector industries are in that category. Because mean expected
earnings are almost identical in the two sectors, it is not surprising that
demographic characteristics cannot explain intersector differences in
actual earnings. To do so it is necessary to identify variables that have

TABLE 49

Results of Regression of Hourly Earnings on Demographic
Characteristics Across All Industries
($N = 138$)

	$\bar{R}^2$	Regression Coefficient	t Value [a]
Linear: unweighted	.572	1.456	13.58
weighted	.641	1.448	15.67
Logs: [b] unweighted	.576	1.462	13.69
weighted	.698	1.547	17.83

Note: Demographic characteristics are measured by expected hourly earnings. Industry 879, "welfare and religious services" was excluded from all regression analyses because of special problems of measuring and interpreting the compensation of priests, nuns, and other religious workers.

Source: Appendix Table I–1.

[a] These are equal to the regression coefficient divided by its standard error. These values indicate extremely high statistical significance.

[b] All logarithms of variables are in natural logs.

different values in the two sectors and are thought to be significantly related to earnings. The most promising is the extent of unionization.[8]

Unionization (X_2)

It is well-known that the workers in much of the Industry sector are highly organized, whereas unions are weak or nonexistent in most service industries. For the Industry sector as a whole, nearly 50 per cent of all employed persons were union members in 1960. For the Service sector as a whole, the comparable figure was less than 10 per cent.[9] It is widely (though far from universally) believed that workers in unionized industries receive higher wages than do those in other industries.[10]

[8] Another variable that is often mentioned along with unionization is industry concentration; however, the evidence presented by L. W. Weiss in "Concentration and Labor Earnings," *American Economic Review,* March 1966, convincingly rejects the hypothesis of a systematic relation between concentration and earnings, *ceteris paribus.* Adrian Throop reports a similar finding in his Stanford Ph.D. dissertation, 1967, "Sources of Inflationary Bias in the American Economy," Chapter 5.

[9] These estimates were derived from the data assembled from a number of sources by H. Gregg Lewis and presented in *Unionism and Relative Wages in the United States,* Chicago, 1963.

[10] For comprehensive reviews of this subject, see H. Gregg Lewis, *ibid.,* and George H. Hildebrand, "The Economic Effects of Unionism," in *A Decade of*

TABLE 50

Results of Regression of Hourly Earnings on Demographic
Characteristics and Unionization Across All Industries
($N = 138$)

Form of X_2	$\bar{R}^2$	Demographic Characteristics (X_1)		Unionization (X_2)	
		Regression Coefficient	t Value	Regression Coefficient [a]	t Value
Linear					
$U = $ 0 to 100	.748	1.449	18.71	.0075	7.64
$U = $ 0 to 60	.746	1.451	18.69	.0081	7.58
$U = 20$ to 60	.773	1.426	19.39	.0125	8.93
$U = 20$ to 100	.767	1.423	19.12	.0107	8.66
Reciprocal of $U = 20$ to 100	.774	1.432	19.51	.0108 [b]	
Logarithmic [c]					
$U = $ 0 to 100	.797	1.524	21.38	.33	8.18
$U = $ 0 to 60	.797	1.524	21.43	.36	8.22
$U = 20$ to 60	.819	1.506	22.36	.55	9.58
$U = 20$ to 100	.812	1.504	21.93	.46	9.15
Reciprocal of $U = 20$ to 100	.820	1.510	22.51	.48 [b]	

[a] The linear runs show the change in dollars per hour and the logarithmic runs in per cent associated with a change of one percentage point in unionization.
[b] At the unionization mean of 35.52 per cent, this is the union effect implied by the regression coefficient.
[c] The dependent variable, hourly earnings (X_0) and X_1 are in natural logarithms; unionization (X_2) is not.

The unionization variable used in this study measures, in principle, the fraction of total employment covered by collective bargaining agreements. In practice it is obtained through a variety of methods and sources (see Appendix I), and the figures for some industries are undoubtedly subject to considerable measurement error.

Despite these measurement problems, the regression results reveal a strong and consistent relation between unionization and earnings, after allowing for demographic characteristics (see Table 50). It is doubtful that the elimination of measurement error would make these results

Industrial Relations Research, Neil W. Chamberlain, Frank C. Pierson, and Theresa Wolfson (eds.), New York, 1958.

weaker or less consistent.[11] Unionization and demographic characteristics together explain up to 82 per cent of all interindustry variation in
hourly earnings.

Another important problem concerns the form of the relation between
unionization and earnings. The adjusted coefficients of multiple determination ($\bar{R}^2$) indicate that the best fits are obtained when the unionization variable is limited to the range 20 to 60 per cent (all industries
below or above that range are set equal to 20 or 60, respectively) or
when the reciprocal of unionization is used and limited to the range 20
to 100 per cent.

It should be noted that, if the true relation between earnings and
unionization were linear throughout, the grouping of observations at 20
and 60 per cent would tend to lower the $\bar{R}^2$. In fact, the $\bar{R}^2$ is increased,
and by an amount that is statistically significant.[12]

The results, therefore, suggest the possibility that the relation between
standardized earnings and unionization is not linear throughout. At low
levels, changes in unionization seem to have little effect on earnings.
This also appears to be true once most of the workers in an industry are
covered by collective bargaining agreements. It is possible that measurement error obscures any union effect below 20 per cent, since the measurement of unionization in these industries is particularly poor. However, it should be noted that there is still a statistically significant difference between the fit of unionization 20 to 100 per cent and unionization
20 to 60 per cent in the logarithmic runs.

In the linear runs, the effects of unionization on hourly earnings can
be read directly from the regression coefficients. For instance, in the
third linear run the coefficient .0125 implies that, over the range 20 to

[11] Random errors of measurement in an independent variable bias the regression
coefficient *downward* if the hypothesized relation is positive. See J. Johnston,
Econometric Methods, New York, 1963, pp. 149–150.

[12] Yoel Haitovsky has suggested to me the following test for statistical significance:

$$F_{(1,n-p-1)} = \frac{R^{*2} - R^2}{2 - R^{*2} - R^2} (n - p - 1)$$

If we apply this test to the linear runs, where unionization can take any value from
zero to 100 and where it is restricted to 20 to 60, we obtain the following F value:

$$F = \frac{.776 - .751}{2 - (.776 + .751)} (135) = 7.1,$$

which is highly significant.

I am also grateful to F. Thomas Juster and Jack Johnston for advice concerning
the statistical significance of these results.

60 per cent unionization, an increase of 1.25 cents per hour is associated with an increase of one percentage point in unionization. The first linear run indicates a change of .75 cents per hour per percentage point change in unionization over the full range from 0 to 100 per cent. The run in which the reciprocal of unionization is used results in a different unionization effect at different levels of unionization. The effect shown is the one implied at the mean level of unionization.[13]

In the runs where actual and expected earnings are in natural logarithms, the union effect is given by the regression coefficients, with the decimal point shifted two places to the right. The values shown in Table 50 are the percentage change in earnings associated with a one percentage point change in unionization. The value for the last run is again based on the implied change at the mean level of unionization.

It should be noted that the results concerning unionization are open to more than one interpretation. It is clear that, other things being equal, earnings are higher the higher the level of unionization, but this does not necessarily mean that they are higher for workers of equal skill. The adjustment for color, age, sex, and education cannot capture all differences in labor quality, and it is possible that some of the unmeasured quality differences are correlated with the extent of unionization. This would be true if unions exercised some quality control, or if the higher wages that unionized employers pay permits them to be more selective in their hiring within given demographic groups. Other factors, such as the nonpecuniary advantages and disadvantages of different types of employment also enter into the determination of hourly earnings, but it is doubtful that these have a systematic negative correlation with unionization.[14]

The combined explanatory power of the two independent variables is very high; moreover, the unionization variable does explain most of the Industry-Service differential. The residuals now show almost as high

[13] If the regression equation is

$$X_0 = a + b_1 X_1 + \frac{b_2}{X_2},$$

the effect of a 1-unit change in X_2 would be

$$\frac{\partial X_0}{\partial X_2} = -\frac{b_2}{X_2{}^2}.$$

The mean value of X_2 and the regression coefficient b_2 are substituted to find the effect of unionization on earnings.

[14] It should be emphasized that this analysis is concerned only with the relation between the structure of earnings and unionization, and does not attempt to appraise the over-all impact of unions on the economy.

The Service Economy

TABLE 51

Results of Regression of Hourly Earnings on Demographic Characteristics
and Unionization, Across Industry Sector Only
$(N = 81)$

Form of X_2	$\bar{R}^2$	Demographic Characteristics (X_1)		Unionization (X_2)	
		Regression Coefficient	t Value	Regression Coefficient	t Value
Linear					
$U = $ 0 to 100	.697	1.248	11.65	.0081	6.74
$U = $ 0 to 60	.708	1.248	11.86	.0104	7.06
$U = 20$ to 60	.710	1.203	11.44	.0122	7.13
$U = 20$ to 100	.693	1.197	11.04	.0093	6.60
Reciprocal of $U = 20$ to 100	.726	1.202	11.77	.0061 [a]	7.65
Logarithmic [b]					
$U = $ 0 to 100	.685	1.166	11.24	.33	6.59
$U = $ 0 to 60	.703	1.166	11.57	.42	7.11
$U = 20$ to 60	.711	1.123	11.27	.51	7.38
$U = 20$ to 100	.687	1.118	10.75	.38	6.63
Reciprocal of $U = 20$ to 100	.727	1.122	11.59	.25 [a]	7.88

[a] At the unionization mean of 51.17 per cent this is the union effect implied by the regression coefficient.

[b] The dependent variable, hourly earnings (X_0) and X_1 are in natural logarithms; unionization (X_2) is not.

a proportion of Service as Industry sector industries with observed earnings greater than predicted.

Because unionization is so much more prevalent in the Industry sector than in the Service sector, there is a possibility that the observed union effect really reflects the impact of some other variable that distinguishes the two sectors. One test of this possibility is to run the same regressions for the Industry sector alone. (See Table 51.) We find that the unionization coefficient is still highly significant and has about the same values as in the all-industries run. These values are all higher than those reported by Lewis.[15] They suggest the need to introduce a number of other inde-

[15] H. Gregg Lewis, *Unionism and Relative Wages in the United States.* He estimates the difference between zero and 100 per cent unionization at 10 to 20 per cent.

TABLE 52

Average Hourly Earnings of All Nonagricultural Employed Persons,
by City Size and Region, Standardized for Demographic
Characteristics, 1959 [a]
(dollars per hour)

		Urban Places		Standard Metropolitan Statistical Areas			
Region	Rural	Under 10,000	10,000– 99,999	Under 250,000	250,000– 499,999	500,000– 999,999	1,000,000 and Over
Northeast	2.27	2.28	2.36	2.40	2.40	2.48	2.75
North Central	2.12	2.12	2.32	2.57	2.57	2.77	2.89
South	1.95	1.93	2.09	2.24	2.35	2.41	2.65
West	2.27	2.21	2.36	2.52	2.50	2.64	2.87

Source: Victor R. Fuchs, *Differentials in Hourly Earnings by Region and City Size.*
[a] Standardized earnings equals actual minus "expected" plus $2.50. For definition of "expected" earnings, see text.

pendent variables that may be related to earnings and unionization, and therefore may have biased the union effect upwards. These variables are discussed below.

Other Independent Variables

LOCATION—REGION AND CITY SIZE (X_3). A location variable is introduced to take account of interindustry differences in distribution by region and city size. Numerous writers have observed wages to be higher in the non-South than in the South, and higher in large cities than in small towns or rural areas.[16] Some precise measures of the differentials in hourly earnings for all nonagricultural employed persons in 1959 were developed for seven city sizes in each of the four regions.[17] In addition, measures of "expected" earnings were calculated for each region-city size group following the methods described above for calculating "expected" earnings for industries. The difference between "expected" earnings and the national average of $2.50 per hour was subtracted from actual earnings to obtain average standardized earnings. The results are shown in Table 52.

[16] See, for example, Lowell E. Galloway, "The North-South Wage Differential," *Review of Economics and Statistics,* August 1963, pp. 265–272, and Edwin Mansfield, "City Size and Income, 1949," in *Regional Income,* Princeton for NBER, 1957.
[17] The regions are: Northeast, North Central, South, and West. See V. R. Fuchs, *Differentials in Hourly Earnings by Region and City Size, 1959,* New York, NBER, OP 101, 1967.

TABLE 53

Average Hourly Earnings, by Location Within Standard
Metropolitan Statistical Areas, 1959
(dollars per hour)

Location of Worker	Actual Hourly Earnings (1)	Expected Hourly Earnings [a] (2)	Differential (col. 1 minus col. 2) (3)	Differential Minus Differential for All SMSA's (4)
Works in central city and lives in same SMSA, same county and same city as place of work	2.47	2.41	.06	−.10
Works in ring of SMSA	2.69	2.56	.13	−.03
Works in central city but lives outside the SMSA, or city or county of place of work	3.11	2.72	.39	.23
All workers in SMSA's	2.68	2.52	.16	−

[a] Based on color, age, sex, and education.

A location adjustment factor for each industry was then calculated by weighting the values of Table 52 by the distribution of industry employment across twenty-eight city size-region groups. Those industries that have a disproportionate share of their employment in large cities, and in the non-South, have a location factor greater than $2.50. Those industries located primarily in small towns and in the South have factors below $2.50.

LOCATION WITHIN STANDARD METROPOLITAN STATISTICAL AREAS (X_4). Location and earnings are related in another way; it has been observed that earnings tend to be lower in residential areas, possibly because workers find working near their homes to be more convenient, more congenial, and less expensive.[18] The higher earnings that have been observed for commuters to the central city may also reflect some ability differentials that are not captured by the adjustment for color, age, sex, and education.

Table 53 shows the earnings and earnings differentials for three groups of workers, covering all those who work in Standard Metropolitan Statis-

[18] I am grateful to Albert Rees and to H. Gregg Lewis for calling this point to my attention.

tical Areas. We see that those who live and work in the central city have the lowest earnings, and those who travel to the central city to work have the highest earnings. Workers in the rings of SMSA's are in an intermediate position.

Using the differentials of the last column of Table 53, an adjustment factor was calculated for each industry based on the distribution of its employment among the three groups within SMSA's. This adjustment for location within SMSA's was then multiplied by the ratio of the industry's employment in SMSA's to the industry's total employment. The result was added to $2.50 (the mean earnings for all industries).

ESTABLISHMENT SIZE (X_5). A positive relation between earnings and size of establishment has often been hypothesized. The variable used here measures the fraction of the industry's employment in establishments with more than 250 employees.

EMPLOYMENT GROWTH (X_6). This is measured by the index of employment in 1960 (1950 = 100). Some writers have argued that rapidly growing industries will pay higher than average wages.

UNEMPLOYMENT RATE (X_7). Industries with high unemployment may have to pay higher hourly wages in order to hold labor. On the other hand, a high unemployment rate may indicate a weak labor market and hence lower earnings. This variable is measured by the average of the unemployment rate in 1950 and 1960.

AVERAGE ANNUAL HOURS PER EMPLOYED MALE (X_8). Industries with short hours may have to offer high hourly wages; on the other hand, long hours may indicate a strong demand for labor.

SELF-EMPLOYMENT INCOME AS PERCENTAGE OF TOTAL EARNINGS (X_9). This variable is included because those industries with a large amount of self-employment may have their earnings inflated by the inclusion of the property income of the self-employed. On the other hand, self-employment may have a negative effect on earnings if it involves opportunities to build up equity through capital gains.

The results of regressing hourly earnings on all independent variables are presented in Table 54.[19]

Inclusion of the additional variables raises the explanatory power in every case. The logarithmic run with unionization limited to 20 to 60 per cent has an adjusted coefficient of multiple determination of .88. The significance of such a result in a cross-section regression with 138 observations is very high. It should be noted that the fit of the 20 to 60 run is again significantly better than the 0 to 100 run.

[19] The zero order correlation matrixes are presented in Appendix Table I-3.

TABLE 54

Results of Regression of Hourly Earnings on All Independent Variables, Across All Industries and Industry Sector Only

Form of X_2	$\bar{R}^2$	Demographic Characteristics (X_1)	Unionization (X_2)	Region and City Size (X_3)	Location Within SMSA (X_4)	Establishment Size (X_5)	Employment Growth (X_6)	Unemployment Rate (X_7)	Annual Hours (X_8)	Self-Employment (X_9)
All Industries (N = 138)										
Linear:										
$U = $ 0 to 100	.819	1.247**	.0047**	1.098**	8.466**	.001	.061	-.013	-.058**	.005†
$U = $ 0 to 60	.819	1.249**	.0052**	1.105**	8.352**	.001	.051	-.014	-.060**	.005†
$U = $ 20 to 60	.830	1.232**	.0086**	1.016**	7.668**	.001	.046	-.016	-.053**	.005*
$U = $ 20 to 100	.827	1.232**	.0070**	1.049**	7.854**	.001	.062	-.011	-.052**	.005†
Reciprocal of $U = $ 20 to 100	.829	1.249**	.0072 a**	1.023**	7.582**	.001	.041	-.013	-.054**	.005*
Logarithmic: c										
$U = $ 0 to 100	.868	1.354**	.21**	.670*	6.088**	.026**	.044	-.053*	-.379**	.020*
$U = $ 0 to 60	.868	1.356**	.25**	.703*	6.026*	.026**	.034	-.055*	-.386**	.020*
$U = $ 20 to 60	.879	1.341**	.37**	.608†	5.177*	.026**	.031	-.056*	-.331**	.022*
$U = $ 20 to 100	.875	1.342**	.30**	.599†	5.292*	.027**	.048	-.049*	-.333**	.022*
Reciprocal of $U = $ 20 to 100	.876	1.358**	.31 a**	.618†	5.216*	.026**	.028	-.052*	-.344**	.022*

Industry Sector Only (N = 81)

Linear:

U = 0 to 100	.762	.976**	.0052**	.542†	4.547†	.002	.071	−.010	−.042*	.010
U = 0 to 60	.764	.990**	.0066**	.515†	4.010†	.002	.052	−.010	−.041*	.010
U = 20 to 60	.769	.952**	.0082**	.466†	4.494†	.002	.059	−.013	−.041*	.010
U = 20 to 100	.764	.933**	.0062**	.539†	4.611†	.002	.084	−.011	−.042*	.011†
Reciprocal of U = 20 to 100	.772	.979**	.0040 b**	4.11	4.170†	.002	.050	−.009	−.041*	.010

Logarithmic: c

U = 0 to 100	.749	.950**	.25**	.444†	4.963†	.007	.071†	.000	−.315*	.001
U = 0 to 60	.750	.969**	.30**	.462†	4.494†	.011	.051	.000	−.308*	.002
U = 20 to 60	.762	.933**	.37**	.396	4.847†	.013	.055	.004	−.300*	.004
U = 20 to 100	.757	.908**	.28**	.424	4.875†	.010	.079†	.001	−.310*	.004
Reciprocal of U = 20 to 100	.762	.958**	.18 b**	.339	4.615†	.010	.050	.001	−.301*	.002

Note: † indicates the regression coefficient is significantly different from zero at .05 level of confidence, * at .01, and ** at .001, on two-tailed test.

a At the unionization mean of 35.52 per cent, this is the union effect implied by the regression coefficient.

b At the unionization mean of 51.17 per cent, this is the union effect implied by the regression coefficient.

c All variables except unionization in natural logarithms.

Inclusion of the additional variables tends to lower the effect of unions on earnings. The best estimates of that effect that emerge from this analysis are that, over the range 20 to 60 per cent unionization, a change of one percentage point in unionization leads to an increase of .8 to .9 cents per hour, or about .37 per cent in earnings. At lower or higher levels of unionization, no effect on earnings is observed.[20]

The runs for the Industry sector alone show almost exactly the same relation between earnings and unionization as do the all-industries regressions. This strengthens our confidence in the relationship and in the conclusion concerning the role of unionization in explaining the intersector difference in earnings.

None of the other variables are as highly and consistently significant as are unionization and demographic characteristics. The two location variables are usually significant in the expected direction, but more so in the linear than in the logarithmic runs, and much more so for the all-industries runs than for the Industry sector alone. This last point suggests that geographical wage differentials may be much smaller for workers in the Industry sector than for those in the Service sector.[21]

Establishment size is significant only in the all-industries logarithmic run; and employment growth is not significant at all. Self-employment income is significant in the all-industries run; the regression coefficients suggest that an industry with 100 per cent of its earnings in self-employment income would have 2 per cent higher hourly earnings than would an industry with no self-employment, all other things being equal.

Both the unemployment rate and annual hours show negative coefficients. These results must be interpreted guardedly. First, there is a negative bias associated with the annual hours variable because a similar variable is implicit in the denominator of the dependent variable. Second, the unemployment rate and the annual hours variable show considerable multicollinearity ($r = .50$). It appears that earnings tend to be lower in industries with long hours, but also tend to be lower in industries with high unemployment rates. Much more investigation of these relationships is needed before any firm conclusions are warranted.

The key role of unionization in explaining the Industry-Service differential in earnings is brought out clearly in Table 55 where the gross sector earnings differential is decomposed according to the regression re-

[20] The less reliable runs with unionization values not restricted indicate a union effect of .47 cents per hour, or .21 per cent per percentage point change over the 0 to 100 range.

[21] Direct analysis of geographical wage differentials by industry, now under way at the NBER, indicates that this is indeed true.

TABLE 55

Decomposition of Industry–Service Earnings Differential According to Regression Results

Variable	Weighted Means		Percentage Difference [a]	Regression Coefficient	Contribution to Sector Differential in Hourly Earnings (percentage points)
	Industry	Service			
X_1 Demographic characteristics	2.5083	2.4946	0.5	1.34	0.7
X_2 Unionization 20–60	48.3919	20.2414	28.2 [b]	0.37	10.4
X_3 Region and city size	2.5006	2.4869	0.5	0.61	0.3
X_4 Location within SMSA	2.5076	2.4948	0.5	5.18	2.6
X_5 Establishment size	52.8330	16.8296	103.4	0.03	3.1
X_6 Employment growth	1.2671	1.3210	–4.2	0.03	–0.1
X_7 Unemployment rate	4.8430	3.3969	35.1	–0.06	–2.1
X_8 Annual hours	19.7745	20.5138	–3.67	–0.33	1.2
X_9 Self-employment	7.6344	21.7752	–96.2	0.02	–1.9
Total contribution of nine independent variables					14.2
X_0 Hourly earnings					15.2
Unexplained residual					1.0

[a] The difference between the Industry and Service means is divided by the average of the two means.
[b] The percentage change in earnings implied by the regression co- efficient is applied to the absolute difference because this variable was not run in logarithmic form.

sults.[22] The contribution of each independent variable to the differential is obtained by finding the weighted mean of the variable for each sector and multiplying the percentage difference between the means by the regression coefficient for that variable. For instance, the percentage difference in the sector means for X_1 (demographic characteristics) is .5 per cent. The regression results show that earnings rise 1.34 per cent for every one percentage point difference in this variable; therefore, a sector differential in earnings of .7 per cent (.5 $\times$ 1.34) would be expected on account of this variable alone.

The contribution of the unionization variable, 10.4 percentage points, is obtained by using the absolute difference between the sector means because this variable was not converted to logarithms. We see that of the total sector earnings differential of 15.2 per cent, more than two-thirds is explained by the sector differential in unionization. The second most important variable in terms of explaining the sector difference in earnings is establishment size. All the variables taken together explain 14.2 percentage points, leaving an unexplained residual of only one percentage point.

Differences in Earnings for Three Groups of Industries

One way of extending and testing the preceding analysis is to run regressions and make comparisons for separate groups of industries. The 138 industries were divided into three groups according to the percentage of the industry's employment that is male. This variable is a good proxy for the "heaviness" or difficulty (in a physical sense) of work. Earnings may be related to physical difficulty; by running regressions across industries with similar sex mixes, we are, in effect, allowing for this possible relationship.

The three groups of industries are: those with less than 60 per cent male ($N = 28$); those with 60 to 79.9 per cent male ($N = 47$); and those with 80 per cent or more male ($N = 63$).

The regression results are shown in Table 56. The equations are the same as those used for the all-industries run, except that employment growth was dropped as an independent variable because it had no effect on any of the results. Also, only the results for the two unionization forms with the highest explanatory power are reported.

We see that the equations do an excellent job of explaining inter-industry variation in earnings within each group of industries. The lowest

[22] The logarithmic run with unionization restricted to 20 to 60 per cent, which gives the highest $\bar{R}^2$, is used.

Differences in Hourly Earnings 155

Results of Regression Analysis for Three Groups of Industries Classified by Percentage Male

Variables	Per Cent Male (linear runs)			Per Cent Male (logarithmic runs)		
	Under 60 (N = 28)	60–79.9 (N = 47)	80 and Over (N = 63)	Under 60 (N = 28)	60–79.9 (N = 47)	80 and Over (N = 63)
	Unionization = 20 to 60 Per Cent					
$\bar{R}^2$	.852	.861	.842	.916	.858	.842
X_1 Demographic characteristics	1.1833**	1.8715**	1.7796**	1.4040**	1.6130**	1.8311**
X_2 Unionization	.0108†	.0119**	.0049†	.0067*	.0037**	.0017
X_3 City size and region	1.4356†	1.8430*	.0571	.8573	2.2261**	–.0460
X_4 Location within SMSA	7.6885	5.9657	9.6469**	.3380	6.5215†	10.2162**
X_5 Establishment size	.0032	–.0037	–.0000	.0311†	.0026	.0245*
X_7 Unemployment rate	–.0347	–.0141	.0292†	–.0934	.0364	.0585†
X_8 Annual hours	–.0481	–.0679	–.0601**	–.2809	–.2091	–.4293**
X_9 Self-employment	.0074	–.0040	–.0088*	.0194	.0082	–.0069
	Reciprocal of Unionization = 20 to 100 Per Cent [a]					
$\bar{R}^2$	.846	.871	.844	.914	.869	.842
X_1 Demographic characteristics	1.1982**	1.9973**	1.8029**	1.4327**	1.7289**	1.8693**
X_2 Unionization	.0163	.0145**	.0028†	1.10*	.47**	.09
X_3 City size and region	1.5146†	1.5367†	.0555	.9250	1.9609**	–.0563
X_4 Location within SMSA	7.8707	4.9233	9.5246**	.1853	5.7684†	10.2825**
X_5 Establishment size	.0034	–.0039†	–.0001	.0332†	.0026	.0226†
X_7 Unemployment rate	–.0313	–.0144	.0306†	–.0933	.0410	.0633†
X_8 Annual hours	–.0494	–.0760†	–.0593**	–.3309	–.2390	–.4323**
X_9 Self-employment	.0072	–.0044	–.0084**	.0208	.0095	–.0078

Note: † indicates the regression coefficient is significantly different from zero at .05 level of confidence, * at .01, and ** at .001, on two-tailed test.

[a] Effect on earnings at mean levels of unionization: under 60 per cent male = 25.30 per cent; 60–79.9 per cent male = 31.53 per cent; 80 per cent male and over = 45.33 per cent.

TABLE 57

Effect of Unionization on Hourly Earnings, Various Regressions

Form of X_2	All Industries Regressions	Weighted Average of Regressions Across Industries, Grouped by Percentage Male
Linear runs		
$U = 20$ to 60 per cent	.0086	.0080
Reciprocal of $U = 20$ to 100 per cent	.0072	.0064
Logarithmic runs [a]		
$U = 20$ to 60 per cent	.37	.30
Reciprocal of $U = 20$ to 100 per cent	.31	.24

Source: Tables 54 and 56.
[a] All variables in natural logarithms except unionization.

adjusted coefficient of multiple determination is .84, and some are as high as .91. The effect of unionization on earnings seems to be stronger in the two groups with smaller percentage males. In fact, for the industries with 80 per cent or more males, the unionization coefficient is not always statistically significant.

These runs also afford an opportunity to examine the union effect on earnings after allowing for the fact that unionization is correlated with the percentage male. By comparing a weighted (by man-hours) average of the unionization coefficients in each group with the coefficients from the all-industries run, we can see whether this correlation significantly affects the relation between earnings and unionization.

Table 57 indicates that the results are similar when the regressions are run across industries grouped by percentage male. The effect of unions on earnings is reduced about one-fifth compared with results that were obtained when each regression was run across all industries, but this difference is not statistically significant.

Summary

Average hourly earnings in the Industry sector were 39 cents, or 17 per cent higher than in the Service sector in 1959. Multiple regression analysis across industries was used to identify the sources of interindustry and intersector differences in earnings. A demographic characteristics variable ("expected" earnings) based on color, age, sex, and education explains more than half of the interindustry variation in earnings, but explains none of the sector differential because "expected" earnings were equal in the two sectors.

The principal explanatory variable of the sector differential is unionization. Approximately half of the workers in Industry are union members; fewer than one-fifth of the Service workers are organized. Multiple regression analysis across industries reveals a significant positive relation between hourly earnings and extent of unionization after taking account of demographic characteristics, location of industry, and many other variables.

The effect of unions on wages seems to be most pronounced in the range of 20 to 60 per cent. Below and above that range no systematic relation between changes in unionization and hourly earnings was observed. Within that range, hourly earnings rise by about .3 or .4 per cent with each increase of one percentage point in unionization.

Differences in size of establishments is the second most important variable in explaining the Industry-Service earnings differential. Service sector employment is mostly in small establishments, and the multiple regression analysis reveals a significant relation between industry earnings and the fraction of employment in establishments with more than 250 employees.

Although service earnings are typically low, a few industries show high earnings, and two groups—wholesale trade and finance, insurance and real estate—show high earnings relative to those that would be "expected" based on demographic characteristics. In general, it was found that the industries in the Service sector are much more heterogeneous than those in the Industry sector with respect to both actual and "expected" earnings.

7

CYCLICAL FLUCTUATIONS

One of the most intriguing aspects of the development of a service economy is the prospect it offers of increasing stability over the business cycle. The tendency for employment and earnings to be less sensitive to the business cycle in service industries than in goods-producing industries has been noted by many observers.[1] This chapter explores the hypothesis of stability in services in some detail. Monthly data for 1947 through 1965 are presented for various service industries and comparisons are made with manufacturing and other goods-producing industries. Time series on output and on output per man-hour are included as well as on employment, and relative measures of the amplitude of fluctuation are calculated.

A Priori Considerations

Before looking at the data, it is useful to review some of the factors that might contribute to differences in stability between service industries and, say, manufacturing. Since the demand for employment is derived from the demand for output, the factors affecting the stability of output will be considered first; a discussion of those that bear only on employment will follow.

Probably the most important difference between goods output and service output is that the former can be stored and the latter cannot. True, some goods output, such as perishable food, cannot be stored for very long. Most of the output of farms and mines can be stored, however, and much of the output of manufacturing takes the form of durable goods. Wesley Mitchell observed that "The characteristic of goods that

[1] See, for example, Arthur F. Burns, "Progress Towards Economic Stability," *American Economic Review,* March 1960, No. 1, pp. 6–7; also Daniel Creamer, *Personal Income During Business Cycles,* Princeton University Press for the National Bureau of Economic Research, 1956, p. 47.

seems to have most influence upon cyclical amplitudes is durability." [2]

In the case of consumer durable goods, true consumption (i.e., the use of the goods or of their services) depends upon the stocks in the hands of consumers, not on the rate of purchase of new goods. The latter, which is comparable to investment in capital goods, may evidence wide cyclical swings in response to changes in availability of credit, expectations, and other investment determinants, while the true consumption rate remains relatively stable. In addition, cyclical swings in the rate at which businessmen add to or deplete their inventories of goods may increase the amplitudes of fluctuation of industries producing such goods. In the case of services, consumption and output must coincide; inventories are nonexistent.

Another potentially relevant factor is the income elasticity of demand for goods and services. Some evidence, presented in Chapter 2, suggests that demand for services might be more elastic than for goods. If agricultural goods are excluded, however, the difference does not appear to be large. A higher income elasticity for services, other things being equal, would lead to greater cyclical instability in service output. The effect of this differential, however, is diminished to the extent that consumption patterns are determined by permanent income rather than by transitory or cyclical changes.[3] Furthermore, income elasticity refers to consumption rather than purchases. In the long run the two are identical, but, as has been noted, in the short run the existence of stocks in the hands of consumers tends to dampen the link between consumption and output for durable goods.

One other factor that might affect cyclical fluctuations in measured output of goods and services is the possibility of substitution between market and nonmarket production in response to cyclical changes in labor market conditions. When jobs are easy to find, unemployment usually falls and additional workers are attracted to the labor force. This increased employment in the market production of goods and services may be offset to some extent by a decrease in "nonmarket" or "home" production because the newly employed have less time available for such activities. This substitution between home and market production is par-

[2] Wesley C. Mitchell, *What Happens During Business Cycles: A Progress Report,* New York, NBER, 1941, p. 115. Mitchell went on to say that durability is "a somewhat ambiguous term." Arthur F. Burns has suggested that the high unit cost of most durable goods is a key element in the greater cyclical swings in their sales. This is another way of pointing up the difference between acquiring a stock and purchasing a flow of services.

[3] See Milton Friedman, *A Theory of the Consumption Function,* Princeton for NBER, 1957.

ticularly characteristic of women and other secondary workers.[4] If, as seems likely, this substitution occurs more often for services (e.g., restaurants, laundries, household cleaning, beauty care, nursing care) than for goods, there would be a tendency for the differential between fluctuations in measured output and true output to be greater for services than for goods. That is to say, if market production of goods is more volatile than market production of services, the difference is likely to be even greater if nonmarket production is taken into account.[5]

Given the cyclical behavior of output, there are several questions to be asked concerning the relative stability of employment in goods and services. First, there are large numbers of self-employed in the Service sector; as will be shown, their employment is almost completely insensitive to moderate cyclical fluctuations in output. Second, the role of salaried employees as opposed to hourly workers is much larger in services than it is in goods. Also, the educational level of service workers is higher than that of workers in Industry, and the costs of hiring are probably greater.[6] This means that dismissals or layoffs during recessions that are expected to be short-lived, will be less frequent. Finally, it should be noted that a substantial number of service industry employees are classified as "wage and salary workers" but are actually compensated on a "piecework" basis. Their wages, in whole or in part, are determined by their output and take the form of commissions, tips, or a share of "profits." Employers have little reason to dismiss such employees when business falls off. This group includes real estate, insurance, and security brokers, waiters and waitresses, barbers and beauticians, and most retail salesmen of durable goods. Because their earnings are more sensitive to cyclical fluctuations in spending than are their hours of work, we can think of these workers as having "flexible" wages.[7]

There is some "piecework" employment in manufacturing, as well as in the Service sector, but the effect on measured employment is not the same because of differences in the production process. When demand

[4] See Jacob Mincer, "Labor Force Participation of Married Women," in *Aspects of Labor Economics,* Universities—National Bureau Conference 14, Princeton for NBER, 1962, pp. 66–67; and "Market Prices, Opportunity Costs, and Income Effects," in *Measurement in Economics: Studies in Mathematical Economics and Econometrics in Memory of Yehuda Grunfeld,* Stanford, 1963, pp. 70–78.

[5] I am grateful to Michael Grossman for calling this point to my attention.

[6] The higher *level* of education of service industry employees should not be confused with *changes* in the level of education, which have been greater in the Industry sector.

[7] I am grateful to Jacob Mincer for this formulation.

falls in manufacturing, the employer will probably cut back on production, regardless of whether labor is paid on an hourly or piecework basis, and this cutback will result in less employment. The effect in services is different because the amount and timing of the output and employment required is not known in advance, and because there are practically no raw material costs for the employer to consider. In both situations a decrease in demand means a fall in the marginal revenue product of labor. In manufacturing, the wage per hour tends to remain the same, and there is a reduction in man-hours. In the case of waiters, barbers, salesmen, and so on, employment tends to remain unchanged, and the necessary adjustment is achieved through a fall in hourly earnings.

These considerations suggest that for equal cyclical changes in output there will be a greater accompanying change in employment in manufacturing than in services. If this tendency is present, the result may be greater cyclical swings in productivity in services than in manufacturing, even though output may fluctuate more in manufacturing.

One final point to be mentioned is the larger role of nonprofit organizations in services than in the Industry sector. Nonprofit organizations, public and private, account for over one-third of Service sector employment, but for only a small percentage of Industry employment. It will be recalled that one of Mitchell's main points about cyclical fluctuations stressed their relation to the "business economy." [8]

To sum up, we should expect to find larger cyclical fluctuations in output and employment in the Industry sector than in services. This sector differential should be greater for employment than for output, and should be more noticeable for durable than for nondurable goods. If employment is very stable relative to output in services, it is possible that productivity might fluctuate more in services than in the Industry sector.

Employment

This section discusses the amplitude of fluctuation of employment in the nine nonagricultural major industrial groups. The employment concept used is comprehensive. It includes part-time as well as full-time workers, supervisory as well as production workers, self-employed as well as employees. It does not, however, include unpaid family workers. Data on wage and salary earners, based on establishment reports, were obtained

[8] Wesley C. Mitchell, *Business Cycles, The Problems and Its Setting,* New York, NBER, 1927, pp. 458 and 468.

from the Bureau of Labor Statistics.[9] Estimates of the self-employed by industry were provided by the Bureau of Labor Statistics from unpublished work sheets of the Current Population Survey.

Chart 12 shows monthly series for the period 1947 through 1965 adjusted for seasonal fluctuations. Table 58 shows the average annual rate of change of each series during business cycle expansions and contractions and the net difference between rates of change in expansions and contractions. The net difference may be regarded as a measure of the cyclical amplitude of the series, net of trend. The larger the difference in rates of change between expansions and contractions, the greater the cyclical volatility of the series. The figures in parentheses indicate the average deviation of each phase or cycle from the mean of all the phases or cycles. A brief explanation of how these measures were calculated follows.

For the years covered by these time series, the National Bureau has identified seven business cycle turning points covering four contractions and three expansions. They are: Peak—November, 1948; Trough—October, 1949; Peak—July, 1953; Trough—August, 1954; Peak—July, 1957; Trough—April, 1958; Peak—May, 1960; Trough—February, 1961. These are known as reference cycle dates. The period between a peak and the following trough is called a contraction; the period between a trough and the following peak is called an expansion.[10] One contraction or one expansion is known as a phase, and a cycle consists of two successive phases. The cycle can be defined from trough to trough or from peak to peak; the choice is largely a matter of convention.[11]

The rates of change for each expansion are measured from a three-month average centered on a trough to a three-month average centered on the following peak. Rates of change in contractions are measured in a similar way from peak to trough. These rates are affected by the trend

[9] A description of the sources for the employment series and all the other series presented in this chapter can be found in Appendix J.

[10] For a description of the NBER method of dating business cycle turns see Arthur F. Burns and Wesley C. Mitchell, *Measuring Business Cycles,* New York, National Bureau of Economic Research, 1946, Chapter 4. See also, Geoffrey Moore, "What Is a Recession," *American Statistician,* October 1967.

[11] One argument for the trough to trough view of the cycle is that the forces leading to a contraction often develop as an integral part of the preceding expansion, whereas the forces leading to an expansion are more often exogenous. An argument for the peak to peak view is that the amplitude of an expansion (particularly with respect to physical production and related variables) depends in considerable degree on the amplitude of the previous contraction, whereas the amplitude of a contraction is not similarly dependent upon that of the previous expansion. The measures used in this study are based on an average of both approaches.

of the series as well as its cyclical behavior. For instance, government employment shows a positive rate of growth during contractions of 2.2 per cent per annum because of the strong underlying upward trend. Since this trend is also present during expansions, the net difference between rates of change in two adjacent phases indicates the magnitude of the cyclical component net of trend. The final figure, 1.4 per cent per annum, is the average of the net difference between all possible adjacent phase comparisons.[12]

This measure shows the cyclical volatility of each series when the cycle is defined by the NBER reference dates for the general business cycle. If the time series conforms to the general business cycle in the timing of peaks and troughs, these are clearly the appropriate dates to use. To the extent that a series has substantially different cyclical peaks and troughs, the present measure tends to understate the amount of cyclical fluctuation. Most of the cyclical movements in the series examined in this chapter conform reasonably well to the general business cycle. One exception is the series for construction employment; its cyclical volatility

---

[12] Assume the value of X at time i is composed of a trend component T and a cycle component C. Also assume that the relationship is multiplicative. Then

$$X_1 = T_i C_i \tag{1}$$

and

$$\ln X_i = \ln T_i + \ln C_i. \tag{2}$$

Differentiate (2) with respect to time.

$$\frac{dX_i}{dt}\frac{1}{X_i} = \frac{dT_i}{dt}\frac{1}{T_i} + \frac{dC_i}{dt}\frac{1}{C_i}. \tag{3}$$

Rewrite (3) as

$$m = r + c. \tag{4}$$

This defines the monthly rate of growth of the series assuming continuous compounding. The cyclical component will be positive in expansions and negative in contractions. Therefore

$$m_e = r + c_e \tag{5}$$

$$m_c = r - c_c. \tag{6}$$

Subtract (6) from (5) to get

$$m_e - m_c = c_e + c_c. \tag{7}$$

Multiply (7) by 12 to get the annual rate of change net of trend. Then average for all cycles.

CHART 12

Employment, Industry Groups, 1947–65

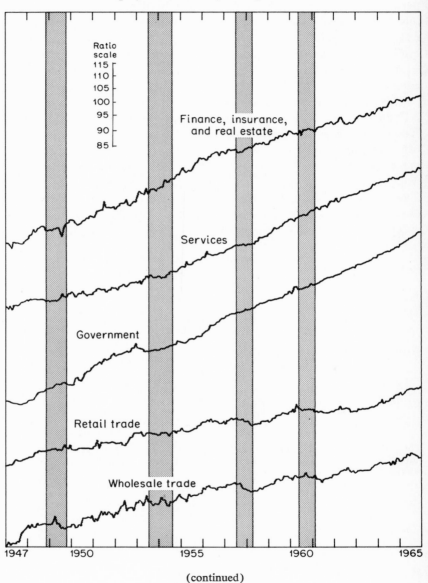

(continued)

CHART 12 (concluded)

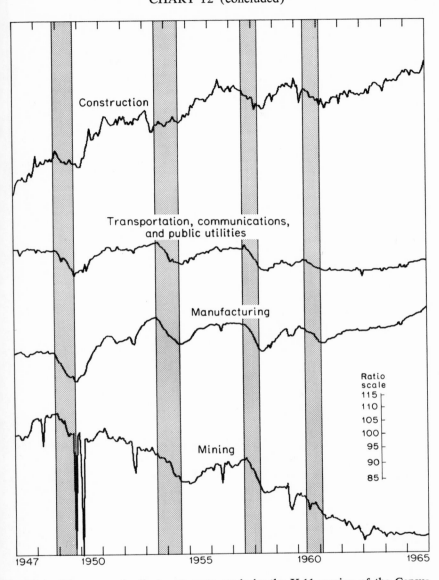

Construction

Transportation, communications,
and public utilities

Manufacturing

Mining

Ratio
scale
115
110
105
100
95
90
85

1947   1950   1955   1960   1965

Note: The seasonal adjustments were made by the X-11 version of the Census
method II seasonal adjustment program.

TABLE 58

Average Rates of Change of Employment During Business Cycles,
Nine Nonagricultural Major Industry Groups, 1947–65 [a]
(per cent per annum)

| Industry | Average Rate of Change in | | Average Cyclical Change Net of Trend |
	Expansions	Contractions	
Finance, insurance, and real estate	3.1(0.5)	2.4(1.0)	0.7(0.8)
Government	3.6(0.4)	2.2(0.1)	1.4(0.4)
Services [b]	3.4(1.0)	1.8(0.8)	1.6(1.3)
Retail trade	2.0(0.7)	−0.8(1.7)	2.8(2.3)
Wholesale trade	2.5(0.1)	−1.7(1.4)	4.2(1.3)
Construction	3.1(0.5)	−2.6(3.0)	5.7(2.6)
Transportation, communications, and public utilities	1.9(0.6)	−7.6(1.3)	9.5(1.4)
Mining	0.5(1.8)	−12.0(4.3)	12.5(4.6)
Manufacturing	3.8(1.4)	−9.5(1.4)	13.3(2.0)

Source: See Appendix J.

[a] Numbers shown in parentheses are average deviations defined as

$$\frac{\sum\limits_{i=1}^{n} |X_i - \bar{X}|}{n}$$

[b] Professional, personal, business and repair services. Domestic servants are excluded.

is much greater when measured over expansions and contractions in the specific series.[13]

Inspection of Table 58 reveals that the service industries are all characterized by small cyclical swings in employment. The smallest move-

[13] The average rates of change are: expansions, +5.9 per cent; contractions, −13.1 per cent; and cyclical change net of trend, 19.0 per cent. The dates of peaks and troughs for construction employment and other specific series are given in Appendix Table J-2. I am grateful to Sophie Sakowitz of the National Bureau's business cycle unit for the identification of these turning points by the methods described in *Measuring Business Cycles*, Chapter 4. It should be noted that some of the series, notably government; finance, insurance and real estate; and services have such strong upward trends that no true contractions can be observed. Nevertheless, even in these series there is evidence of conformity to the business cycle; the rates of growth are more rapid during periods of general business expansion than during general business contractions.

TABLE 59

Average Rates of Change of Employment During Business Cycles,
Sector Aggregates, 1947–65
(per cent per annum)

Sector	Average Rate of Change in		Average Cyclical Change Net of Trend
	Expansions	Contractions	
Total nonagricultural employment	3.0(0.2)	−3.4(1.0)	6.4(1.0)
Nonagricultural self-employment	0.7(1.6)	0.8(2.0)	−0.1(3.0)
Nonagricultural wage and salary employment	3.4(0.5)	−3.8(1.0)	7.2(0.1)
Service sector (total employment)	2.9(0.5)	0.7(0.7)	2.2(0.1)
Industry sector (total employment)	3.2(1.1)	−8.3(1.6)	11.5(1.8)
Service sector (wage and salary employment)	3.2(0.2)	0.5(0.6)	2.7(0.6)
Industry sector (wage and salary employment)	3.4(1.2)	−8.6(1.4)	12.0(1.8)

Note: Numbers shown in parentheses are average deviations. For definition see notes to Table 58.
Source: See Appendix J.

ments are found for finance, insurance and real estate; government; and the services proper. Retail employment shows slightly more cyclical sensitivity, and wholesaling slightly more than retailing, but still far less than the four major groups classified in the Industry sector.

The sector differential is confirmed and developed further in Table 59 where similar measures are presented for various sector aggregates. We see that self-employment does not conform to the business cycle, but this explains only a minor part of the cyclical stability of service employment. There is a significant sector differential for wage and salary employment alone. Industry employment fluctuated more than four times as much as did Service employment during the post-World War II business cycles. Furthermore, the very small average deviations (shown in parentheses) indicate that this sector differential is consistent from cycle to cycle and is highly significant in a statistical sense.[14]

[14] Similar calculations were made with transportation, communication, and public utilities classified in the Service sector; the Industry-Service difference was unaffected by this change. However, if freight transportation is treated separately, it shows considerable cyclical volatility.

TABLE 60

Mean Percentage Deviations from Trend of Employment, Major Industry
Groups and Sectors, 1947–65

Industry	Mean Percentage Deviation (in Absolute Terms)	
	Loga-rithmic Trend	75-Month Moving Average
Retail trade	1.0	1.0
Government	1.1	1.1
Wholesale trade	1.1	1.1
Finance, insurance, and real estate	1.6	0.9
Services	2.0	0.7
Transportation, communications, and public utilities	2.1	1.9
Mining	3.0	3.0
Manufacturing	3.1	2.6
Construction	3.9	2.9
Service sector	0.6	0.6
Industry sector	2.8	2.3

Source: See Appendix J.

As a check on these findings, two entirely different measures of fluctu-ations were calculated. The first is the average deviation of the smoothed monthly observations from a logarithmic trend fitted to all observations, 1947 through 1965.[15] Such a measure is independent of such concepts as cycles and turning points. The second is the average percentage devi-ation from a 75-month moving average.[16] This provides an alternative approach to eliminating the trend. The results, presented in Table 60,

[15] Smoothing is done by the "MCD span" moving average, defined as the num-ber of months necessary for the ratio $\bar{I}/\bar{C}$ to fall below 1. $\bar{I}$ denotes average per-centage change in the irregular component of a series without regard to sign, and $\bar{C}$ denotes average percentage changes in the trend-cycle component. The MCD is calculated by the X-11 variant of the Census method II seasonal adjustment program.
[16] These calculations were made at the National Bureau by Dennis Thornton, using a program he had written for Ilse Mintz's study of turning points in foreign business cycles.

TABLE 61

Average Rates of Change of Employment During Business Cycles,
Selected Industries, 1947–65
(per cent per annum)

Industry	Average Rate of Change in		Average Cyclical Change Net of Trend
	Expansions	Contractions	
Food stores	1.1(1.0)	1.2(1.7)	−0.1(2.5) [a]
Apparel stores	1.7(1.1)	−2.8(1.2)	4.5(1.8)
Auto dealers	2.3(0.5)	−2.9(3.2)	5.2(3.1)
Nondurable manufacturing	1.4(0.5)	−3.6(0.7)	5.0(0.5)
Durable manufacturing	5.6(2.4)	−14.2(2.3)	19.8(3.2)

Note: Numbers shown in parentheses are average deviations. For definitions see notes to Table 58.

Source: See Appendix J.

[a] Based on turning points in deflated retail sales, the average rates of change for food stores are: expansions, +1.6 per cent; contractions, +0.4 per cent; and cyclical change, 1.2 per cent.

provide substantial confirmation of the results based on cyclical analysis. The ranking of the industries differs somewhat between the two measures based on deviations from trend, but both are very highly correlated with the results based on cyclical analysis. Even more important in the present context is the finding that every group in the Service sector shows less deviation from trend than every group in the Industry sector.

It may be noted that the differentials are relatively smaller for the deviations from trend than for the cyclical changes shown in Table 58. This is probably because the deviations from trend consist of three components: (a) difference between the true trend and the trends actually fitted, (b) irregular movements, and (c) cyclical movements. There may be no systematic difference between industries in the two sectors with respect to the first two components. If there is none, the deviations from trend understate the differential attributable to cyclical differences alone.

The role of durability is explored in Chart 13 and Table 61, where measures of cyclical change are presented for durable and nondurable manufacturing, separately, and for three different types of retail stores. Food retailing involves mostly highly perishable commodities, apparel is

CHART 13

Employment, Selected Industries, 1947–65

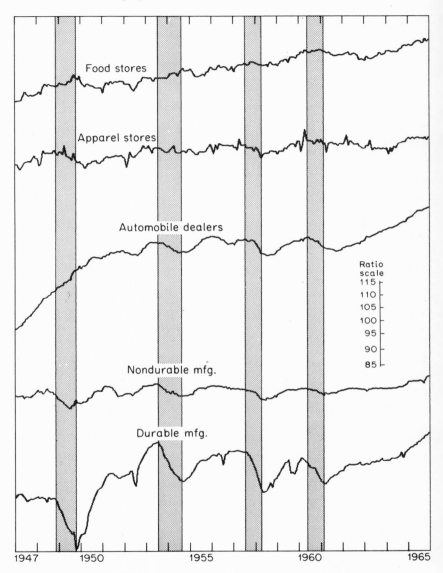

Food stores

Apparel stores

Automobile dealers

Ratio
scale
115
110
105
100
95
90
85

Nondurable mfg.

Durable mfg.

1947   1950   1955   1960   1965

more durable, and automobiles still more durable. We find that the cyclical swings correspond closely to the degree of durability in both manufacturing and retailing. Indeed, employment in food stores is almost completely insensitive to the business cycle.

Output

The difficulties encountered in measuring real output in the service industries have been discussed in the preceding chapters. Few satisfactory measures are available on an annual basis, and even fewer are available in the form of the monthly or quarterly series needed to analyze cyclical movements. This section, therefore, is limited to monthly series for wholesaling and retailing. The output measures are the conventional ones of deflated sales; changes in the quality or quantity of service associated with a constant dollar's worth of sales are not reflected in output.[17]

Comparisons are made with manufacturing output as measured by the Federal Reserve Board index of manufacturing production. In this case also there are shortcomings; some components of output are estimated from man-hour series. Therefore, a series of deflated manufacturing sales is also used.

Given the problems of measurement, not much confidence should be placed in minor differences in cyclical amplitude. The gross differences that emerge, however, probably reflect underlying economic realities rather than defects in the data.

Movements in output of manufacturing, wholesaling, and retailing, are compared in Chart 14 and the first part of Table 62. We see that, for all industries, there is considerably more fluctuation in output than in employment, and that manufacturing output shows more cyclical volatility than does output in wholesale or retail trade. Wholesaling shows greater fluctuations than retailing over the NBER dates.[18] There is a close correspondence between manufacturing output as measured by the FRB index and that measured by deflated sales, but the latter series shows less cyclical fluctuation.[19]

---

[17] Conceptually it is preferable to deflate sales by each store type separately and then average the results using margins as weights. Some experimentation revealed that the difference between a series obtained in this manner and the one actually used is negligible for cyclical analysis.

[18] Very similar results are obtained when changes for each series are based on turning points in that series. See Appendix Table J-3.

[19] Analysis of deviations from trend, 1947–65, reveals a similar pattern. The mean percentage deviation for the FRB index is 4.5; it is 4.0 for deflated manufacturing sales, and 2.5 for retailing.

CHART 14

Output, Industry Groups, 1947–65

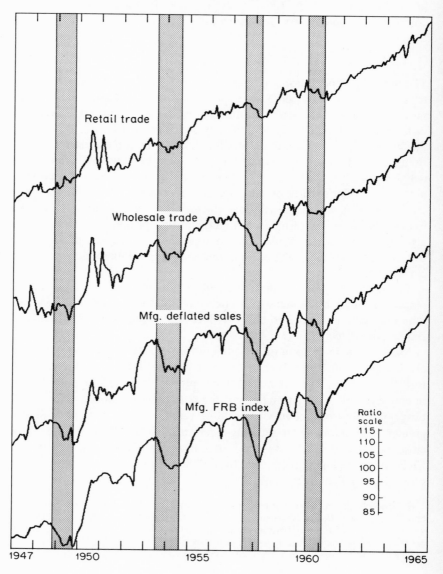

TABLE 62

Average Rates of Change of Output During Business Cycles,
Selected Industries, 1947–65
(per cent per annum)

| Industry | Average Rate of Change in | | Average Cyclical Change Net of Trend |
	Expansions	Contractions	
Retail trade	4.6(0.8)	−2.3(3.7)	6.9(4.4)
Wholesale trade	5.5(1.4)	−4.7(3.1)	10.2(3.1)
Manufacturing (FRB index)	8.7(1.9)	−11.8(4.9)	20.5(4.6)
Manufacturing (deflated sales)	7.0(1.6)	−9.7(3.2)	16.7(3.0)
Nondurable manufacturing (FRB)	5.9(1.3)	−2.3(2.5)	8.2(3.5)
Durable manufacturing (FRB)	11.1(3.1)	−19.5(6.9)	30.6(5.8)
Food stores	4.4(0.6)	1.1(1.8)	3.4(2.0)
Apparel stores	4.1(2.0)	−1.2(1.2)	5.3(2.6)
Auto dealers	5.1(1.8)	−7.9(12.6)	13.0(14.3)

Note: Numbers shown in parentheses are average deviations. For definition see notes to Table 58.
Source: See Appendix J.

The second part of Table 62 and Chart 15 shows the relation between cyclical fluctuations of output and durability. The cyclical change, net of trend, of durable manufacturing is almost four times as great as nondurable manufacturing. The cyclical change of output in auto retailing is more than double that of apparel retailing, which, in turn, is almost double that of food retailing. This confirms our expectations concerning the role of durability.

Output Per Man-Hour

This section presents amplitude measures of output per man-hour for the same series presented in the output section. Output per man-hour is calculated by dividing the output series by a man-hour series. (Neither series is adjusted for seasonal fluctuations.) The latter is obtained by multiplying the employment series of the first section by an average hours series obtained from the Bureau of Labor Statistics and the Current Population Survey.[20]

[20] See Appendix J for a full description.

CHART 15
Output, Selected Industries, 1947–65

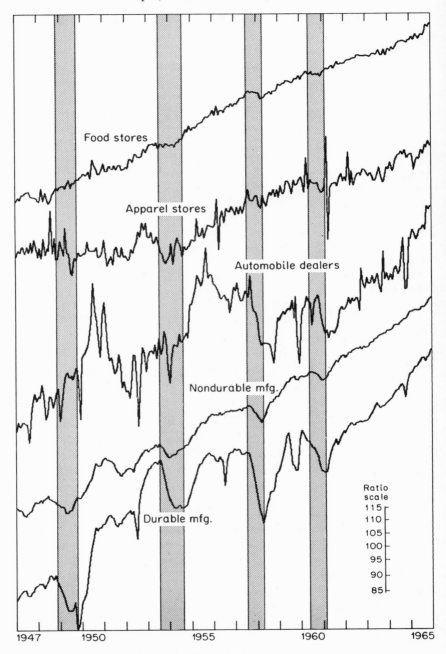

Food stores

Apparel stores

Automobile dealers

Nondurable mfg.

Durable mfg.

Ratio
scale
115
110
105
100
95
90
85

1947   1950   1955   1960   1965

CHART 16

Output Per Man-Hour, Industry Groups, 1947–65

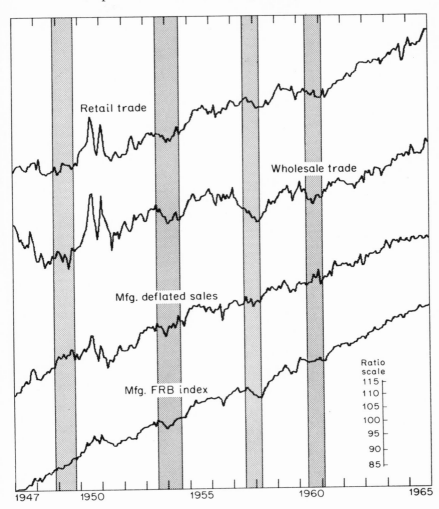

After output per man-hour was calculated, it was seasonally adjusted; the results are presented in Charts 16 and 17. The measures of cyclical volatility shown in Table 63 indicate some important differences between output per man-hour and employment and output. In particular, cyclical fluctuations of output per man-hour are greater in wholesaling than in manufacturing. The cyclical change in retailing is greater than in manu-

CHART 17

Output Per Man-Hour, Selected Industries, 1947–65

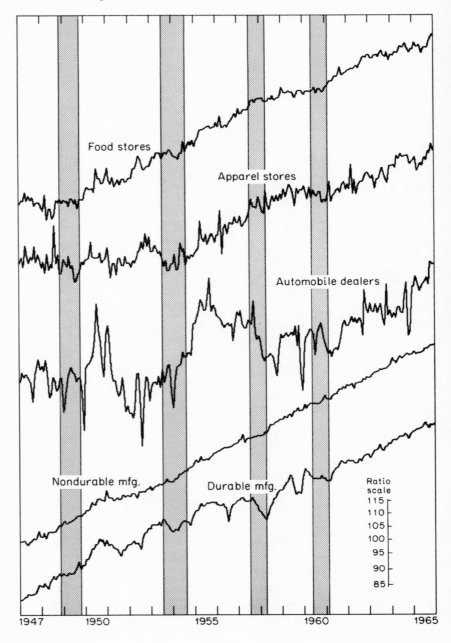

TABLE 63

Average Rates of Change of Output Per Man-Hour During Business Cycles,
Selected Industries, 1947–65
(per cent per annum)

Industry	Average Rate of Change in		Average Cyclical Change Net of Trend
	Expansions	Contractions	
Retail trade	3.1(0.3)	−0.7(2.1)	3.8(2.0)
Wholesale trade	3.0(1.3)	−2.4(2.3)	5.4(2.0)
Manufacturing (FRB index)	4.2(1.2)	0.3(2.3)	3.9(2.8)
Manufacturing (deflated sales)	2.4(0.8)	2.1(0.7)	0.3(1.2)
Nondurable manufacturing (FRB)	4.0(0.7)	3.4(0.9)	0.6(1.4)
Durable manufacturing (FRB)	4.5(1.4)	−2.5(3.9)	7.0(4.3)
Food stores	3.8(1.3)	2.2(0.9)	1.6(1.8)
Apparel stores	3.0(2.1)	0.9(1.3)	2.1(1.6)
Auto dealers	2.9(1.8)	−4.7(9.8)	7.6(11.2)

Note: Numbers shown in parentheses are average deviations. For definition see notes to Table 58.
Source: Appendix J.

facturing when output is measured by deflated sales and is approximately equal when the FRB index is used to measure output.[21]

Calculation of percentage deviations from trend confirms this conclusion. The average deviation for retailing is 2.3 per cent; it is 1.3 or 1.5 per cent for manufacturing depending upon the output series used. Chart 18 compares the trend deviations for retailing and manufacturing (FRB index) and the greater cyclical movements of retailing can be observed.

One of the factors accounting for the greater cyclical variability of output per man-hour in retailing than in manufacturing is the different timing of cyclical changes in output and employment in the two industries. Chart 19 shows that in manufacturing, output and employment tend to move together over the cycle. In retailing, however, the peaks and troughs of employment tend to lag behind those of output. (See Chart 20.) This lack of coincidence in timing accentuates the cyclical changes in productivity.

[21] When specific cycle turning points are used, the gap between trade and manufacturing is even larger. See Appendix Table J-4.

CHART 18

Percentage Deviations From Trend, Output Per Man-Hour, Retail Trade
and Manufacturing, 1947–65

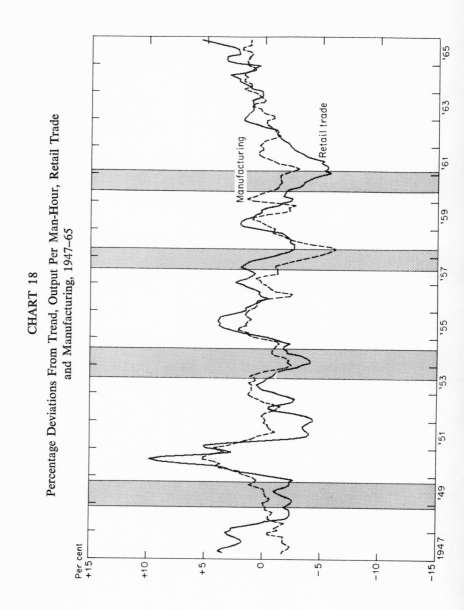

CHART 19

Percentage Deviations From Trend, Manufacturing, Output, and Employment, 1947–65

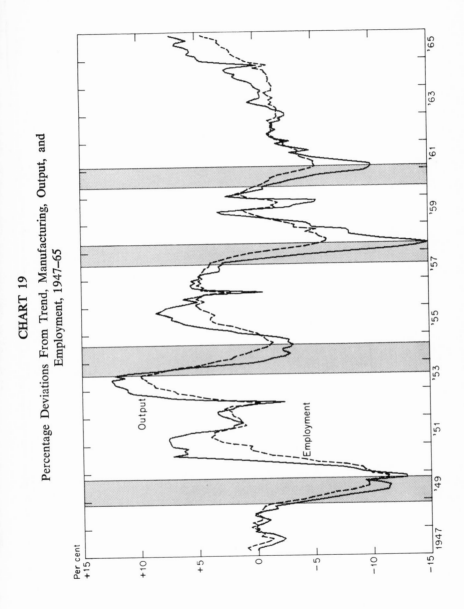

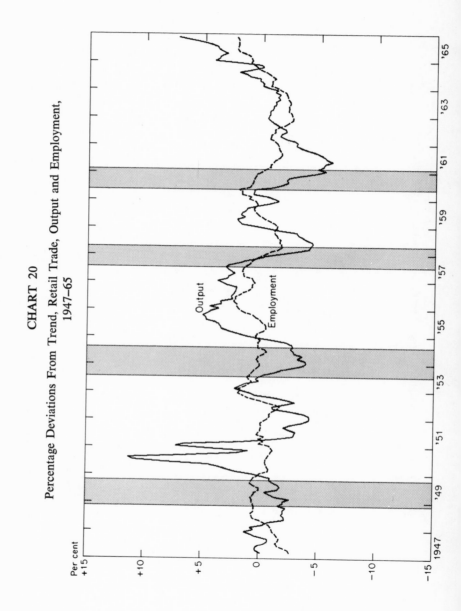

CHART 20

Percentage Deviations From Trend, Retail Trade, Output and Employment,
1947–65

TABLE 64

Effect of Changing Distribution of Employment on Average Cyclical
Volatility of Total Nonagricultural Employment, 1929–65
(per cent per annum)

Weight Base	Average Rate of Change in		Average Cyclical Change Net of Trend
	Expansions	Contractions	
1929	2.96	−4.05	7.01
1947	3.04	−3.82	6.86
1956	3.08	−3.57	6.65
1965	3.12	−3.03	6.15

Note: Cyclical measures for each major group (Table 58) are weighted by the distribution of persons engaged in each year.

Implications for Cyclical Stability

Given the greater cyclical stability of service industry employment, and given the trend toward greater employment in services, it is interesting to ask what are the implications for over-all stability of employment. We have taken the average cyclical volatility measures of Table 58 for the nine major industry groups and weighted them by the distribution of total nonagricultural employment in 1929, 1947, 1956, and 1965. (See Table 64.) This yields a hypothetical measure of changes in the cyclical amplitude of employment that could be attributed solely to the changes in the industrial distribution of employment. The average cyclical change net of trend shows a decrease from 7.01 per cent per annum in 1929 to 6.15 per cent in 1965, purely as a result of the changes in weights. Thus, the change in industrial distribution of employment between 1929 and 1965 may be said to account for a 15 per cent decrease in the cyclical volatility of total nonagricultural employment, if the volatility of each industry group remained unchanged.[22]

Table 65 presents a similar calculation for output per man. In this case, the shift in weights increases over-all sensitivity to the business cycle, from 5.3 per cent per annum to 6.4 per cent. The cyclical volatility measures of output and employment in manufacturing are taken as proxies

---

[22] This is, of course, only one way that structural change affects cyclical stability. For a discussion of other implications, including the effect of structural shifts on investment demand, see Bert G. Hickman, *Growth and Stability of the Postwar Economy*, Washington, D.C., 1960, pp. 182–203, 274–276.

TABLE 65

Effect of Changing Distribution of Output and Employment on Average
Cyclical Volatility of Output Per Man, Nonagricultural Economy, 1929–65
(per cent per annum)

Weight Base	Average Rate of Change in		Average Cyclical Change Net of Trend
	Expansions	Contractions	
1929	3.6	−1.7	5.3
1947	3.7	−2.1	5.8
1956	3.8	−2.4	6.2
1965	3.8	−2.6	6.4

Note: Weighted average rate of change in expansions or contractions given by

$$(\dot{O}_g O_g + \dot{O}_s O_s) - (\dot{E}_g E_g + \dot{E}_s E_s)$$

where $\dot{O}_g$ and $\dot{E}_g$ equal rates of change of output and employment in manufacturing; $\dot{O}_s$ and $\dot{E}_s$ equal same in retail trade taken from Tables 58 and 62; O_g, E_g, O_s, E_s equal shares of output and employment in Industry and Service sectors in each year.

for the Industry sector; the cyclical volatility measures for retail trade are taken as proxies for the Service sector. The weights are based on the sector shares of output and employment in each of the four years. The volatility measures are for reference cycle dates for all series.

Unlike the case of employment, in this instance the shift in weights results in a steady increase in cyclical sensitivity since 1929. The last column shows that, if the specific cyclical volatility of output per man remained unchanged, we could expect a 20 per cent increase in over-all volatility because of the growing importance of the Service sector.

8

SOME IMPLICATIONS
OF THE GROWTH
OF A SERVICE ECONOMY

The preceding chapters have delineated the shift of employment to services, have suggested some of the reasons for this shift, and have hinted at some of the implications. In this chapter we will take a longer and closer look at some aspects of the growth of a service economy. It will be argued that this growth has important implications for society, and that it also has important implications for economic analysis.

To be sure, such an attempt to look into the future is subject to many qualifications. A shift in the relative importance of different industries is only one of many changes that are occurring simultaneously in the economy, and these other changes may tend to offset the effects of interindustry shifts. Also, these shifts themselves may set in motion changes with implications different from those discussed here. Nevertheless, given the rapid growth of the service industries, it is useful to consider differences between them and the rest of the economy.

As Chapters 2 and 3 make clear, the dramatic shift to services has occurred in employment—not in output. A question arises, therefore, about the validity of the emphasis given here to the growth of a service economy. It is probably true that for some economic questions the industrial distribution of employment is of no greater significance than the industrial distribution of output or of physical capital. A million dollars' worth of capital input can be said to have as much economic significance as a million dollars' worth of labor input. But labor is human and physical capital is not; it is appropriate, therefore, to give labor primary attention in any broad study concerned with total social development.

Changes in the industrial distribution of employment have implications for where and how men live, the education they need, and even the health hazards that they face. Indeed, it has been written that "When man changes his tools and his techniques, his ways of producing and distributing the goods of life, he also changes his gods." [1]

A hypothetical example may help to clarify the point. Suppose we had an economy in which inputs of physical capital and human labor were roughly equal in economic importance; i.e., the annual value of the services flowing from each was approximately equal. Suppose further that 90 per cent of the physical capital and 10 per cent of the labor were employed in Industry, and 10 per cent of the capital and 90 per cent of the labor in the production of services. Although the sectors would be equal in economic importance, it seems reasonable to expect that the dominant tone of the society would be set by the service component. The kind of work people do, the kinds of organizations they work for, the location of the work, and many other critical aspects of their lives would be different than if capital and labor were equally divided between the two sectors. [2]

Implications for the Economy

Labor Force

Differences between the Industry and Service sectors are most noticeable with respect to labor force characteristics. Some of these differences are shown in Table 66 and expanded upon in Tables 67–70. Probably the most significant one is that many occupations in the Service sector do not make special demands for characteristically male qualities, such as physical strength. This means that women can compete on more nearly equal terms with men. We find women holding down almost one-half of all service jobs compared with only one-fifth of those in the Industry sector. More detailed information on the sex distributions in the two sectors is presented in Table 67.

We see that over half of all man-hours in the Industry sector are worked in industries with negligible (under 15 per cent) female employment. By contrast, in the Service sector more than 60 per cent of the man-hours are worked in industries with at least 30 per cent female employment.

We also find proportionately more older workers in services, despite the fact that this is the more rapidly growing sector and would therefore

---

[1] Harvey Cox, *The Secular City*, New York, 1965, p. 8.

[2] Another possible source of difference is that there may be more socially desirable externalities associated with the production of services than with the production of goods. See Arthur Treadway, "What Is Output?—Problems of Concept and Measurement," in *Production and Productivity in the Service Industries*, V. R. Fuchs, ed., NBER, in press.

TABLE 66

Labor Force Characteristics, Industry and Service Sectors, 1960 [a]

	Percentage of U.S. Total in		Percentage of Sector Employment	
	Industry	Service	Industry	Service
1. All employed [b]	43	50	100	100
2. Females	27	71	20	46
3. Over 65	25	59	3	5
4. Part-timers	34	59	18	27
5. Self-employed [c]	16	50	5	13
6. Union members	82	17	57	9
7. More than 12 years of school	30	68	14	28
8. Fewer than 9 years of school	49	37	34	22

Source: Rows 1–5, *U.S. Census of Population, 1960;* row 6, H. G. Lewis, *Unionism and Relative Wages in the United States,* 1963, p. 251; rows 7–8, NBER tabulations of the 1960 U.S. Census of Population 1/1,000 sample.

[a] For sector definitions, see Table 1.
[b] Civilian employment, includes unpaid family workers.
[c] Excludes unpaid family workers.

TABLE 67

Distribution of Industries and Man-Hours by Percentage
of Female Employment, Industry and Service Sectors, 1960

Percentage Female	Number of Industries		Percentage of Industries		Percentage of Man-Hours	
	I	S	I	S	I	S
0 to 15.0	39	12	48.1	21.1	56.6	15.1
15.1 to 30.0	23	16	28.4	28.1	21.5	23.3
30.1 to 45.0	9	14	11.1	24.6	12.7	17.2
45.1 to 60.0	6	7	7.4	12.3	4.7	16.2
60.1 and over	4	8	4.9	14.0	4.4	28.2

Source: Appendix Table I–2.

tend to have a disproportionately large number of young workers. One reason why women and older workers are attracted to the Service sector is that it provides greater opportunities for part-time employment. Almost three out of every ten workers in the Service sector in 1960 worked fewer than thirty-five hours a week. Sector differences in the role of part-timers in 1948 and 1963 are presented in greater detail in Table 68. We see that trade and services in particular have employed large numbers of part-timers and that the number has grown appreciably in the postwar period. If data were available on those working fewer than thirty-five hours per week *voluntarily,* the difference between the sectors would probably be even greater than that shown.

Table 66 shows that self-employment is relatively twice as important in the Service sector as in Industry. Moreover, the Census of Population may understate the number of self-employed in Services relative to Industry because corporate employees are classified as wage and salary workers regardless of the size of the corporation. The officers of small, owner-managed corporations are, for analytical purposes, similar to partners or individual proprietors, and should be considered self-employed. About three-quarters of such corporations are in the service industries.

It has been widely believed that opportunities for self-employment are

TABLE 68

Percentage of Wage and Salary Workers Working Fewer Than 35 Hours, By Industry, 1948 and 1963

	May 1948	May 1963	Change, 1948–63
Industry sector	9.6	10.6	+1.0
Service sector	16.3	23.8	+7.5
Mining, forestry, and fisheries	11.3	7.9	−3.4
Construction	16.2	16.9	+0.7
Manufacturing	9.1	9.4	+0.3
Transportation and public utilities	6.3	9.7	+3.4
Wholesale and retail trade	14.7	24.1	+9.4
Finance, insurance, and real estate	7.8	12.5	+4.7
Service industries [a]	23.7	30.7	+7.0
Public administration	5.3	8.7	+3.4

Source: 85th Congress, First Session, House Education and Labor Committee, Hours of Work, Hearings before the Select Subcommittee on Labor, on HR 355, HR 3102, and HR 3320, Washington, D.C., 1963, Part I, p. 78.

[a] These include personal, professional, business, and repair services.

TABLE 69

Distribution of Industries and Man-Hours By Self-Employment Income
as Percentage of Total Earnings, Industry and Service Sectors, 1960

Self-Employment Earnings as Percentage of Total Earnings		Number of Industries		Percentage of Industries		Percentage of Man-Hours	
		I	S	I	S	I	S
0 to 9.99		69	9	85.2	15.8	78.2	33.9
10 to 19.99		8	10	9.9	17.5	7.5	16.6
20 to 29.99		3	17	3.7	29.8	13.8	21.2
30 and over		1	21	1.2	36.8	.4	28.4

Source: Appendix Table I–2.

diminishing in the United States. But if one excludes the decline of agriculture, this is no longer true.[3] Table 69 shows that self-employment plays a large role in many service industries. Indeed, self-employment income represents over 30 per cent of total earnings in twenty-one service industries that account for 28.4 per cent of total man-hours worked in the Service sector.

The role of self-employment in the future will be determined by several conflicting trends. The growth of nongovernmental services will tend to favor it, but this may be offset by the growth of government employment and by the influx of young workers and women into the labor force, since these groups are predominantly wage and salary workers. There may also be some tendency toward larger firms within each individual industry, but there is little reason to think that the door to self-employment will be closed as long as services continue to grow.

Given the importance of females, part-time employment, and self-employment in the Service sector, it is not surprising to find a vast difference in the importance of unions in the two sectors. This difference is shown in some detail in Table 70. We see that no Service industry was as much as 40 per cent unionized in 1960, and that only a few reached the 20 per cent level. In the Industry sector, on the other hand, 75 per cent of the man-hours were worked in industries with at least 40 per cent unionization.

[3] See John E. Bregger, "Self-Employment in the United States 1948–1962," Special Labor Force Report No. 27, *Monthly Labor Review,* January 1963, and Irving Leveson, "Nonfarm Self-Employment in the U.S.," unpublished Ph.D. dissertation, Columbia University, January 1968.

TABLE 70

Distribution of Industries and Man-Hours By Percentage
Unionized, Industry and Service Sectors, 1960

Percentage of Employment Unionized	Number of Industries		Percentage of Industries		Percentage of Man-Hours	
	I	S	I	S	I	S
0 to 19.99	6	52	7.4	91.2	6.4	95.0
20 to 39.99	23	5	28.4	8.8	19.1	5.0
40 to 59.99	33	0	40.7	0	50.3	0
60 and over	19	0	23.5	0	24.3	0

Source: Appendix Table I–2.

The continued growth of services may mean a decline in union influence in the United States. On the other hand, if unions are successful in
organizing the Service sector to the same extent as the Industry sector,
we may see a significant change in the nature of the union movement.
The spread of unionism to service workers would probably also have
implications for labor quality, productivity, and unemployment in those
industries.

Although unionization is not widespread, in services, considerable attention has been directed to strikes in that sector in recent years. Walk-
outs by teachers, sanitation workers, and hospital employees have pro-
voked relatively more comment and intervention than much longer strikes
by workers in mining, manufacturing, and construction. This is probably
related in part to the perishable nature of service output. One possible
implication of the spread of unionism to services is growing pressure for
compulsory arbitration and other modifications in traditional approaches
to collective bargaining.

The last two rows of Table 66 reveal interesting sector differences in
education. The service industries make greater use of workers with
higher education and relatively less use of those with only limited schooling. This is not true for all service industries, of course, but it is true for
the sector on average.[4]

There is another implication concerning labor which is not readily
apparent in the statistics but which is potentially of considerable impor-

[4] As indicated in footnote 6, Chap. 7, we are discussing the higher *level* of education of service industry employees. This should not be confused with *changes* in
the level of education, which have been greater in the Industry sector.

tance. For many decades we have been hearing that industrialization has alienated the worker from his work, that the individual has no contact with the final fruit of his labor, and that the transfer from a craft society to one of mass production has resulted in the loss of personal identification with work.

Whatever validity such statements may have had in the past, a question arises whether they now accord with reality. The advent of a service economy may imply a reversal of these trends. Employees in many service industries are closely related to their work and often render a highly personalized service that offers ample scope for the development and exercise of personal skills.[5]

This is true of some goods-producing occupations as well, but the direct confrontation between consumer and worker that occurs frequently in services creates the possibility of a more completely human and satisfying work experience. To be sure, within many service industries there is some tendency for work to become less personalized (e.g., teaching machines in education, self-service counters in retailing, and laboratory tests in medicine); but with more and more people becoming engaged in service occupations, the net effect for the labor force as a whole may be in the direction of the *personalization* of work.

It should be stressed that deriving satisfaction from a job well done and taking pride in one's work are only possibilities, not certainties. Teachers can ignore their pupils; doctors can think more of their bank balances than of their patients. The salesman who must go through life with an artificial smile on his face while caring little for his customers and less for what he sells is often held in low regard. But at their best many service occupations are extremely rewarding, and the line between "work" and "leisure" activity is often difficult to draw.

Some service occupations, especially some personal services, are not well-regarded in this country. In a country with a high average level of income, however, one should expect that a large amount of personal service will be consumed and that a large number of people will be so employed. This would be true even if the income distribution were completely egalitarian. High per capita income implies high average output per man. This is likely to mean *very* high output per man in some industries (where capital can be substituted for labor, and technological change is rapid). Employment, therefore, will probably expand primarily in those industries, such as personal services, where output per man advances slowly. Our attitudes toward personal services are not immu-

---

[5] For example, health, education, entertainment, personal services, repair services.

table laws of nature; they can be changed. Such a change would, I suspect, reduce unemployment and increase consumer satisfaction.

Industrial Organization

The shift of employment to the Service sector carries with it important implications for industrial organization in the United States because the size of the "firm" and the nature of ownership and control are typically different in Services than Industry.

In Industry, with some notable exceptions, such as construction, most of the output is accounted for by large corporations. Ownership is frequently separate from management, and significant market power held by a few firms in each industry is not uncommon.

In the Service sector, on the other hand, and again with some exceptions, firms are typically small, usually owner-managed and often noncorporate. Furthermore, nearly all firms in the Industry sector are organized for profit, whereas nonprofit operations, public and private, account for one-third of the Service sector's employment.

Table 71 summarizes some of the available information concerning

TABLE 71

Percentage Distribution of Employment, by Size of Firm or Employer, Manufacturing and Selected Service Industries

	Number of Employees	
Industries	Fewer than 20	Fewer than 500
1. Manufacturing (1958)	7	38
2. Wholesale trade (1958)	47	93
3. Retail trade (1958)	56	78
4. Selected services (1958)	57	87
5. Finance, insurance, and real estate (1956)	41	67
6. Hospitals (nongovernmental, 1963)	n.a.	52
7. Local government (1962)	n.a.	49

Source: Rows 1–4, Bureau of the Census, *Enterprise Statistics: 1958 Part 1, General Report*, p. 30, adjusted to include self-employed proprietors by assuming that they are in firms with fewer than twenty employees; row 5, Betty C. Churchill, "Size of Business Firms," *Survey of Current Business*, September 1959, p. 19, adjusted for self-employed proprietors as rows 1–4; row 6, American Hospital Association, *Hospitals*, Guide Issue, 1964, estimated from distributions by number of beds; row 7, Census of Government, *Compendium of Government Employment*, 1962, estimated in part.

TABLE 72

Distribution of Industries and Man-Hours, by Percentage of Employment
in Establishments With Over 250 Employees, Industry
and Service Sectors, 1960

Percentage of Employment in Establishments With Over 250 Employees		Number of Industries		Percentage of Industries		Percentage of Man-Hours	
		I	S	I	S	I	S
0 to 19.99		10	44	12.3	77.2	17.4	70.3
20 to 39.99		22	9	27.2	15.8	22.6	16.0
40 to 59.99		15	1	18.5	1.8	17.3	3.7
60 to 79.99		20	2	24.7	3.5	18.6	8.4
80 and over		14	1	17.3	1.8	24.1	1.6

Source: Appendix Table I–2.

the distribution of employment in different service industries by size of
employer. The size distribution in manufacturing is included for comparison. In wholesale trade, retail trade, and selected services, accounting
for more than 50 per cent of the Service sector, half of the employment
is in companies with fewer than twenty workers. In finance, insurance,
and real estate, 40 per cent is in very small firms. Another large
fraction of Service sector employment is accounted for by self-employed
professionals and domestic servants, not shown in the table. They represent the extreme in small size of employer.

Private (i.e., nongovernmental) hospitals are considerably larger than
the typical service firm; but even so, more than half the total employment
of these institutions is in hospitals with fewer than 500 employees. Similarly, most private schools and colleges are relatively small.

Government, which is often referred to as a "huge bureaucracy," actually includes many small employers. It is worth noting that employment
at the local level of government now exceeds that of state and federal
(civilian) government combined. One-half of this local employment is
in governmental units with fewer than 500 employees.

Table 72 presents some additional detail concerning the size of establishments in the two sectors. In Industry, employment is evenly distributed among all types of industries, ranging from those in which most of
the employment is in small establishments to those in which very little
of the employment is in small establishments. Service sector employment

is heavily concentrated in industries characterized by small-scale operations.

Because of the importance of small firms and nonprofit organizations in the Service sector, the growth of this sector has tended to limit the pervasiveness of business corporations in the economy. In the first half of this century, the corporation's role grew steadily, but its relative importance apparently reached a peak about 1956 when corporations accounted for over 57 per cent of total national income. Since then there has been a tendency for this fraction to remain stable, or even to show some decline, despite changes in the tax laws which encourage incorporation.

Other things being equal, the shift to services tends to increase the relative importance of small firms in the economy. There are, however, forces within many industries that tend to increase the size of the average "firm." The pressure for consolidation of school districts and other local government units is a notable example. Bank mergers is another. The net effect of these countertendencies is difficult to predict.

Industries in which small firms account for the bulk of the output typically do not present industrial control problems of the "trust-busting" variety. On the other hand, the growth of such industries may increase the need to guard against the restrictive practices of trade associations and professional organizations. Small firms may pose another problem for the economy because it is alleged that they do not allocate sufficient resources to research and other activities with large external benefits.

The growing importance of the nonprofit sector will probably pose some disturbing questions about how to promote efficiency and equity in such organizations (for example, the problems associated with increasing costs in voluntary hospitals). When nonprofit operations represent only a minor exception to an essentially private-enterprise economy, the problem is not very serious. But if we ever reach the stage where nonprofit operations tend to dominate the economy, we probably will be faced with the need for radically new instruments of regulation and control.

Sector Differences and Rates of Growth

Table 73 presents summary measures of industry characteristics by sector, and for groups of industries within each sector, classified according to their rate of growth of employment, 1929–65. There were, for instance, thirteen industries in the Industry sector and twelve in the Service sector that had above average rates of growth in employment. The median measures for these industries for each characteristic are

TABLE 73

Industry Characteristics, by Sector and Rate of Growth
of Employment, 1929–65 [a]
(median values)

	Employment Growth, 1929–65 [b]					
	Above Average		Below Average		All Industries	
	Indus-try	Serv-ice	Indus-try	Serv-ice	Indus-try	Serv-ice
No. of Industries [c]	13	12	20	6	33	18
Characteristic:						
Per cent female	14.6	37.8	12.1	44.5	12.9	38.3
Per cent 65 years of age and over	1.9	4.6	2.6	6.7	2.2	5.6
Per cent working less than 35 hrs. per wk.	6.7	13.0	10.2	28.3	8.7	17.1
Self-employment income as % of total earnings	5.9	19.2	4.2	22.1	4.6	19.7
Per cent unionized	51.0	1.5	52.5	20.5	52.0	4.5
Per cent with 12 yrs. schooling and over	54.7	69.2	34.2	37.2	41.2	61.4
Per cent in large establishments (over 250 employees)	61.9	11.5	50.0	8.0	58.7	9.1

Source: See Appendix Table C–6 and Appendix I.
[a] Figures for industry characteristics based on data for 1960.
[b] Median rate of growth = 1.44 per cent per annum.
[c] These industries roughly correspond to the Office of Business Economics classification, and the rates of growth of employment were calculated from that source. A few industries were combined in order to obtain comparability with the Census of Population classification that was the primary source of the characteristics data, and a few industries were excluded because of lack of comparability over time. See note to Table 3.

shown in columns 1 and 2. A similar comparison for slow-growing industries is presented in columns 3 and 4.

We see that the sector differences discussed earlier in this chapter are still evident. In nearly every instance the critical difference is between the sectors, not between fast-growing and slow-growing industries. The only exception is the percentage of employees with twelve or more years of schooling. This percentage is still higher for the Service sector for all groups, but the differential within each sector between fast-growing and slow-growing industries is greater than the differential between the sectors for industries with similar growth rates. With this one exception, the hypothesis that the observed sector differentials are really differences between fast- and slow-growing industries is refuted.

Implications for Economic Analysis

The growth of the Service sector has important implications for economic analysis. In some respects, the current situation is analogous to the shift from agriculture to industry. In retrospect, it is apparent that this shift had considerable influence on economic analysis: land became less important as an input in production and distribution models, and physical capital became much more important. The need for a theory of imperfect competition became more apparent. Short-run supply curves could no longer be thought of as completely inelastic, and the possibilities of increasing returns had to be examined with greater rigor.

Although all the necessary theoretical tools can be found in one form or another in the writings of the earliest economists, the development and refinement of concepts are often related to changes in the economy itself. Analytical work requires compromises with reality. The compromises that may be appropriate, or the second-order effects that may be neglected, in an economy dominated by agriculture and manufacturing may turn out to be inappropriate, or too important to be neglected, in an economy dominated by the service industries. I shall try to illustrate this point by reference to the analysis of productivity and growth.

The Consumer as a Factor in Production

One lesson that our study of productivity in the service industries keeps forcing upon us is the importance of the consumer as a cooperating agent in the production process. To the best of my knowledge, this point is neglected in the analysis of productivity in goods-producing industries, as well it might be. After all, productivity in the automobile industry is not affected by whether the ultimate drivers are bright or stupid, or whether they drive carefully or carelessly.

In services, however, the consumer frequently plays an important role in production. Sometimes, as in the barber's chair, the role is essentially passive. In such cases the only conceptual adjustment called for is to recognize that the time of the consumer is also a scarce resource.[6] But in

[6] See Gary S. Becker, "A Theory of the Allocation of Time," *Economic Journal*, September 1965.

the supermarket and laundromat the consumer actually works, and in the doctor's office the quality of the medical history the patient gives may influence significantly the productivity of the doctor. Productivity in banking is affected by whether the clerk or the customer makes out the deposit slip—and whether it is made out correctly or not. This, in turn, is likely to be a function of the education of the customer, among other factors. Productivity in education, as every teacher knows, is determined largely by what the student contributes, and, to take an extreme case, the performance of a string quartet can be affected by the audience's response. Thus we see that productivity in many service industries is dependent in part on the knowledge, experience, and motivation of the consumer. Consider, for instance, what would happen to service-industry productivity in the United States if technology and capital and labor inputs remained as they are, but the consumers were exchanged for 190 million consumers chosen at random from India.

In a similar vein, productivity can be and often is affected by the level of honesty of the consumer. If, for example, consumers can be trusted to refrain from stealing merchandise, to report prices and costs properly at check-out counters, and to honor verbal commitments for purchases and other contracts, there can be tremendous savings in personnel on the part of producers of services.[7] These savings are probably important when comparisons are made with productivity in other countries or with the same country at different points in time. It may be that qualities such as honesty are themselves functions of the general level of productivity and income. A full analysis of productivity, therefore, requires consideration of these interrelations.

Labor-Embodied Technological Change

A second example of an analytical implication of the growth of service-industry employment concerns the labor embodiment of technological change. This refers to a situation where technological change or an advance in knowledge affects productivity through new additions to the labor force. For example, if newly trained doctors, after receiving the same amount of schooling as their predecessors, know more about disease and are more effective in treating sick people, we should attribute the increase in output to labor-embodied technological change.

Most previous discussions of embodiment have concentrated on physi-

---

[7] Changes in the honesty of employees have implications for productivity in the Industry sector as well as in services; changes in the honesty of consumers have implications primarily for services.

cal capital.[8] It has typically been assumed that capital is a fixed factor and that labor is variable, as in the following statement by Salter. "By investing in fixed capital equipment an entrepreneur gives 'hostages to fortune'; a decision to employ fixed capital equipment is irrevocable in contrast to labor, which can be discharged at will." [9] This may be a reasonably satisfactory description of the situation in manufacturing (though probably less so now than formerly), but it will not do for much of the Service sector. In fact, given the growing opportunity to rent capital equipment (e.g., computers), the reverse is sometimes closer to the truth. If one argues that rented capital equipment represents an irrevocable commitment for society, if not for the particular firm or industry using it, the same can be said for the supply of labor, and the distinction loses all force.

Let us imagine, for instance, a technological change in some government activity—a change that requires new labor skills. Civil service rules may prohibit the firing of old employees, and it may be difficult to train them in the new techniques. The full benefits of the advance, therefore, will not be realized immediately. If this type of technological change occurs at an even rate, the rate of change in productivity in government will be unaffected even though the level will be less than optimal.[10] But such changes probably do not occur at a smooth rate. If the output of the government agency is accelerating rapidly, it is likely that new additions of capital and labor are being made and that they can incorporate the latest technological change, thus raising the average level of productivity. This may be one reason that changes in output and changes in productivity are sometimes found to be positively correlated.

The argument applies not only to government but to all industries in which individuals are attached to specific organizations for long periods of time (through contract, moral commitment, or high hiring costs) and cannot easily be replaced by others. Such long-term attachments are common in many service industries. To be sure, sometimes the existing labor force can be trained or adapted to take advantage of technological change, but in many cases this is not easy to accomplish. Economics

[8] See W. E. G. Salter, *Productivity and Technical Change*, Cambridge, Mass., 1960; R. M. Solow, "Technical Progress, Capital Formation, and Economic Growth," *American Economic Review Proceedings*, May 1962, pp. 76–86; and E. F. Denison, "The Unimportance of the Embodied Question," *American Economic Review*, March 1964, pp. 90–93. For reference to labor embodiment see Gary S. Becker, *Human Capital*, New York, NBER, 1964, p. 143.

[9] *Productivity and Technical Change*, p. 38.

[10] Current methods of measuring output in government *assume* no change in productivity. This discussion is concerned with the effects on true productivity.

professors who lack knowledge of modern mathematical techniques provide a good example close to home.

The question may be raised why, if technological change is embodied in new entrants to the labor force, do we usually find that older workers earn more than do new entrants with the same number of years of schooling? The answer is, of course, that employers place a value on the experience and the maturity of the older worker which more than offsets the value of the labor-embodied technological change. If one could compare two workers of equal experience and maturity, one with the education of twenty years ago and the other with the current model, there is little doubt that the latter would command higher earnings. This is particularly evident in fields experiencing rapid technological change, such as engineering, where recent graduates often earn as much as old-timers do despite the maturity and experience of the latter.

The concept of labor embodiment is likely to be most relevant when formal schooling and job security are important, as in the professional and technical occupations. Three-fourths of all professional and technical workers are employed in the Service sector.

Changes in Demand and Productivity

Another area where the growth of services may require some refinement of concepts is the analysis of the relation between changes in demand and changes in productivity. In many service industries it is not enough to know by *how much* demand has changed in order to predict the effect on productivity. At least two other dimensions of demand in addition to quantity must be specified.

One source of variation arises because output is frequently uneven, with peaks coming at particular hours of the day, particular days of the week, and even particular weeks of the month. Such fluctuations are important for retailing, banking, barber and beauty shops, places of amusement, and some local government services. During nonpeak times there is usually idle capacity. An increase in demand, if it occurs at these times, may result in very substantial gains in productivity. On the other hand, an increase in demand occurring at times of peak demand will probably not result in any increase in productivity.

A second source of variation is the "size of transaction." [11] This refers

---

[11] Armen Alchian has a general theoretical discussion of this concept in "Costs and Output," in *The Allocation of Economic Resources, Essays in Honor of Bernard Francis Haley,* Stanford, 1959, but he does not apply it specifically to the service industries. See also Jack Hirschleifer, "The Firm's Cost Function: A Successful Reconstruction," *Journal of Business,* July 1962.

to the volume of business done with a single customer at a single purchase. David Schwartzman and Jean Wilburn have found examples of service industries where increased demand that takes the form of increases in the average size of transaction results in greater increases in measured productivity than does an equivalent increase in demand that takes the form of more transactions.[12] George Benston has reported a similar finding for banking, and I suspect that this is true of many service industries.[13]

The "Real" Gross National Product

My final example of how the growth of services may affect economic analysis concerns the gross national product in constant dollars. This statistic is the keystone of many studies of productivity and economic growth. Unfortunately, it is probably becoming increasingly less useful for such purposes. The reason is simple. Measures of real output in the Service sector have always been unsatisfactory; as this sector becomes more important, the aggregate measure must become less satisfactory in the absence of significant improvements in the measures for individual industries.

Another trend working in the same direction is the decrease in market labor as a fraction of all time spent in productive activity. A small increase in the fraction of the adult population in the labor force has been more than offset by decreases in average hours per week and increases in vacations and holidays. Some of the increased free time may be spent in pure leisure, but probably the bulk of it is spent in the nonmarket production of goods and services and in consumer participation in the market production of services. As I have already suggested, how well or poorly these activities are carried out will surely influence economic well-being. Furthermore, both the output and inputs involved should be included in any comprehensive measure of productivity.

Economists have long been aware that the value of real GNP as a measure of output and economic well-being differs depending upon the level of economic development. There has been a presumption that the measure becomes more useful the more highly developed the economy.[14]

Up to a point it is probably true that the higher real GNP is, the more

---

[12] There is some question whether the former should be called increased output or not. Under present conventions for measuring output in many service industries, it is recorded as such.

[13] "The Cost of Bank Operations," unpublished Ph.D. dissertation, University of Chicago, 1964.

[14] Simon Kuznets wrote, "The importance of domestic activities relative to those that are part of the business system declines in the long run," *National Income and Its Composition, 1919–1938*, New York, NBER, 1941, p. 432.

reliable it is as a measure of economic welfare. But the trend may now be in the other direction, because at high levels of GNP per capita a large fraction of productive effort is devoted to services (where real output is very difficult to measure) and to other activities that are not measured at all.

An increase in home production at the expense of labor in the market reduces measured output because the former is mostly excluded from the gross national product.[15] If the outputs and inputs of home production were included, growth of this type of activity would probably tend to reduce measured productivity because of the absence of specialization and economies of scale. On the other hand, true economic welfare might be increased by such a shift if, as seems likely, labor in the market involves more disutility or less utility than labor in home production.

One example of the difficulty of measuring productivity and economic welfare at high levels of GNP per capita can be found in mortality statistics. At low or moderate levels of economic development, there is usually a negative correlation between real GNP per capita and death rates. However, we now have a situation in which GNP per capita in the United States is 50 per cent above the Swedish level, but life expectancy is considerably lower in the United States, and the death rate for males 50–54 is double the Swedish rate. The reasons for this huge difference are not known, but are probably related to the pace of work, diet, exercise, as well as the output of the health industry.

I conclude that even as we increase our efforts to measure real output in the Service sector, we must recognize that these efforts are likely to leave considerable margins of uncertainty. Future studies of growth and productivity will probably find it necessary to develop auxiliary measures of "output" and economic welfare to be used in conjunction with the gross national product.

[15] For a discussion of the shift of capital stock from business to the household economy, see F. Thomas Juster and Robert E. Lipsey, "Consumer Asset Formation in the United States," *Economic Journal,* December 1967.

THEORETICAL DISCUSSION OF SECTOR SHIFTS IN EMPLOYMENT

In a tautological sense, the difference between the rates of growth of employment in the Service sector and in the rest of the economy (called "goods" for short) is equal to the difference in the rates of growth of output minus the difference in the rates of growth of output per man, i.e.,

$$(\dot{E}_s - \dot{E}_g) \equiv (\dot{O}_s - \dot{O}_g) - (\dot{P}_s - \dot{P}_g) \tag{1}$$

where E equals employment, O equals output, P equals output per man, the dot denotes percentage rates of change, and the subscripts s and g indicate the service and goods sectors.

This formulation is an oversimplification because it fails to specify the determinants of the differential changes in output and output per man and it assumes that these differentials are independent of one another. By pursuing each of these questions, we can identify the information that would be needed to provide a more satisfactory nontautological explanation of sector differentials in employment growth.

Assuming tastes constant, the change in output of each sector depends upon the change in per capita real income ($\dot{Y}$), the income elasticities of demand (n) for goods and services, the change in the price ($\dot{R}$) of goods relative to services and the elasticity of substitution (e_{sg}) between goods and services.

$$(\dot{O}_s - \dot{O}_g) = f[\dot{Y}, n_s, n_g, (\dot{R}_s - \dot{R}_g), e_{sg}] \tag{2}$$

The differential rate of change of price depends upon the differential rate of change of the nominal price ($\dot{N}$) and the rate of growth of real wages ($\dot{W}$) (a good measure of the value of time) and the time intensity of goods relative to services, (t).[1]

$$(\dot{R}_s - \dot{R}_g) = f[(\dot{N}_s - \dot{N}_g), \dot{W}, t_s, t_g] \tag{3}$$

---

[1] See Gary S. Becker, "A Theory of the Allocation of Time," *Economic Journal*, September 1965, pp. 493–517.

The differential rate of change of the nominal price will, under competitive conditions, be approximately equal to the differential rate of change of output per unit of total factor input $(\dot{T})$ with the sign reversed.[2] The latter will depend upon the rates of change of technology $(\dot{A})$ (sometimes referred to as the advance of knowledge) and the economies of scale (c) that can be realized from changes in output, i.e.,

$$(\dot{N}_s - \dot{N}_g) = -(\dot{T}_s - \dot{T}_g) = f[(\dot{A}_s - \dot{A}_g), \dot{O}_s, \dot{O}_g, c_s, c_g] \tag{4}$$

The differential rate of change of output per man $(\dot{P}_s - \dot{P}_g)$ depends upon the same variables as does the differential for output per unit of total factor input, plus the differential in the rate of change of capital (physical and human) per man $(\dot{K})$ in the two sectors, the initial level of hours per man (H), and the change in hours (ΔH).[3]

$$(\dot{P}_s - \dot{P}_a) = f[(\dot{T}_s - \dot{T}_g), (\dot{K}_s - \dot{K}_g), H_s, H_g, \Delta H_s, \Delta H_g] \tag{5}$$

Combining the five equations we find that

$$(\dot{E}_s - \dot{E}_g) = f[\dot{Y}, (\dot{A}_s - \dot{A}_g), (\dot{K}_s - \dot{K}_g), n_s, n_g, c_s, c_g, e_{sg}, t_s, t_g, H_s, H_g, \Delta H_s, \Delta H_g] \tag{6}$$

The above assumes that the price of labor (W) and the price of capital (I) change at the same rate, and that the differential change in capital intensity is attributable only to factor bias in the character of technological change (B). If relative factor prices change, the change in capital per man could be a function of sector differences in the elasticity of substitution of capital for labor (m) and the factor proportions in the initial year (K) as well.

$$(\dot{K}_s - \dot{K}_g) = f[(\dot{B}_s - \dot{B}_g), K_s, K_g, \dot{W}, \dot{I}, m_s, m_g] \tag{7}$$

Moreover, when $\dot{W}$ differs from $\dot{I}$, and K_s differs from K_g, the differential rate of change of price $(\dot{R}_s - \dot{R}_g)$ will depend upon these variables as well as those indicated in (3).

We know that $\dot{W}$ did differ from $\dot{I}$ over the period 1929–65 and that K_s was not equal to K_g. Therefore, we combine (6) and (7) and obtain

$$(\dot{E}_s - \dot{E}_g) = f[\dot{Y}, (\dot{A}_s - \dot{A}_g), (\dot{B}_s - \dot{B}_g), K_s, K_g, \dot{W}, \dot{I}, n_s, n_g, c_s, c_g \ e_{sg}, m_s,$$

$$m_g, t_s, t_g, H_s, H_g, \Delta H_s, \Delta H_g] \tag{8}$$

[2] See p. 83.

[3] Both the initial level and the change in hours are relevant because the changes in output per man-hour that presumably accompany changes in hours are likely to vary depending upon the initial level.

This says that the sector differential in rates of growth of employment depends upon:

1. The rate of growth of per capita real income in the total economy.
2. The difference in rates of growth of technological change.
3. The differences in the factor bias of technological change.
4. The capital/labor ratios in the two sectors.
5. The rate of growth of the price of labor.
6. The rate of growth of the price of capital.
7. The income elasticities of demand for goods and services.
8. The potential economies of scale in goods and services.
9. The elasticity of substitution between services and goods.
10. The elasticities of substitution between capital and labor in each sector.
11. The time intensities of goods and services.
12. The initial level of hours per man in each sector and the changes in hours.

Additional realism could be introduced by recognizing that the price of labor (W), probably did not change at the same rate in both sectors because of the greater impact of unionization and minimum wage legislation on the goods-producing industries. Thus we should have two prices for labor in the equation, $\dot{W}_s$ and $\dot{W}_g$.

NOTATION AND DEFINITIONS, CHAPTER THREE

Let O = real output (gross product in 1958 dollars)
E = employment (persons engaged in production)
C = total labor compensation
L = labor input (adjusted for hours and quality)
Y = gross product in current dollars
T = total factor input in real terms
K = capital input
W = price of a unit of labor input
P = price of a unit of total factor input
α = labor's share of output
β = capital's share of output
A = a family of productivity measures

$\dot{O}, \dot{E}, \dot{A}$, etc. = annual rates of change of O, E, A, etc.

Subscript i = industry i
a = all industries
g = industry sector
s = service sector

$\dot{A}_1 = \dot{O} - \dot{E}$ = output per man
$\dot{A}_2 = \dot{O} - \dot{L}$ = output per unit of labor input
$\dot{A}_3 = \dot{O} - \dot{T}$ = output per unit of total factor input
$\dot{A}_4 = \dot{O} - (\alpha\dot{L} + \beta\dot{K})$ = output per unit of labor and capital combined

$$\dot{L}_i - \dot{L}_a = (\dot{C}_i - \dot{W}_i) - (\dot{C}_a - \dot{W}_a). \qquad (1)$$

$\dot{W}_i$ assumed to equal $\dot{W}_a$; therefore

$$\dot{L}_i - \dot{L}_a = \dot{C}_i - \dot{C}_a.$$

$$\dot{T}_i - \dot{T}_a = (\dot{Y}_i - \dot{P}_i) - (\dot{Y}_a - \dot{P}_a). \qquad (2)$$

$\dot{P}_i$ assumed to equal $\dot{P}_a$; therefore

$$\dot{T}_i - \dot{T}_a = \dot{Y}_i - \dot{Y}_a.$$

$$\dot{A}_{4g} - \dot{A}_{4s} = (\dot{O}_g - \dot{O}_s) - [\alpha(\dot{L}_g - \dot{L}_s) + \beta(\dot{K}_g - \dot{K}_s)]. \qquad (3)$$

DEFINITIONS AND SOURCES
OF MEASURES OF OUTPUT AND INPUT

Gross Product in Current Dollars: Data for 1947, 1956, and 1965 from Jack J. Gottsegen, "Revised Estimates of GNP by Major Industries," *Survey of Current Business,* April 1967. Data for 1929 were estimated from the 1947 data by assuming the same rate of change between 1929 and 1947 for gross product as for national income by industry. This was done using the level of industry detail in Table 15, except that estimates were made separately for finance and insurance, for real estate, for services excluding households and institutions, and for households and institutions. The assumption of equal rates of change for gross product and national income may result in minor errors when gross product components such as sales taxes or depreciation changed at rates different from national income.

Gross Product in Constant (1958) Dollars: Data for 1947, 1956, and 1965 were derived from the same source as the gross product in current dollars. The 1929 estimates were obtained where possible by applying the 1929–47 rates of change of gross product by industry estimated by Martin L. Marimont, "GNP by Major Industries," *Survey of Current Business,* October 1962. The data for 1929 used by Marimont were derived from John W. Kendrick, *Productivity Trends in the United States,* Princeton for NBER, 1961. The estimate for real estate was obtained by applying the 1957 ratio of GNP in real estate to GNP in housing services to the 1929 GNP in housing services. The 1929 gross product for government enterprise was estimated from national income originating data and gross product for all government.

Employment. Estimates of the number of persons engaged in production were taken from Table 6.6 of the general source. "Persons engaged in production" includes wage and salary workers in full-time equivalents and self-employed who are assumed to be full-time, but ex-

Unless otherwise indicated, the source is U.S. Department of Commerce, Office of Business Economics, *The National Income and Product Accounts of the United States, 1929–1965,* Statistical Tables.

cludes unpaid family workers. Employment in households and institutions was estimated to be the sum of employment in private households plus the number of employees in educational services n.e.c., and in nonprofit organizations n.e.c., plus a portion of employment in medical and health services, estimated in the following manner. The compensation of employees in the households and institution sector other than those in the medical and health industry was subtracted from total compensation of employees in households and institutions. The remainder represents compensation of employees in the medical and health industry that are included in the households and institutions sector. The ratio of this compensation to total compensation for all medical and health service employees was applied to the number of full-time equivalent employees in medical and health services to obtain the number that are in the households and institutions sector, on the assumption that the average compensation per employee was the same in both sectors. It was further assumed that none of the self-employed in the medical and health service industry are in households or institutions.

Labor Compensation. Labor compensation in this book is the sum of compensation of employees and labor income of the self-employed. It was assumed that returns to labor of the self-employed were a percentage of proprietors' income (income of unincorporated enterprises plus inventory valuation adjustment of unincorporated enterprises), which varied by industry but was the same in all years for any one industry. The percentages, based on tax return data on net worth of unincorporated enterprises, were derived by Irving Leveson in "Nonfarm Self-Employment in the U.S.," unpublished Ph.D. dissertation, Columbia University, 1967, Chapter 4. The shares of labor in entrepreneurial income were assumed to be 60 per cent in agriculture; 80 per cent in finance, insurance, and real estate; 90 per cent in mining; manufacturing; transportation, communications, and public utilities; and wholesale and retail trade, and 95 per cent in construction and services.

Industrial Classification. Data for 1929–47 were published by the OBE according to the 1942 and 1945 Standard Industrial Classifications and from 1948–65 according to the 1957 Standard Industrial Classification. The major change for our purposes was a shift of automobile repair services from retail trade to services. The new classification was adopted and adjustments made for all series. The adjustments involved the assumption that the change in an auto repair series relative to the same series for 1929–48 equaled the relative change from 1948 to 1963. Changes from 1948–63 were taken from Appendix G and those for 1929–48, from unpublished tables of David Schwartzman.

TABLE C–1

Persons Engaged, by Sector, 1929–65
(millions)

Year	Agri-culture	Industry	Service	Service Subsector
1929	9.2	18.4	18.6	12.3
1930	9.0	16.8	18.3	11.9
1931	9.0	14.6	17.4	11.2
1932	8.9	12.4	16.3	10.4
1933	8.9	12.6	16.6	10.3
1934	9.0	14.1	18.3	11.0
1935	9.1	14.7	19.0	11.3
1936	9.0	16.0	21.0	11.9
1937	8.9	17.1	21.2	12.6
1938	8.5	15.2	21.5	12.5
1939	8.3	16.4	22.0	12.8
1940	8.0	17.6	22.8	13.3
1941	7.9	20.7	24.4	14.0
1942	7.8	23.5	26.7	13.8
1943	7.5	25.2	30.9	13.4
1944	7.2	24.2	33.1	13.2
1945	7.0	22.5	33.4	13.7
1946	7.0	23.0	27.4	15.9
1947	7.0	24.3	26.4	16.7
1948	7.0	25.3	26.5	16.6
1949	6.8	23.8	26.8	16.5
1950	6.8	24.9	27.4	16.7
1951	6.3	26.6	30.0	17.4
1952	6.2	27.0	31.0	17.7
1953	6.0	27.8	31.3	17.9
1954	5.9	26.1	31.0	17.8
1955	5.7	26.8	31.6	18.2
1956	5.4	27.5	32.5	18.8
1957	5.2	27.3	33.0	19.1
1958	5.0	25.5	33.2	19.1
1959	4.9	26.3	33.8	19.5
1960	4.7	26.4	34.7	20.0
1961	4.7	25.8	35.1	20.1
1962	4.5	26.4	36.0	20.4
1963	4.4	26.7	36.7	20.7
1964	4.2	27.2	37.8	21.4
1965	4.0	28.2	39.0	22.1

Appendix C

TABLE C-2

Sector Shares of Persons Engaged, 1929–65
(per cent)

Year	Agri-culture	Industry	Service	Service Subsector
1929	19.9	39.7	40.4	26.5
1930	20.4	38.1	41.5	27.0
1931	21.9	35.6	42.5	27.4
1932	23.6	33.1	43.3	27.7
1933	23.4	33.0	43.5	27.0
1934	21.8	34.0	44.3	26.5
1935	21.3	34.3	44.4	26.3
1936	19.7	34.7	45.6	26.0
1937	18.8	36.3	44.9	26.7
1938	18.9	33.7	47.9	27.6
1939	17.8	35.1	47.1	27.5
1940	16.6	36.3	47.1	27.5
1941	14.9	39.0	46.0	26.4
1942	13.4	40.6	46.0	23.7
1943	11.8	39.5	48.6	21.0
1944	11.2	37.5	51.2	20.5
1945	11.2	35.7	53.1	21.7
1946	12.2	40.1	47.7	27.6
1947	12.1	42.1	45.8	29.0
1948	11.9	43.0	45.1	28.2
1949	11.8	41.5	46.7	28.7
1950	11.4	42.1	46.4	28.2
1951	10.0	42.3	47.7	27.5
1952	9.6	42.1	48.3	27.5
1953	9.2	42.7	48.1	27.5
1954	9.4	41.4	49.2	28.3
1955	8.9	41.8	49.3	28.4
1956	8.3	42.0	49.7	28.8
1957	7.9	41.7	50.4	29.2
1958	7.9	40.0	52.1	29.9
1959	7.5	40.5	52.0	30.0
1960	7.2	40.2	52.7	30.4
1961	7.1	39.4	53.5	30.6
1962	6.8	39.5	53.8	30.4
1963	6.5	39.4	54.1	30.6
1964	6.0	39.3	54.7	31.0
1965	5.7	39.6	54.8	31.1

TABLE C-3

Selected Measures of Output and Input, by Sector and Major Industry Group, Selected Years

	GNP, Current Dollars (billion dollars)				GNP, Constant (1958) Dollars (billion dollars)			
	1929	1947	1956	1965	1929	1947	1956	1965
Total economy	101.4	229.5	418.3	678.5	198.3	313.5	446.8	613.1
Agriculture	9.3	20.8	19.7	25.4	16.7	17.9	22.0	25.1
Industry	44.5	105.5	202.6	310.4	85.6	148.1	214.7	292.1
Service	47.6	103.2	196.0	342.7	96.0	147.5	210.1	295.9
Service subsector	27.0	63.8	110.6	185.2	58.7	86.0	117.3	166.2
Industry								
Mining	3.4	6.8	13.4	14.0	8.6	10.2	13.6	14.8
Contract construction	4.0	8.8	20.0	30.7	10.4	12.9	21.8	23.2
Manufacturing	24.7	66.9	126.8	196.7	50.3	91.8	134.1	188.7
Transportation	7.7	13.6	21.2	28.5	10.0	21.1	22.8	27.8
Communications and public utilities	3.7	6.9	17.1	31.3	4.1	8.5	17.7	30.4
Government enterprise	1.0	2.5	4.1	9.2	2.2	3.6	4.7	7.2
Service								
Wholesale and retail trade	15.8	43.4	70.4	111.4	34.3	52.7	73.8	105.5
Finance, insurance, real estate, and services	27.5	43.1	89.0	163.5	48.7	66.2	95.0	139.5
Finance, insurance, and services excluding households and institutions	11.2	20.4	40.2	73.8	24.4	33.3	43.5	60.7
General government	4.3	16.7	36.6	67.8	13.0	28.6	41.3	50.9

(continued)

TABLE C–3 (concluded)

	Employment (millions)				Labor Compensation (billion dollars)			
	1929	1947	1956	1965	1929	1947	1956	1965
Total economy	46.2	57.7	65.4	71.2	63.0	156.5	278.3	439.1
Agriculture	9.2	7.0	5.4	4.0	5.1	12.2	10.0	12.9
Industry	18.4	24.3	27.5	28.2	29.3	73.0	137.5	202.9
Service	18.6	26.4	32.5	39.0	28.5	71.3	130.8	223.2
Service subsector	12.3	16.7	18.8	22.1	20.5	48.0	80.9	132.4
Industry								
Mining	1.0	1.0	0.9	0.7	1.6	3.3	5.0	5.0
Contract construction	2.3	3.0	3.7	4.0	3.6	8.0	17.6	26.8
Manufacturing	10.6	15.4	17.7	18.4	16.8	45.8	88.2	131.8
Transportation	3.0	3.0	2.8	2.5	5.0	10.2	15.1	20.0
Communications and public utilities	1.0	1.2	1.5	1.5	1.6	3.6	7.5	11.8
Government enterprise	0.4	0.7	0.9	1.1	0.8	2.0	4.1	7.5
Service								
Wholesale and retail trade	7.7	10.6	11.9	13.1	11.9	31.1	49.1	74.1
Finance, insurance, real estate, and services	8.2	9.7	11.6	14.8	12.2	23.4	45.1	81.4
Finance, insurance, and services excluding households and institutions	4.6	6.1	6.9	9.0	8.6	16.9	31.8	58.3
General government	2.8	6.1	9.0	11.0	4.3	16.7	36.6	67.8

TABLE C-4

Annual Rates of Change of Output and Input Measures, by Sector and Major Industry Group, 1929–65 and Selected Subperiods

(per cent per annum)

	GNP, Current Dollars					GNP, Constant Dollars (1958)				
	1929–65	1929–47	1947–65	1947–56	1956–65	1929–65	1929–47	1947–65	1947–56	1956–65
Total economy	5.28	4.54	6.02	6.67	5.37	3.14	2.54	3.73	3.94	3.52
Agriculture	2.79	4.47	1.11	-0.60	2.82	1.13	0.39	1.88	2.29	1.46
Industry	5.40	4.80	6.00	7.25	4.74	3.41	3.05	3.77	4.13	3.42
Service	5.48	4.30	6.67	7.13	6.21	3.13	2.39	3.87	3.93	3.80
Service subsector	5.35	4.78	5.92	6.11	5.73	2.89	2.12	3.66	3.45	3.87
Industry										
Mining	3.93	3.85	4.01	7.54	0.49	1.51	0.95	2.07	3.20	0.94
Contract construction	5.66	4.38	6.94	9.12	4.76	2.23	1.20	3.26	5.83	0.69
Manufacturing	5.76	5.54	5.99	7.10	4.88	3.67	3.34	4.00	4.21	3.80
Transportation	3.64	3.16	4.11	4.93	3.29	2.84	4.15	1.53	0.86	2.20
Communications and public utilities	5.93	3.46	8.40	10.08	6.72	5.57	4.05	7.08	8.15	6.01
Government enterprise	6.16	5.09	7.24	5.50	8.98	3.29	2.74	3.85	2.96	4.74
Service										
Wholesale and retail trade	5.43	5.61	5.24	5.37	5.10	3.12	2.39	3.86	3.74	3.97
Finance, insurance, real estate, and services	4.95	2.50	7.41	8.06	6.76	2.92	1.71	4.14	4.01	4.27
Finance, insurance, and services excluding households and institutions	5.24	3.33	7.14	7.54	6.75	2.53	1.73	3.34	2.97	3.70
General government	7.66	7.54	7.78	8.72	6.85	3.79	4.38	3.20	4.08	2.32

(continued)

TABLE C-4 (concluded)

	Employment					Labor Compensation				
	1929-65	1929-47	1947-65	1947-56	1956-65	1929-65	1929-47	1947-65	1947-56	1956-65
Total economy	1.20	1.23	1.17	1.39	0.95	5.40	5.06	5.73	6.40	5.07
Agriculture	-2.29	-1.52	-3.06	-2.84	-3.28	2.56	4.82	0.30	-2.27	2.86
Industry	1.19	1.56	0.83	1.36	0.29	5.37	5.06	5.68	7.04	4.33
Service	2.05	1.93	2.17	2.31	2.02	5.72	5.09	6.34	6.75	5.94
Service subsector	1.64	1.72	1.56	1.33	1.80	5.18	4.72	5.64	5.81	5.47
Industry										
Mining	-1.16	-0.25	-2.07	-1.07	-3.08	3.19	4.03	2.34	4.65	0.03
Contract construction	1.51	1.47	1.54	2.30	0.79	5.56	4.41	6.70	8.72	4.68
Manufacturing	1.55	2.10	1.00	1.54	0.46	5.73	5.59	5.87	7.27	4.46
Transportation	-0.55	0.02	-1.13	-0.92	-1.33	3.85	3.96	3.73	4.34	3.12
Communications and public utilities	1.06	0.78	1.33	2.51	0.16	5.64	4.63	6.64	8.24	5.03
Government enterprise	2.78	2.77	2.78	3.02	2.55	6.35	5.35	7.36	8.04	6.68
Service										
Wholesale and retail trade	1.48	1.80	1.17	1.25	1.08	5.07	5.32	4.82	5.06	4.57
Finance, insurance, real estate, and services	1.66	0.93	2.39	2.08	2.69	5.27	3.62	6.92	7.29	6.55
Finance, insurance, and services excluding households and institutions	1.89	1.59	2.19	1.46	2.92	5.33	3.77	6.89	7.07	6.72
General government	3.83	4.37	3.30	4.28	2.32	7.64	7.50	7.78	8.71	6.85

TABLE C–5

Average Weekly Hours of Full-Time Employed Persons, by Major Industry Groups, 1929 and 1965

Major Industry Groups	1929	1965
Mining	42.1	42.3
Construction	42.6	38.5
Manufacturing	48.0	39.1
Transportation	50.1	45.5
Communications and public utilities	46.8	41.1
Government enterprise	44.9	37.4
Trade	55.0	47.0
Finance, insurance, and real estate	45.5	40.1
Services excluding households and institutions ⎱	52.8	41.1
Households and institutions ⎰		34.9
General government	37.4	33.8

Source: 1929 (except manufacturing and trade), John Kendrick, *Productivity Trends in the United States:* 1965 (except trade), Kendrick, NBER manuscript; 1929 manufacturing, Ethel B. Jones, "New Estimates of Hours of Work per Week and Hourly Earnings 1900–1957," *Review of Economics and Statistics,* November 1963; 1929 and 1965 trade, David Schwartzman, NBER manuscript.

TABLE C–6

Persons Engaged, by Detailed Industry, 1929 and 1965

Industry	Persons Engaged (thousands) 1929	1965	Percentage Change Per Annum 1929–65
Industries			
Metal mining	130	87	−1.12
Coal mining	627	150	−3.97
Crude petroleum and natural gas	168	308	1.68
Mining and quarrying of nonmetallic minerals	92	125	0.85
Contract construction	2,306	3,971	1.51
Food and kindred products	1,078	1,793	1.41
Tobacco manufactures	147	88	−1.43
Textile mill products	1,264	932	−0.85

(continued)

TABLE C–6 (continued)

Industry	Persons Engaged (thousands)		Percentage Change Per Annum
	1929	1965	1929–65
Apparel and other fabricated textile products	793	1,371	1.52
Paper and allied products	285	641	2.25
Printing, publishing and allied industries	630	1,052	1.42
Chemicals and allied products	401	912	2.28
Petroleum refining and related industries	128	184	1.01
Rubber and miscellaneous plastic products	176	469	2.72
Leather and leather products	372	355	−0.13
Lumber and wood products, except furniture	620	697	0.33
Furniture and fixtures	442	449	0.04
Stone, clay, and glass products	402	645	1.31
Primary metal industries and fabricated metal products	1,549	2,586	1.44
Machinery, except electrical	769	1,795	2.35
Electrical machinery	519	1,659	3.23
Transportation equipment and ordnance, except motor vehicles	150	1,141	5.49
Motor vehicles and equipment	541	842	1.23
Railroad transportation	1,845	738	−2.55
Local, suburban, and highway transportation	438	288	−1.16
Motor freight transportation and warehousing	381	914	2.43
Water transportation	168	208	0.59
Air transportation	2	232	13.20
Pipelines transportation	25	19	−0.76
Transportation services	175	87	−1.94
Telephone and telegraph	535	778	1.04
Radio broadcasting and television	4	97	8.86
Electric, gas, and sanitary services [a]	495	638	0.70
Federal government enterprise [a]	299	694	2.34
State and local government enterprise [a]	110	417	3.70

(continued)

TABLE C-6 (concluded)

Industry	Persons Engaged (thousands)		Percentage Change Per Annum
	1929	1965	1929–65
Services			
Wholesale trade	1,744	3,362	1.82
Retail trade [b]	5,955	9,767	1.37
Banking [c]	386	763	1.89
Credit agencies, holding and other investment companies [c]	137	304	2.21
Security and commodity brokers [c]	143	129	−0.21
Insurance carriers [d]	358	843	2.38
Insurance agents, brokers and service [d]	183	279	1.17
Real estate [d]	368	766	2.04
Hotels and other lodging places	518	707	0.86
Personal services	1,008	1,438	0.99
Miscellaneous business services	209	1,145	4.72
Auto repair, auto services and garages [b]	122	467	3.73
Motion pictures	153	173	0.34
Amusement and recreation, except motion pictures	295	437	1.09
Medical and other health services	750	2,475	3.32
Legal services	194	349	1.63
Educational services	287	1,022	3.53
Nonprofit membership organizations	351	1,157	3.31
Miscellaneous professional services	83	617	5.57
Private households	2,348	1,476	−1.29
Federal general government	528	4,567	5.99
State and local general government	2,247	6,461	2.93

Source: Table 6–6 of general source.

[a] Electric, gas, and sanitary services, Federal government enterprises, and state and local government enterprises were combined for use in Table 73. See note to Table 73.

[b] In 1929 Retail trade included auto services. For comparability with 1965 data, persons engaged in auto services were estimated for 1929 at 122 and shown separately.

[c] Banking, credit agencies, holding and other investment companies, and security and commodity brokers were combined for use in Table 73. See note to Table 73.

[d] Insurance carriers, insurance agents, brokers and services, and real estate were combined for use in Table 73. See note to Table 73.

ESTIMATES OF SECTOR
DIFFERENTIALS IN THE GROWTH
OF CAPITAL PER WORKER

Two attempts were made to estimate sector differentials in the growth of capital per worker (Tables D-1 and D-2). One is based on Internal Revenue Service data from the *Statistics of Income*. This utilizes book value of net depreciable assets, plus inventories—all in current dollars. Estimates were made for the Industry sector and the Service subsector. For 1929 no balance sheet data were available for the noncorporate portions of each sector; estimates were based on the relation between

TABLE D-1

Sector Differential Trend in Capital Per Worker Estimated From
Book Values in Current Dollars, 1929–60

	1929	1960	Average Annual Rate of Change 1929 to 1960 (per cent)
Capital ($ billions)			
Industry	110.0	306.8	3.3
Service subsector	26.8	87.6	3.8
Employment (millions)			
Industry	17.9	25.5	1.1
Service subsector	12.3	20.0	1.6
Capital per worker (dollars)			
Industry	6,140	12,030	2.2
Service subsector	2,180	4,380	2.2

TABLE D-2

Sector Differential Trend in Capital Per Worker Estimated From
Net Cumulative Investment in 1954 Dollars, 1947–60

	1947	1960	Average Annual Rate of Change 1947 to 1960 (per cent)
Capital ($ billions)			
Industry [a]	189.9	284.2	3.1
Service subsector [b]	90.4	117.0	2.0
Employment (millions)			
Industry [a]	22.6	24.6	0.7
Service subsector [b]	16.6	19.8	1.3
Capital per worker (dollars)			
Industry [a]	8,400	11,550	2.4
Service subsector [b]	5,450	5,910	0.6

[a] Industry excludes mining, radio broadcasting and television, and local utilities and public services n.e.c.
[b] Service subsector excludes medical and health services.

corporate and noncorporate capital in 1960, and corporate and, noncorporate income in 1960 and 1929.

Numerous other adjustments were required because of the absence of detailed information, e.g., an estimate was made for capital in real estate to be subtracted from finance, insurance, and real estate. It should be noted that the data are based on historical cost less book depreciation, and are unadjusted for price changes. Given the rough nature of these estimates, only an impressionistic report of the results is warranted.

The Internal Revenue Service data suggests that the *level* of capital per worker was and is considerably higher in Industry than in the Service subsector, but that the rate of change was fairly similar between 1929 and 1960.

The alternative estimate is based on Bert Hickman's estimates of the net value in constant (1954) dollars of the stock of plant and equipment in various industries in 1947 and 1960.[1] These estimates were derived by cumulating annual estimates of net investment. The industries

[1] Bert G. Hickman, *Investment Demand in U.S. Economic Growth,* Washington, D.C., 1965, pp. 230–231.

covered by Hickman do not correspond exactly to the sector definitions used in this book, and no figures are presented for the pre-World War II period. These data can be used, however, to obtain some rough notions about possible differential trends in capital per worker.

The capital figures shown in Table D-2 are based on Hickman's estimates plus adjustments for inventories. Inventories in manufacturing were added to the Industry capital, and inventories in wholesale and retail trade were added to the Service capital. Also, construction was transferred to Industry from the sector labeled by Hickman, "commercial and other" (which corresponds roughly to the Service subsector), by assuming that the level of net depreciable assets per worker in construction in 1947 and 1960 was equal to the average level in "commercial and other" in those years.

Changes in employment (persons engaged) for corresponding industries were also calculated, and a differential trend in capital per worker was estimated. This differential was 1.8 per cent per annum between 1947 and 1960. This implies a differential of .8 per cent per annum for the period since 1929, if we assume that there was no differential trend in capital per worker between 1929 and 1947. This result is almost equal to the differential trend obtained if we assume that output per unit of capital grew at the same rate in both sectors.

DISCUSSION OF THE 1/1,000
SAMPLE OF THE U.S. CENSUS
OF POPULATION AND HOUSING

The data of this sample are contained on 80-column punch cards and a magnetic tape with 120 alpha-numeric characters for each record. There is a separate card or tape record for each person included in the sample. The sample is self-weighting; universe totals may be obtained by adding three zeroes to the uninflated counts.

Each punch card contains information on the characteristics of a person, his household, family and subfamily, of the associated person, and of the housing unit in which he lives. Availability of the information in this form permits detailed cross-classification of persons by more than seventy economic, social, and demographic characteristics.[1]

In this study, persons employed in "agriculture, forestry, and fisheries" were excluded. All other employed persons were cross-classified (into 168 cells) by age, color (white and nonwhite), sex, and years of school completed.

Age Classes	Years of School Completed
14–19	Under 5
20–24	5–8
25–34	9–11
35–44	12
45–54	13–15
55–64	16 and over
65 and over	

Actual annual and hourly earnings and hours per person were computed for each of the 168 age, color, sex, and education cells. The hours

[1] For additional information concerning the sample, see U.S. Bureau of the Census, *U.S. Census of Population and Housing: 1960, 1/1,000, 1/10,000, Two National Samples of the Population of the United States, Description and Technical Documentation,* Washington (n.d.).

data are for a single week in April 1960. Earnings and number of weeks worked are for the entire year 1959. Annual hours were estimated for each individual, and then aggregated for the various cells and groups. The following midpoints were applied to the Census data.

Hours		Weeks	
Class	*Midpoint*	*Class*	*Midpoint*
1–14	7.5	Under 14	7.0
15–29	22.0	14–26	20.0
30–34	32.0	27–39	33.0
35–39	37.0	40–47	43.5
40	40.0	48–49	48.5
41–48	44.5	50–52	51.0
49–59	54.0		
60 and over	64.0		

Earnings	
Class	*Midpoint*
1–999	500
1,000–1,999	1,500
2,000–2,999	2,500
3,000–3,999	3,500
4,000–4,999	4,500
5,000–5,999	5,500
6,000–6,999	6,500
7,000–9,999	8,200
10,000–14,999	12,000
15,000–24,999	18,500
25,000 and over	40,000

Persons with no earnings in 1959 are excluded. This procedure leaves out persons who were only unpaid family workers in 1959, as well as new entrants to the labor force in 1960. Persons who had earnings in 1959 but left the labor force before April 1960 were also omitted. These exclusions are in addition to the exclusions of those unemployed or with a job but not at work in the survey week 1960. The latter two groups could not be included because no information concerning hours is available for them.

National average hourly earnings by color, age, sex, and education for nonagricultural employed persons are presented in Table E-1, and

Table E-2 indicates the sample sizes. Sample sizes are frequently small for 14-to-19-year olds and nonwhites, and the earnings figures for such cells are subject to considerable sampling error. The use of such figures to calculate "expected" and "standardized" earnings for groups, however, does not necessarily introduce any bias into the estimates, and, provided the sample size of the group is not small, the sampling errors of the individual color-age-sex-education cells are unimportant.

TABLE E-1

Average Hourly Earnings of Nonagricultural Employed Persons, by Color, Age, Sex, and Education, 1959

| | Years of School Completed | | | | | | |
Age	0–4	5–8	9–11	12	13–15	16 and Over	Total
White males							
14–19	0.98 [a]	1.51	1.45	1.40	1.61	[b]	1.44
20–24	1.48 [a]	1.71	1.77	1.90	2.09	2.26	1.90
25–34	1.78	2.18	2.41	2.57	2.79	3.30	2.62
35–44	2.00	2.43	2.76	3.02	3.50	4.69	3.13
45–54	1.95	2.54	2.78	3.16	4.03	5.33	3.18
55–64	2.11	2.50	2.90	3.34	4.17	5.14	3.04
65 and over	1.90	2.26	2.84	3.72	3.62	5.15	2.92
Total	1.95	2.40	2.58	2.78	3.33	4.31	2.87
White females							
14–19	1.11 [a]	1.35	1.53	1.28	1.26	0.74 [a]	1.35
20–24	1.47 [a]	1.20	1.44	1.54	1.66	2.13	1.57
25–34	1.46 [a]	1.37	1.61	1.78	2.02	2.55	1.82
35–44	1.40 [a]	1.44	1.58	1.88	2.09	2.77	1.81
45–54	1.18 [a]	1.43	1.65	1.83	2.20	3.01	1.85
55–64	1.35	1.46	1.54	1.88	2.26	3.06	1.81
65 and over	1.22 [a]	1.12	1.57	1.82	1.59	2.64	1.52
Total	1.31	1.41	1.58	1.74	2.02	2.77	1.76
Nonwhite males							
14–19	0.73 [a]	1.22	1.00	1.04	2.78	[b]	1.09
20–24	1.29 [a]	1.15	1.35	1.37	1.30 [a]	2.48 [a]	1.30
25–34	1.36	1.66	1.84	2.00	2.03	2.36	1.84
35–44	1.49	1.85	2.13	2.35	2.25	3.65	2.06
45–54	1.59	1.79	1.99	2.34	2.24 [a]	3.13 [a]	1.90
55–64	1.37	2.04	2.29 [a]	1.77 [a]	2.13 [a]	2.30 [a]	1.82
65 and over	1.50 [a]	1.61 [a]	1.47 [a]	1.85 [a]	2.43 [a]	1.80 [a]	1.60
Total	1.46	1.74	1.88	2.00	2.04	2.87	1.83

(continued)

Age	Years of School Completed						
	0–4	5–8	9–11	12	13–15	16 and Over	Total
Nonwhite females							
14–19	1.36 [a]	1.08 [a]	1.10	1.44 [a]	2.00 [a]	[b]	1.23
20–24	0.72 [a]	0.61 [a]	1.06	1.33	1.43 [a]	1.97 [a]	1.15
25–34	0.94 [a]	1.01	1.32	1.35	1.59	2.35 [a]	1.35
35–44	0.77 [a]	1.01	1.16	1.42	1.61 [a]	2.66 [a]	1.25
45–54	0.66	0.86	0.93	1.36	1.70 [a]	2.70 [a]	1.03
55–64	0.81	1.03	1.14 [a]	1.01 [a]	1.34 [a]	2.76 [a]	1.08
65 and over	0.62 [a]	1.19 [a]	0.77 [a]	1.47 [a]	1.72 [a]	3.04 [a]	1.05
Total	0.74	0.96	1.15	1.36	1.58	2.53	1.20
Males							
14–19	0.92 [a]	1.46	1.42	1.38	1.63	[b]	1.41
20–24	1.42	1.58	1.72	1.87	2.05	2.26	1.84
25–34	1.63	2.11	2.36	2.53	2.75	3.26	2.56
35–44	1.81	2.36	2.71	2.99	3.45	4.66	3.04
45–54	1.82	2.47	2.74	3.13	3.99	5.29	3.09
55–64	1.91	2.47	2.88	3.30	4.13	5.10	2.96
65 and over	1.83	2.21	2.76	3.66	3.58	5.08	2.83
Total	1.80	2.32	2.52	2.74	3.28	4.27	2.79
Females							
14–19	1.14 [a]	1.29	1.48	1.28	1.31	0.74 [a]	1.34
20–24	1.25 [a]	1.04	1.37	1.53	1.64	2.12	1.54
25–34	1.27 [a]	1.27	1.55	1.73	1.95	2.53	1.74
35–44	1.16	1.33	1.52	1.81	2.06	2.76	1.74
45–54	0.94	1.34	1.59	1.81	2.19	3.00	1.77
55–64	1.15	1.41	1.51	1.86	2.24	3.05	1.75
65 and over	1.06	1.13	1.50	1.81	1.59	2.66	1.49
Total	1.09	1.32	1.53	1.72	1.99	2.75	1.70
Whites							
14–19	1.02 [a]	1.48	1.48	1.34	1.43	0.74 [a]	1.40
20–24	1.48	1.62	1.70	1.75	1.92	2.21	1.78
25–34	1.74	2.06	2.25	2.37	2.64	3.19	2.46
35–44	1.91	2.22	2.48	2.66	3.19	4.40	2.81
45–54	1.79	2.28	2.47	2.71	3.44	4.72	2.80
55–64	1.97	2.26	2.50	2.82	3.53	4.52	2.70
65 and over	1.77	2.00	2.50	3.20	2.96	4.55	2.58
Total	1.84	2.18	2.33	2.44	2.97	4.00	2.58
Nonwhites							
14–19	0.82 [a]	1.18	1.05	1.19 [a]	2.15 [a]	[b]	1.14
20–24	1.13 [a]	1.04	1.25	1.36	1.36	2.15 [a]	1.25
25–34	1.31	1.46	1.64	1.75	1.84	2.36	1.67
35–44	1.38	1.53	1.79	1.97	2.03	3.26	1.77
45–54	1.33	1.46	1.58	1.95	2.05 [a]	2.92 [a]	1.59
55–64	1.22	1.67	1.79	1.50 [a]	1.83 [a]	2.56 [a]	1.57
65 and over	1.27	1.50	1.22 [a]	1.76 [a]	2.25 [a]	2.35 [a]	1.45
Total	1.30	1.47	1.61	1.75	1.85	2.73	1.61

(continued)

TABLE E-1 (concluded)

	Years of School Completed						
Age	0–4	5–8	9–11	12	13–15	16 and Over	Total
Total							
14–19	0.97 [a]	1.43	1.44	1.33	1.46	0.74 [a]	1.38
20–24	1.37	1.48	1.64	1.73	1.89	2.21	1.73
25–34	1.59	1.97	2.18	2.32	2.58	3.15	2.38
35–44	1.71	2.11	2.41	2.62	3.14	4.35	2.72
45–54	1.61	2.19	2.41	2.67	3.40	4.67	2.71
55–64	1.76	2.21	2.47	2.78	3.49	4.47	2.62
65 and over	1.67	1.97	2.42	3.15	2.94	4.49	2.50
Total	1.66	2.09	2.26	2.40	2.92	3.96	2.50

Source: *U.S. Censuses of Population and Housing: 1960, 1/1,000 Sample.*
[a] Based on fewer than fifty observations.
[b] No observations.

TABLE E-2

Number of Nonagricultural Employed Persons, by Color, Age, Sex, and Education, 1959

	Years of School Completed						
Age	0–4	5–8	9–11	12	13–15	16 and Over	Total
White Males							
14–19	17	302	834	436	77	0	1,666
20–24	35	337	631	1,184	510	222	2,919
25–34	140	1,225	1,680	2,534	1,001	1,356	7,936
35–44	213	1,746	2,032	2,661	983	1,214	8,849
45–54	250	2,402	1,608	1,578	684	772	7,294
55–64	328	1,981	840	622	407	350	4,528
65 and over	179	625	201	207	112	139	1,463
Total	1,162	8,618	7,826	9,222	3,774	4,053	34,655
White Females							
14–19	10	93	509	519	88	1	1,220
20–24	22	94	257	948	366	155	1,842
25–34	24	285	603	1,220	342	321	2,795
35–44	49	637	855	1,570	403	328	3,842
45–54	72	941	782	1,052	445	386	3,678
55–64	84	734	412	437	260	206	2,133
65 and over	48	246	94	98	64	54	604
Total	309	3,030	3,512	5,844	1,968	1,451	16,114

(*continued*)

Appendix E

TABLE E-2 (concluded)

Age	Years of School Completed						
	0–4	5–8	9–11	12	13–15	16 and Over	Total
Nonwhite Males							
14–19	4	60	62	26	2	0	154
20–24	22	105	94	98	27	6	352
25–34	79	217	197	196	67	58	814
35–44	129	295	205	146	47	37	859
45–54	155	274	108	70	21	20	648
55–64	124	155	38	22	9	6	354
65 and over	47	42	12	6	3	3	113
Total	560	1,148	716	564	176	130	3,294
Nonwhite Females							
14–19	3	29	57	23	3	0	115
20–24	8	35	63	73	29	11	219
25–34	15	119	156	146	50	37	523
35–44	34	230	147	115	27	29	582
45–54	75	200	83	59	15	22	454
55–64 .	54	118	30	16	4	12	234
65 and over	20	24	7	2	2	2	57
Total	209	755	543	434	130	113	2,184

Source: Same as Table E-1.

RELIABILITY OF HOURS
DATA IN 1/1,000 SAMPLE

One way of determining the reliability of hours data in the 1/1,000 sample is to compare them with hours data from other sources. Table F-1 compares the sample with the Current Population Survey data for the same month (April 1960). The distributions are similar, and the means, which are calculated from more detailed but noncomparable distributions, are also similar. The CPS shows a lower mean, a smaller concentration in the 35–40 hours class, and a greater concentration in the 15–34 hours class. This is probably due to the inclusion of Good Friday in the CPS survey week. The 1/1,000 sample is less sensitive to this bias be-

TABLE F-1

Comparison of Means and Distribution of Hours in the 1/1,000 Sample
and Current Population Survey, Nonagricultural Employed
Persons, 1959 and April 1960

	Hours Worked Per Week (per cent)				
	1–14	15–34	35–40	41 and Over	Average Hours
1/1,000 Sample					
April 1960	3.7	10.7	52.7	32.0	40.7 [a]
Current Population Survey					
April 1960	5.7	17.8	47.5	29.0	39.5 [a]
1959	5.6	15.0	48.8	30.6	40.0 [b]

Source: CPS data from U.S. Bureau of Labor Statistics, *Labor Force and Employment in 1960*, Special Labor Force Report No. 14, by Robert Stein and Herman Travis, Table D–1.

[a] Average computed from more detailed distribution.
[b] Computed from distributions by single hours.

cause, whereas each person is asked his hours in a single week, different workers are enumerated for different weeks in April 1960.

The 1/1,000 sample hours data do not differ greatly from establishment reports either. The April 1960 average hours of all employed persons in manufacturing with some earnings and weeks worked in 1959 in the 1/1,000 sample is 40.3; the average hours of manufacturing production workers for April 1960 in the BLS series is 39.4.[1]

There is a question as to how much inaccuracy is introduced by using hours for a single month in 1960 to estimate hours in 1959. Table F-1 indicates that the distribution and mean for 1959 were very similar to those for April 1960. The BLS series for manufacturing production workers shows a mean of 40.3 hours for 1959. It was possible to compare the average weekly hours worked by production workers in April 1960 with the 1959 annual average for 80 of the 138 *Census of Population* industries used in the regression analysis in Chapter 6. The differences, typically 1 or 2 per cent, were small relative to interindustry variation in hourly earnings.

An important source of inaccuracy at the individual level is the tendency of persons to report regular or standard hours rather than hours actually worked. However, since persons working either more or less than usual hours will tend to report regular hours, average hours for groups may not be seriously affected. The Monthly Labor Survey found that when this source of error was substantially reduced by additional probing, average hours were only .4 below the average in the Current Population Survey for all nonagricultural employed persons in the first half of 1965.[2]

In the absence of reliable hours data, weekly earnings might be studied in place of hourly earnings. If there were no correlation between hours and weeks worked across individuals, weeks worked would give a good indication of time spent at work. However, as Table F-2 indicates, there is a clear tendency for persons working many weeks per year to work long hours per week also. Therefore, if we know that one person worked more weeks than another, we would expect that he worked more man-hours per year by a greater relative amount than indicated by the relative number of weeks worked. Information on hours, therefore, adds

[1] U.S. Bureau of Labor Statistics, *Employment and Earnings Statistics for the United States, 1909–64,* Bulletin No. 1312-3, Washington, 1964, p. 42.

[2] Robert L. Stein and Daniel B. Levine, "Research in Labor Force Concepts," *Proceedings of the Social Statistics Section of the American Statistical Association,* 1965, pp. 218–226.

TABLE F–2

Average Weeks Worked in 1959, by Hours Worked Per Week in
April 1960, for Color-Sex Groups, Employed Persons, 1960

	Hours Worked Per Week, April 1960							
	1–14	15–29	30–34	35–39	40	41–48	49–59	60+	Total
	Average Weeks Worked, 1959					.			
White males	34.3	36.6	42.0	46.2	47.6	48.2	48.7	49.3	46.6
White females	30.3	34.6	38.7	43.1	44.1	43.4	42.9	44.8	41.1
Nonwhite males	34.2	34.9	38.5	40.7	45.7	46.2	46.4	46.7	43.8
Nonwhite females	31.4	33.9	40.6	41.2	43.4	42.5	43.8	46.1	39.8

Note: Excludes persons with zero weeks worked or zero earnings in 1959.
Source: *U.S. Censuses of Population and Housing: 1960, 1/1,000 Sample.*

to our knowledge of differences among groups in time spent at work, and
hence improves our estimate of earnings per unit of time worked.

The use of hours data is particularly important because of our interest
in distinguishing workers by color and sex. Table F-3 shows that average hours per week are considerably lower for females than for males
and lower for nonwhites than for whites within each sex. Table F-3 also
shows that the color-sex differences in hours derived from the 1/1,000
sample correspond very closely to the color-sex differences reported in
the Current Population Survey in 1959. Since we are using the 1/1,000
sample (April 1960) as a proxy for the 1959 annual average, this strong
correlation is reassuring.

In summary, it appears that the use of the hours data from the
1/1,000 sample adds to our understanding of earnings differentials and,
while the errors for any individual may be large, there is no evidence
of important systematic biases for groups.

TABLE F-3

Comparison of Means and Distribution of Hours in the 1/1,000 Sample
and Current Population Survey, by Sex and Color of Nonagricultural
Employed Persons, 1959 and April 1960

	Hours Worked Per Week			
	1–34	35–40	41 and Over	Average [a] Hours
Per Cent of Total				
1/1,000 Sample (April 1960)				
White male	11.9	47.7	40.4	41.9
White female	26.9	56.7	16.4	35.2
Nonwhite male	17.4	56.7	25.9	38.8
Nonwhite female	36.3	47.1	16.5	33.2
Current Population Survey (1959 Average)				
White male	14.7	47.8	37.4	42.5
White female	29.6	51.1	19.2	36.1
Nonwhite male	21.8	53.4	24.8	38.9
Nonwhite female	38.6	41.6	19.8	33.9

Source: CPS data from U.S. Bureau of Labor Statistics, *Labor Force and Employment in 1959*, Special Labor Force Report No. 4, by Joseph S. Zeisel, Table D-7.

[a] For the 1/1,000 sample, averages are computed from more detailed distributions; for the Current Population Survey, averages are computed from distributions by single hours.

MEASURES OF OUTPUT
AND INPUT IN DETAILED
SERVICE INDUSTRIES

Selected Services, Industry Classification

Two types of adjustments were necessary to achieve comparability of industries over time. The first consisted of shifting detailed kinds of business between industries. This was necessary because of modifications in the industrial classification adopted by the Census Bureau. The other adjustment concerned the inclusion of units other than stores in retail trade. Nonstore retailers, consisting of mail-order houses, vending-machine operators, and house-to-house selling organizations, had to be allocated by kind of business, beginning in 1954, when they were first shown separately. Administrative offices, warehouses, and auxiliaries, also shown separately, were included in each year. The eighteen selected service industries as defined in this paper are described in the following paragraphs, and the Standard Industrial Classification codes used in the 1963 *Census of Business* are indicated.

BARBER SHOPS (SIC 724). barber shops.

BEAUTY SHOPS (SIC 723). beauty shops and combination barber and beauty shops.

LAUNDRIES (SIC 7211, 7212, 7213, 7214, 7215). power laundries, industrial laundries, linen supply, diaper service, self-service laundries, and self-service dry cleaning. (Self-service dry cleaning was included in laundries because separate information was not available prior to 1963.)

DRY CLEANING (SIC 7216, 7217). cleaning and dyeing plants (except rug cleaning), and cleaning and pressing shops.

SHOE REPAIR (SIC 725). shoe repair, shoeshine, and hat cleaning establishments.

AUTO REPAIR (SIC 75). auto repair shops, parking, auto and truck rentals, and auto laundries.

MOTION PICTURE THEATERS (SIC 783). regular motion picture theaters and drive-ins.

HOTELS AND MOTELS (SIC 7011). year-round hotels, seasonal hotels, motels, tourist courts, and motor hotels.

LUMBER, BUILDING MATERIALS, HARDWARE, FARM EQUIPMENT DEALERS (SIC 52). lumber yards, building materials dealers, heating and plumbing equipment dealers, paint, glass, and wallpaper stores, electrical supply stores, hardware stores, farm equipment dealers.

GENERAL-MERCHANDISE GROUP STORES (SIC 53, excluding part of nonstore retailers). department stores, limited-price variety stores, general-merchandise stores.

FOOD STORES (SIC 54). groceries, delicatessens, meat markets, fish markets, fruit stores, vegetable markets, candy, nut, and confectionery stores, dairy products stores, retail bakeries, egg and poultry stores.

AUTOMOTIVE DEALERS (SIC 55, excluding 554). passenger car dealers, tire, battery, and accessory dealers, home and auto supply stores, aircraft, motorcycle, boat, and household trailer dealers. (Dealers primarily engaged in selling trucks are classified under wholesale trade.)

GASOLINE SERVICE STATIONS (SIC 554). gasoline service stations.

APPAREL, ACCESSORY STORES (SIC 56). men's, women's, and children's wear stores, custom tailors, specialty stores, furriers, family clothing stores, shoe stores.

FURNITURE, HOME FURNISHINGS, EQUIPMENT STORES (SIC 57). furniture stores, floor-covering stores, drapery, curtain, and upholstery stores, china, glassware, and metalware stores, household appliance stores, radio and television stores, music stores.

EATING, DRINKING PLACES (SIC 58). restaurants, lunchrooms, cafeterias, refreshment places, caterers, drinking places (alcoholic beverages).

DRUG STORES, PROPRIETARY STORES (SIC 591). drug stores, proprietary stores.

OTHER RETAIL STORES (SIC 59, excluding 591). liquor stores, book stores, stationery stores, sporting goods stores, bicycle shops, farm and garden supply stores, jewelry stores, fuel and ice dealers, florists, cigar stores, news dealers, photographic supply stores, optical goods stores, etc.

Current Dollar Output

Current dollar output is defined as receipts from customers for services rendered and merchandise sold, whether or not payment was received. Receipts of income from investments, rental of real estate, and similar items are excluded. Beginning in 1954, state and local sales taxes and federal excise taxes collected by the establishment and paid directly to a tax agency are included. The only exception to this is motion picture theaters, for which taxes are included beginning in 1939. Sales of each of the ten retail trades were taken as the sum of each component kind of business. For total retail trade, output was derived by adding the margins (sales minus cost of goods sold) of the ten retail trades. The margins as a percentage of sales were derived from Internal Revenue Service tabulations for corporations in 1957, published in the *Statistics of Income, 1957–58, Corporation Income Tax Returns* and used for all years. It was determined that there were no significant differences between margins as a percentage of sales for corporations and all firms. The aggregation procedure is not sensitive to possible inaccuracies in the margin percentages.

Prices

Price indexes for all of the eight services, except hotels, are components of the U.S. Bureau of Labor Statistics Consumer Price Index. For hotels and motels, the average room rate for hotels in large cities was taken from Horwath and Horwath, *Hotel Operations in 1963,* p. 21. The drawback to this measure stems from the fact that it is affected by quality of room and extent of multiple occupancy.

For the ten retail trades, price indexes were supplied by David Schwartzman, who computed them primarily from components of the Consumer Price Index. Components of the Wholesale Price Index and other sources were also used. For each kind of business an index was obtained by weighting components by the share of commodity sales in 1948 given in the *Census of Business.*

Real Output

Real output was obtained by deflating current dollar output by the price indexes.

Employment

Employment is defined as the number of full-time equivalent wage and salary workers plus the number of proprietors. The number of proprietors in retail trade was adjusted for changes in coverage, as will be described. Proprietors were assumed to be full-time workers, as were employees in administrative offices, warehouses, and auxiliaries of retail stores. Wage and salary workers were converted into full-time equiv-

TABLE G-1

Output and Input in Selected Service Industries, Sectors and
Total Economy, Selected Years, 1939–63

	Current Output (million dollars)	Price Index (1954 = 100)	Real Output (million 1954 dollars)	Employment (thousands)	Labor Compensation (million dollars)
Auto Repair					
1939	441	57.6	766	166.0	179
1948	1,561	79.6	1,961	246.2	612
1954	2,223	100.0	2,223	244.9	792
1958	3,853	111.9	3,443	378.2	1,357
1963	5,444	122.4	4,448	414.4	1,781
Barber Shops					
1939	231	39.9	579	186.3	177
1948	404	75.8	533	155.2	360
1954	552	100.0	552	147.3	430
1958	783	122.3	640	183.7	633
1963	907	139.5	650	180.3	753
Beauty Shops					
1939	250	50.2	498	190.3	139
1948	434	92.0	472	163.3	276
1954	654	100.0	654	168.0	367
1958	1,028	113.8	903	246.4	615
1963	1,618	125.7	1,287	345.2	1,028
Dry Cleaning					
1939	323	63.9	505	169.4	175
1948	1,128	86.6	1,303	303.7	654
1954	1,497	100.0	1,497	314.1	832
1958	1,671	110.5	1,512	311.8	942
1963	1,765	118.1	1,494	268.1	937
Hotels and Motels					
1939	900	46.1	1,952	360.0	280
1948	2,368	74.2	3,191	444.3	800
1954	2,862	100.0	2,862	440.2	1,015
1958	3,644	118.0	3,088	524.8	1,348
1963	4,667	128.7	3,626	544.2	1,637

(continued)

TABLE G-1 (continued)

	Current Output (million dollars)	Price Index (1954 = 100)	Real Output (million 1954 dollars)	Employment (thousands)	Labor Compensation (million dollars)
			Laundries		
1939	528	52.7	1,002	281.7	268
1948	1,323	80.2	1,650	304.9	721
1954	1,605	100.0	1,605	329.2	828
1958	1,943	114.0	1,704	345.5	1,004
1963	2,493	133.1	1,873	346.5	1,196
			Motion Picture Theaters		
1939	803	52.4	1,532	116.8	135
1948	1,614	85.8	1,881	170.2	314
1954	1,407	100.0	1,407	144.9	304
1958	1,172	116.9	1,003	134.9	291
1963	1,063	146.3	727	105.7	268
			Shoe Repair		
1939	119	45.2	263	72.3	75
1948	219	88.2	248	64.1	159
1954	202	100.0	202	43.3	133
1958	232	115.4	201	44.7	157
1963	208	132.5	157	33.5	152
			Apparel, Accessory Stores		
1939	3,259	49.2	6,628	421.3	583
1948	9,803	101.1	9,692	624.7	1,734
1954	11,214	100.0	11,214	646.4	2,108
1958	12,706	103.2	12,311	686.5	2,357
1963	14,204	108.2	13,129	658.8	2,623
			Automotive Dealers		
1939	5,549	48.8	11,373	435.9	597
1948	20,104	89.6	22,432	694.9	2,248
1954	29,918	100.0	29,918	773.8	3,209
1958	31,824	110.4	28,833	792.7	3,488
1963	45,402	118.2	38,408	859.5	4,579

(continued)

Appendix G

TABLE G-1 (continued)

	Current Output (million dollars)	Price Index (1954 = 100)	Real Output (million 1954 dollars)	Employment (thousands)	Labor Compensation (million dollars)
	Drug Stores, Proprietary Stores				
1939	1,562	66.2	2,360	225.4	288
1948	4,014	90.7	4,428	300.6	823
1954	5,252	100.0	5,252	316.2	1,053
1958	6,779	109.0	6,218	361.1	1,274
1963	8,487	112.6	7,537	364.6	1,550
	Eating, Drinking Places				
1939	3,527	41.6	8,482	1,046.0	881
1948	10,683	92.4	11,560	1,567.4	3,064
1954	13,101	100.0	13,101	1,587.4	3,694
1958	15,201	110.0	13,818	1,819.8	4,275
1963	18,412	124.5	14,785	1,932.7	5,250
	Food Stores				
1939	9,560	41.4	23,075	1,134.6	1,166
1948	29,438	93.0	31,654	1,327.1	3,526
1954	40,646	100.0	40,646	1,384.7	4,251
1958	49,693	106.1	46,823	1,481.5	4,883
1963	58,021	107.5	53,983	1,490.1	6,060
	Furniture, Home Furnishings, Equipment Stores				
1939	1,798	54.5	3,300	255.0	365
1948	7,252	100.6	7,210	465.6	1,425
1954	9,450	100.0	9,450	483.1	1,868
1958	10,481	97.4	10,765	509.9	2,072
1963	11,481	95.9	11,972	459.4	2,229
	Gasoline Service Stations				
1939	2,822	61.5	4,592	445.4	443
1948	6,483	85.9	7,549	446.8	1,084
1954	10,744	100.0	10,744	513.7	1,484
1958	14,178	108.0	13,128	654.3	1,926
1963	17,760	112.5	15,788	682.1	2,314

(continued)

TABLE G-1 (continued)

	Current Output (million dollars)	Price Index (1954 = 100)	Real Output (million 1954 dollars)	Employment (thousands)	Labor Compensation (million dollars)
			General Merchandise Group Stores		
1939	6,475	51.9	12,478	849.1	982
1948	17,135	99.6	17,206	1,153.9	2,748
1954	19,241	100.0	19,241	1,229.4	3,300
1958	23,665	102.3	23,144	1,333.2	4,021
1963	31,937	105.1	30,381	1,433.9	4,979
			Lumber, Building Materials, Hardware, Farm Equipment Dealers		
1939	2,735	44.7	6,123	301.4	403
1948	11,152	86.4	12,906	543.3	1,536
1954	13,366	100.0	13,366	539.2	1,887
1958	14,720	108.6	13,556	551.4	2,117
1963	14,792	112.1	13,199	466.2	2,119
			Other Retail Stores		
1939	4,156	53.4	7,778	546.5	678
1948	12,930	92.2	14,025	678.8	1,816
1954	16,628	100.0	16,628	737.9	2,466
1958	19,872	105.4	18,856	847.0	2,868
1963	23,258	109.8	21,178	869.7	3,481
			Eight Services [a]		
1939	3,600	50.7	7,100	1,543	1,430
1948	9,050	80.5	11,240	1,852	3,900
1954	11,000	100.0	11,000	1,832	4,700
1958	14,330	114.7	12,490	2,170	6,350
1963	18,170	127.4	14,260	2,238	7,750
			Ten Retail Trades [a]		
1939	11,200	48.3	23,200	5,661	6,390
1948	34,260	93.9	36,480	7,803	20,000
1954	43,800	100.0	43,800	8,212	25,320
1958	51,710	105.9	48,820	9,037	29,280
1963	62,750	110.6	56,720	9,217	35,180

(continued)

TABLE G-1 (concluded)

	Current Output (million dollars)	Price Index (1954 = 100)	Real Output (million 1954 dollars)	Employment (thousands)	Labor Compensation (million dollars)
		Eighteen Selected Service Industries [a]			
1939	14,800	48.8	30,300	7,204	7,810
1948	43,310	90.8	47,720	9,655	23,900
1954	54,800	100.0	54,800	10,044	30,020
1958	66,040	107.7	61,310	11,207	35,630
1963	80,920	114.0	70,980	11,455	42,940
		Manufacturing [a]			
1939	–	–	47,700	10,100	14,700
1948	74,700	87.3	85,600	16,000	51,000
1954	106,200	100.0	106,200	16,800	74,400
1958	123,700	112.5	110,000	16,300	87,900
1963	167,000	115.7	144,300	17,400	114,500
		Service [a]			
1939	–	–	91,500	22,000	29,200
1948	113,500	85.0	133,500	26,500	76,100
1954	169,000	100.0	169,000	31,000	113,000
1958	219,300	113.4	193,300	33,200	145,700
1963	297,100	126.1	235,600	36,700	194,700
		Industry [a]			
1939	–	–	78,200	16,400	24,600
1948	121,200	87.1	139,100	25,300	82,100
1954	170,700	100.0	170,700	26,100	116,800
1958	202,600	111.9	181,100	25,500	138,800
1963	267,300	116.4	229,600	26,700	177,000
		Total Economy [a]			
1939	–	–	184,900	46,600	57,500
1948	258,700	88.8	291,700	58,800	172,200
1954	360,400	100.0	360,400	63,100	240,400
1958	443,900	111.6	395,500	63,700	296,000
1963	587,400	119.6	488,200	67,800	383,400

[a] Output in current and constant dollars for these aggregates corresponds to gross product originating rather than to total sales, except for the eight services and for their portion of the eighteen selected services.

alents for 1948, 1954, and 1958 by assuming that the average hourly earnings of part-time workers were the same as the average hourly earnings of full-time workers in the same industry. The number of full-time workers was multiplied by the ratio of payroll of all wage and salary workers to payroll of full-time wage and salary workers. For 1939, the procedure was based on annual rather than weekly earnings, since payroll and employment data were available on an annual basis only. For 1963, the 1958 relation between the total number of wage and salary workers and the number of full-time equivalent wage and salary workers was used because the number of employees working the full workweek was not given. Because 1963 data on employees of administrative offices, warehouses, and auxiliaries were not yet published, they were assumed to be the same percentage of full-time equivalent wage and salary workers in 1963 as in 1958. Unpaid family workers are not included.

Coverage Adjustment

In retail trade, establishments with no paid employees were excluded from coverage in the *Census of Business* if receipts for the year did not exceed $100 in 1939, $500 in 1948, and $2,500 in 1954 and 1958. In my earlier study [1] an attempt was made to adjust the count of proprietors to the 1939 coverage base. This adjustment was small, and because of questions concerning its accuracy was not adopted here. The count of proprietors is as reported in each Census.

Total Labor Input

Total labor input is measured by payroll of all employees. Payroll for the entire year was used throughout. The payroll of proprietors was obtained by assuming that labor input was equal to 90 per cent of OBE proprietors' income in all of trade and 95 per cent in services (see Appendix C). The average annual labor income per proprietor in each industry within trade or services was assumed to bear the same relation to every other detailed industry as average annual earnings of proprietors in 1959 according to the 1960 *Census of Population* 1/1,000 sample.

Sectors and Manufacturing

Methods and sources of data for the total economy, Industry sector, Service sector, and manufacturing are the same as described in Appendix C.

[1] *Productivity Differences Within the Service Sector,* New York, NBER Occasional Paper 102, 1967.

Because the Office of Business Economics series did not include 1939, estimates for that year were based on John W. Kendrick, *Productivity Trends in the United States,* Princeton University Press for NBER, 1961. The 1939–48 changes in Kendrick's series were applied to the 1948 real gross product for given major industry groups.

ALTERNATIVE MEASURES
OF REAL OUTPUT
IN SOME SERVICE INDUSTRIES

The following notes on some of the individual retail trades provide some rough alternative measures of real output and compare them with the deflated sales indexes that have been used in this study. Some of these alternatives serve as a check on the quality of the data; others involve a different concept of real output.

Automobile Dealers

A typical transaction in this industry consists of the sale of one car or one truck. The number of such sales may show rates of change different from the deflated value of sales, as shown in the following figures.[1]

Year (1958 = 100)	Deflated Sales	Number of New Cars and Trucks Sold [a]
1939	39.5	69.9
1948	77.8	102.9
1954	103.8	128.5
1958	100.0	100.0
1963	133.3	177.2

The explanation for the differences probably lies in changes in the proportion of low-priced, medium- priced, and expensive cars sold. One way of approaching this problem of measurement would be to look at the retail margins realized on cars in different price ranges. If the percentage margins are typically the same, regardless of price range, then

[1] Source notes for all of the series presented in this Appendix are given in a footnote at the end of the Appendix.

the use of deflated sales as a measure of real output, without regard to the number of cars sold, would seem to be justified.

Drug Stores

There seems to be a very close correspondence between deflated sales of drug stores and the total number of prescriptions filled. The index for industrial production of drugs, soap, and toiletries seems to rise more rapidly than either of the other series. It may be that sales of these commodities have been increasing at a rapid rate in retail stores other than drug stores.

Year (1958 = 100)	Deflated Sales	Number of Prescriptions [b]	Industrial Production of Drugs, Soap, and Toiletries [c]
1939	37.9	32.3	n.a.
1948	71.2	69.8	45.2
1954	84.5	80.4	68.9
1958	100.0	100.0	100.0
1963	121.3	122.5	141.2

Food Stores

Changes in deflated sales of food stores have closely paralleled changes in industrial production of food in the postwar period. The average size of transaction has apparently been rising markedly as people tend to shop less frequently. There would be some increase attributable to higher incomes even if the frequency of shopping was unchanged.

Year (1954 = 100)	Deflated Sales	Industrial Production of Food [c]	Number of Transactions [d]
1948	77.8	86.4	n.a.
1954	100.0	100.0	100.0
1958	115.2	110.4	n.a.
1963	132.8	129.8	87.0

Gasoline Stations

Gas stations are another type of retail outlet for which the size of transaction may be of considerable importance. Casual observation suggests that productivity is much greater when pumping fifteen gallons into one tank than when servicing three cars for five gallons each. Transaction size has probably increased over time as gas tanks have become larger and incomes have risen. The following data seem relevant.

Year (1958 = 100)	Deflated Sales	Number of Privately Owned Cars, Trucks, and Buses [a]	Number of Vehicle Miles Traveled [a]	Gallons of Motor Fuel Consumed [a]	Size of Gasoline Tank (Ford) [e]	Replacement Production of Tires and Batteries [a]
1939	35.0	45.4	42.8	38.8	70.0	53.8
1948	57.5	60.2	59.8	57.1	85.0	83.1
1954	81.8	85.7	84.4	83.1	n.a.	85.2
1958	100.0	100.0	100.0	100.0	100.0	100.0
1963	120.3	121.0	120.0	114.0	100.0	126.7

General Merchandise Stores

The average size of transactions has apparently risen in general merchandise stores also.

Year (1958 = 100)	Deflated Sales (1)	Number of Transactions (3 ÷ 4) (2)	Receipts in Current $ [f] (3)	Average Sale in Department Stores in Current $ [g] (4)
1939	53.9	61.7	27.4	44.4
1948	74.4	78.4	72.4	92.3
1954	83.2	89.0	81.3	91.3
1958	100.0	100.0	100.0	100.0
1963	131.3	117.7	135.0	114.7

Lumber Dealers, Etc.

The following figures suggest either that lumber dealers are losing out to other forms of distribution or that the deflated sales figures for 1963 understate the real amount of goods passing through this type of retail outlet.

Year (1958 = 100)	Deflated Sales	Industrial Production of Lumber and Products [c]	Industrial Production of Construction Materials [c]	Industrial Production of Farm Equipment [c]
1948	95.2	96.0	79.3	143.5
1954	98.6	104.2	92.5	107.3
1958	100.0	100.0	100.0	100.0
1963	97.4	113.9	123.1	128.0

Services

Many of the general points that were made concerning output in retail trades also apply to the services. The attitude and skills of the person supplying the service, the amenities provided to the customer, and the demand made upon the customer's time are clearly factors that should be considered in measuring real output. The principal question in the case of services seems to be: How well does the price index capture the quality dimensions of output? Shifts in the composition of output within a Census industry can also present problems, as indicated in the following two examples.

Hotels and Motels

The postwar period has witnessed a marked shift in the composition of this industry from hotels to motels. In 1948, motels accounted for less than 10 per cent of total industry employment. By 1963 the share in motels was one-third. Receipts per worker have typically been about 5 to 10 per cent higher in motels than in hotels; this shift therefore would tend to raise the rate of change of output per man as currently measured. A factor that probably has considerable effect on output per man is the occupancy rate. Between 1939 and 1948 this rate rose markedly, but since then it has declined. By 1963 it was almost down to the 1939 level.

Year (1958 = 100)	Deflated Sales	Occupancy Rate [h]
1939	63.2	87.0
1948	103.2	123.2
1954	92.7	n.a.
1958	100.0	100.0
1963	117.4	91.3

Motion Picture Theaters

One of the factors tending to raise measured output per man in motion picture theaters has been a shift from regular movie houses to drive-ins. In 1948 the latter accounted for only 3 per cent of the industry's employment, but by 1963 this percentage had grown to over 20 per cent. Receipts per worker have typically been 10 to 20 per cent higher in drive-ins than in regular theaters.

Notes to Appendix H

a Automobile Manufacturers' Association, *Automobile Facts and Figures,* various issues.

b Number of prescriptions per store from Eli Lilly and Company, *The Lilly Digest,* 1961, 1963, multiplied by the number of establishments from the *Census of Business.*

c Board of Governors of the Federal Reserve System, *Industrial Production Indexes,* 1961–63, and *Industrial Production, 1957–1959 Base.*

d 1963, *Progressive Grocer;* 1954, Cox, Reavis, *et al., Distribution in a High Level Economy,* Englewood Cliffs, N.J., 1965.

e Ford Motor Company dealer.

f U.S. Bureau of the Census, *Census of Business.*

g National Retail Merchants Association, *Merchandising and Operating Results,* various issues. Department and specialty stores until 1948—department stores only, subsequently. The 1954 data was estimated by assuming the 1954–56 change in the average sale of "owned" departments applied to all departments.

h Harris, Kerr, and Foster, *Trends in the Hotel-Motel Business, 1963.* Rate refers to both hotels and motels.

DETAILED INDUSTRY
DATA AND SOURCES

Table I-1 presents actual and expected hourly earnings and sample size for the detailed industries analyzed in Chapter 6. Table I-2 presents the other variables used in the interindustry regressions.

The derivation of actual and expected hourly earnings (X_0 and X_1) and of the two location variables is explained in Chapter 6 and Appendix E.

The unionization variable (X_2) was derived from Leonard W. Weiss, Appendix to "Concentration and Labor Earnings," *American Economic Review,* March 1966, Table A-2, with modifications; and H. G. Lewis, *Unionism and Relative Wages in the United States,* Chicago, 1963, Table 76, with modifications.

The per cent of production workers in establishments with more than half of production workers covered by collective bargaining agreements was adjusted to include nonproduction workers, on the assumption that none of the latter are covered. Information on the number of production workers as a per cent of all employed persons was derived from the *Census of Manufactures and Mineral Industries,* except for construction, transportation, communications, and public utilities, which were from *Census of Population* data on occupation by industry.

From the Lewis' data on union membership as a per cent of persons engaged in production, the number of union members was derived and divided by the 1/1,000 sample employment.[1] The number of union barbers was taken from Leo Troy.[2] For industries where Lewis provided insufficient detail, it was assumed that the per cent unionized in any detailed industry was the same as for the industry group of which it was a

---

[1] Despite the differences in year and concept (Lewis' data are for 1953), comparisons with Weiss' series where possible revealed little systematic difference, although individual industries differed significantly.

[2] *Trade Union Membership, 1897–1962,* New York, NBER, Occasional Paper 92, 1965.

TABLE I-1

Actual and Expected Hourly Earnings, by Detailed Industry, 1959

		No. of Persons in Sample	Hourly Earnings (dollars)		
Code	Industry Title		Actual	Expected	Ratio of Actual to Expected
	MINING				
126	Metal mining	72	2.73	2.64	1.03
136	Coal mining	187	2.96	2.44	1.21
146	Crude pet. & nat. gas extrac.	232	3.05	2.76	1.11
156	Nonmetall. mining & quarrying, except fuel	89	2.46	2.52	.98
196	**CONSTRUCTION**	3,625	2.87	2.58	1.11
	MANUFACTURING — *Durable goods*				
206	Logging	140	2.05	2.29	.89
207	Sawmills, planing mills, & mill work	413	1.94	2.31	.84
208	Misc. wood prod.	88	2.09	2.35	.89
209	Furniture & fixtures	359	2.17	2.32	.93
216	Glass & glass prod.	152	2.76	2.47	1.12
217	Cement, & concrete, gypsum & plaster products	174	2.72	2.58	1.05
218	Structural clay products	92	2.54	2.47	1.03
219	Pottery & related products	34	2.35	2.45	.96
236	Misc. nonmetall. mineral & stone prod.	105	2.71	2.51	1.08
237	Blast furnaces, steel works, rolling & finishing mills	570	3.39	2.57	1.32
238	Other primary iron and steel industries	313	2.80	2.45	1.14
239	Primary nonferrous industries	297	2.98	2.63	1.13
246	Cutlery, hand tools, & other hardware	143	2.48	2.39	1.04
247	Fabricated structural metal prod.	327	2.93	2.59	1.14
248	Misc. fabricated metal prod.	821	2.80	2.52	1.11
249	Not specified metal industries	5	2.07	2.63	.79

(continued)

TABLE I-1 (continued)

		No. of Persons in Sample	Hourly Earnings (dollars)		
	Industry				Ratio of Actual to
Code	Title		Actual	Expected	Expected
256	Farm machinery & equip.	116	2.80	2.72	1.03
257	Office, computing, & accounting machines	170	3.05	2.65	1.15
258	Misc. machinery	1,303	2.85	2.67	1.07
259	Electrical machinery, equip., & supplies	1,428	2.80	2.49	1.12
267	Motor vehicles & motor veh. equip.	793	3.05	2.56	1.19
268	Aircraft & parts	675	3.01	2.74	1.10
269	Ship & boat building & repairing	256	2.73	2.61	1.05
276	Railroad & misc. transport. equip.	63	2.43	2.39	1.02
286	Professional equip. & supplies	230	2.96	2.63	1.12
287	Photographic equip. & supplies	59	3.32	2.64	1.26
289	Watches, clocks, & clockwork-operated devices	33	2.83	2.14	1.33
296	Misc. manufacturing industries	368	2.45	2.27	1.08
	MANUFACTURING – *nondurable goods*				
306	Meat products	287	2.42	2.33	1.04
307	Dairy products	298	2.32	2.64	.88
308	Canning & preserving fruits, vegetables, & sea foods	185	2.20	2.33	.95
309	Grain-mill products	142	2.42	2.44	.99
316	Bakery products	322	2.35	2.39	.98
317	Confectionery & rel. prod.	80	2.16	1.87	1.16
318	Beverage industries	207	2.78	2.55	1.09
319	Misc. food preparations & kindred prod.	132	2.54	2.42	1.05
326	Not specified food industries	24	3.15	2.51	1.25
329	Tobacco manufactures	95	2.18	2.00	1.09
346	Knitting mills	176	1.67	1.96	.85
347	Dyeing & finishing textiles, exc. wool & knit goods	52	1.83	2.29	.80

(continued)

TABLE I-1 (continued)

		No. of Persons in Sample	Hourly Earnings (dollars)		
Code	Title		Actual	Expected	Ratio of Actual to Expected
348	Floor covering, exc. hard surface	34	2.67	2.56	1.04
349	Yarn, thread, & fabric mills	559	1.82	2.11	.86
356	Misc. textile mill products	45	2.77	2.39	1.16
359	Apparel & accessories	995	2.17	1.89	1.15
367	Misc. fabricated textile prod.	98	2.10	2.15	.98
386	Pulp, paper, & paperboard mills	281	2.72	2.58	1.05
387	Paperboard containers & boxes	174	2.55	2.40	1.06
389	Misc. paper & pulp prod.	134	2.30	2.24	1.02
396	Newspaper publishing & printing	464	3.02	2.69	1.12
398	Printing, publishing, & allied ind., exc. newspapers	589	2.76	2.46	1.12
406	Synthetic fibers	49	2.84	2.80	1.01
407	Drugs & medicines	105	2.93	2.99	.98
408	Paints, varnishes, & rel. prod.	75	3.01	2.59	1.16
409	Misc. chemicals & allied prod.	563	3.12	2.76	1.13
416	Petroleum refining	245	3.41	2.90	1.17
419	Misc. petroleum & coal prod.	27	2.93	2.81	1.04
426	Rubber products	259	2.88	2.48	1.16
429	Misc. plastic products	108	2.77	2.51	1.10
436	Leather: tanned, curried, & finished	31	2.40	2.23	1.08
437	Footwear, exc. rubber	286	1.97	1.98	.99
438	Leather prod., exc. footwear	70	1.93	2.08	.93
459	Not specified manufacturing indus.	55	3.39	2.51	1.35

(continued)

TABLE I-1 (continued)

		No. of Persons in Sample	Hourly Earnings (dollars)		
	Industry		Actual	Expected	Ratio of Actual to Expected
Code	Title				
	TRANSPORTATION, COMMUNICATIONS & OTHER PUBLIC UTILITIES				
506	Railroads & railway express serv.	941	2.78	2.64	1.05
507	Street railways & bus lines	291	2.36	2.60	.91
508	Taxicab serv.	117	1.42	2.47	.57
509	Trucking serv.	732	2.62	2.48	1.06
516	Warehousing & storage	116	2.67	2.47	1.08
517	Water transportation	199	3.26	2.52	1.30
518	Air transportation	205	3.22	2.70	1.19
519	Petrol. & gasoline pipe lines	24	3.59	2.93	1.23
526	Services incidental to transport	63	3.00	2.52	1.19
536	Radio broadcasting & TV	88	3.81	2.85	1.33
538	Telephone (wire & radio)	654	2.55	2.21	1.16
539	Telegraph (wire & radio)	34	2.37	2.07	1.15
567	Electric light & power	354	2.72	2.68	1.02
568	Gas & steam supply systems	140	2.81	2.52	1.11
569	Electric-gas utilities	134	2.91	2.63	1.11
576	Water supply	106	2.15	2.54	.85
578	Sanitary services	146	2.03	2.38	.85
579	Other & not specified utilities	22	2.35	2.93	.80
	WHOLESALE & RETAIL TRADE				
606	Motor vehicles & equip.	109	2.57	2.80	.92
607	Drugs, chemicals, & allied prod.	95	2.93	2.82	1.04
608	Dry goods & apparel	65	2.81	2.71	1.04
609	Food & rel. prod.	418	2.52	2.58	.97
616	Farm prod. – raw materials	120	2.00	2.65	.75
617	Elec. goods, hardware, & plumbing equip.	223	2.92	2.78	1.05
618	Machinery, equip., & supplies	252	3.24	2.84	1.14
619	Petroleum prod.	163	3.01	2.81	1.07

(continued)

TABLE I-1 (continued)

| | | | Hourly Earnings (dollars) | | |
| | Industry | No. of Persons in | | | Ratio of Actual to |
Code	Title	Sample	Actual	Expected	Expected
626	Misc. wholesale trade	565	3.07	2.66	1.16
629	Not specified wholesale trade	98	3.52	2.80	1.26
636	Food stores, exc. dairy prod.	1,472	1.85	2.29	.81
637	Dairy prod. stores & milk retailing	54	1.79	2.52	.71
638	General merchandise retailing	1,111	2.07	2.18	.95
639	Limited price variety stores	269	1.65	1.95	.85
646	Apparel & access, stores, exc. shoe stores	504	2.16	2.25	.96
647	Shoe stores	96	2.54	2.56	.99
648	Furniture & housefurn. stores	285	2.45	2.65	.93
649	Household appliances, TV, & radio stores	183	2.38	2.71	.88
656	Motor vehicles & access. retailing	751	2.29	2.64	.87
657	Gasoline service stations	552	1.60	2.41	.67
658	Drug stores	327	2.28	2.76	.83
659	Eating & drinking places	1,563	1.52	2.08	.73
666	Hardware & farm equip. stores	237	1.94	2.62	.74
676	Lumber & build. mat. retailing	350	2.26	2.59	.87
678	Liquor stores	85	1.83	2.69	.68
679	Retail florists	59	1.83	2.34	.78
686	Jewelry stores	83	2.39	2.65	.90
687	Fuel & ice dealers	123	2.25	2.54	.88
689	Misc. retail stores	381	2.17	2.57	.84
696	Not specified retail trade	92	2.10	2.45	.86
	FINANCE, INSURANCE, & REAL ESTATE				
706	Banking & credit agencies	915	2.69	2.42	1.11
716	Security & commod. brokerage & invest. companies	137	4.37	3.03	1.44
726	Insurance	1,036	2.93	2.69	1.09
736	Real estate (inc. real est.-ins.-law offices)	529	2.87	2.74	1.05

(continued)

Appendix I

TABLE I-1 (continued)

		No. of Persons in Sample	Hourly Earnings (dollars)		
Industry					Ratio of Actual to
Code	Title		Actual	Expected	Expected
	BUSINESS & REPAIR SERVICES				
806	Advertising	122	3.48	2.55	1.37
807	Misc. business services	588	2.76	2.61	1.06
808	Automob. repair serv. & garages	484	1.91	2.47	.77
809	Misc. repair services	315	2.37	2.63	.90
	PERSONAL SERVICES				
816	Private households	1,635	.84	1.29	.65
826	Hotels and lodging places	493	1.44	2.12	.68
828	Laundering, cleaning, & dyeing serv.	591	1.69	2.03	.83
829	Dressmaking shops	33	1.40	1.75	.80
836	Shoe repair shops	33	1.44	2.39	.60
838	Barber & beauty shops	449	1.65	2.11	.78
839	Misc. personal services	106	2.63	2.85	.92
	ENTERTAINMENT & RECREATION SERVICES				
846	Motion pictures & theaters	177	2.79	2.57	1.09
848	Bowling alleys, & billiard & pool parlors	75	1.54	2.24	.69
849	Misc. entertainment & recreation serv.	242	2.14	2.33	.92
	PROFESSIONAL & RELATED SERVICES				
867	Medical & other health serv., exc. hospitals	813	3.68	3.01	1.22
868	Hospitals	1,548	1.80	2.05	.88
869	Legal services	255	4.72	3.71	1.27
876	Educational services	3,090	2.58	2.85	.91
879	Welfare & religious services	539	1.64	3.19	.52
888	Nonprofit membership organizations	223	2.54	2.55	1.00

(continued)

TABLE I-1 (concluded)

		No. of Persons in Sample	Hourly Earnings (dollars)		Ratio of Actual to Expected
Code	Industry Title		Actual	Expected	
896	Engineering & architectural services	178	3.63	3.35	1.08
897	Accounting, auditing, & bookkeep. serv.	163	3.31	3.25	1.02
898	Misc. profess. & rel. services	109	3.53	3.09	1.14
	PUBLIC ADMINISTRATION				
906	Postal service	565	2.58	2.78	.93
916	Federal public admin.	1,130	2.78	2.76	1.01
926	State public admin.	388	2.35	2.74	.86
936	Local public admin.	929	2.21	2.65	.83
999	INDUSTRY NOT REPORTED	2,318	2.35	2.29	1.03

Note: See Note to Table 46.

part. The final estimates of all industries were submitted to Lewis for review and modified in accordance with his suggestions.

The establishment size variable (X_5) was derived, for the Industry sector, from Leonard, W. Weiss, Appendix to "Concentration and Labor Earnings," *American Economic Review,* March 1966, Table A-2. Service sector data for this variable were from U.S. Bureau of Employment Security, *Employment and Wages,* First Quarter 1960, Table B-1; 1958 *Census of Business,* Retail Trade—Vol. I, Tables 2 and 3A; Wholesale Trade—Vol. III, Tables 1A and 2F; Selected Services—Vol. V, Table 3B; 1960 *Census of Population* 1/1,000 sample. The percentage of employees in establishments of 250 or more employees was not taken directly from the BES data for several reasons. The total number of employees was not used because (1) it does not include proprietors; (2) coverage in the 0–3 size class is incomplete because some state unemployment insurance laws exclude firms with less than four workers. In addition, the figures on the number of employees in establishment sizes of 250 and more were adjusted wherever possible because the BES, while generally using the establishment as the reporting unit, in some cases allows employers to group establishments into one reporting unit (see p. 144 of *Employment and Wages,* First Quarter 1960).

TABLE I-2

Industry Independent Variables, X_2 Through X_9

Industry Code [a]	Union-ization, X_2 (per cent)	Region and City Size, X_3 (dollars)	Location in SMSA, X_4 (dollars)	Establish-ment Size, X_5 (per cent)	Employment Growth, X_6 (ratio of 1960 to 1950)	Unemploy-ment Rate, X_7 (per cent)	Annual Hours, X_8 (hundreds of hours)	Self Employment, X_9 (per cent)
126	71.0	2.28	2.49	60.0	1.026	5.0	18.58	3.06
136	75.0	2.13	2.50	39.0	3.302	9.2	15.57	9.19
146	8.0	2.22	2.49	30.0	1.089	5.0	22.12	18.14
156	24.0	2.27	2.50	12.0	1.106	4.8	21.01	4.63
196	58.0	2.45	2.50	9.0	1.104	9.9	17.98	23.87
206	25.0	2.15	2.50	7.0	0.978	10.7	15.16	40.65
207	20.0	2.24	2.50	22.0	0.715	5.5	18.24	4.59
208	20.0	2.30	2.51	16.0	0.958	5.5	19.79	9.13
209	29.0	2.43	2.49	35.0	1.143	4.6	19.68	6.81
216	57.0	2.48	2.49	79.0	1.163	4.1	19.43	0.01
217	37.0	2.42	2.50	18.0	1.633	4.5	21.02	12.88
218	39.0	2.37	2.50	24.0	1.049	5.1	20.11	14.78
219	35.0	2.38	2.49	56.0	0.797	4.0	20.55	3.04
236	45.0	2.49	2.51	48.0	1.523	3.5	19.57	5.65
237	80.0	2.62	2.50	98.0	0.929	3.6	16.62	1.04

246	46.0	2.52	2.51	57.0	1.086	4.1	20.84	1.13
247	53.0	2.57	2.52	39.0	1.309	5.3	19.72	7.18
248	58.0	2.61	2.50	57.0	1.784	4.1	20.20	4.27
256	65.0	2.51	2.50	68.0	0.737	4.4	19.61	0.86
257	28.0	2.60	2.53	92.0	1.636	2.0	20.37	2.51
258	49.0	2.57	2.51	58.0	1.303	3.4	20.62	6.83
259	52.0	2.61	2.50	90.0	1.727	3.0	20.07	2.44
267	71.0	2.65	2.52	90.0	0.983	5.8	19.34	1.03
268	49.0	2.67	2.50	94.0	2.531	4.5	20.81	0.53
269	59.0	2.49	2.51	76.0	1.517	9.9	19.04	2.76
276	40.0	2.55	2.50	63.0	1.235	8.4	17.28	3.73
286	35.0	2.64	2.50	75.0	2.219	2.6	20.52	8.74
287	27.0	2.50	2.54	82.0	1.369	2.2	20.61	0.01
289	69.0	2.46	2.47	86.0	0.843	5.0	21.06	24.69
306	64.0	2.47	2.49	52.0	1.153	4.2	21.18	4.92
307	27.0	2.42	2.50	21.0	1.518	2.2	23.06	6.48
308	59.0	2.43	2.50	33.0	1.327	12.8	19.74	8.20
309	51.0	2.39	2.52	33.0	1.212	3.3	21.85	4.26
316	29.0	2.56	2.48	31.0	1.330	3.4	22.89	8.45
317	41.0	2.65	2.49	57.0	0.997	5.6	20.04	3.73
318	38.0	2.48	2.52	40.0	1.035	4.1	20.32	12.51
319	51.0	2.50	2.49	27.0	1.242	5.4	20.89	6.52
329	53.0	2.35	2.52	79.0	0.914	7.4	19.55	0.49

(continued)

TABLE I-2 (continued)

Industry Code [a]	Union- ization, X_2 (per cent)	Region and City Size, X_3 (dollars)	Location in SMSA, X_4 (dollars)	Establish- ment Size, X_5 (per cent)	Employment Growth, X_6 (ratio of 1960 to 1950)	Unemploy- ment Rate, X_7 (per cent)	Annual Hours, X_8 (hundreds of hours)	Self Employment, X_9 (per cent)
346	28.0	2.27	2.50	45.0	1.029	4.2	20.07	1.65
347	42.0	2.29	2.48	62.0	4.757	7.9	20.59	0.51
348	53.0	2.34	2.50	82.0	0.638	3.7	21.15	4.63
349	21.0	2.18	2.50	76.0	0.667	3.8	20.17	3.73
356	34.0	2.53	2.49	48.0	0.950	4.6	20.53	0.58
359	55.0	2.45	2.48	28.0	1.068	6.8	19.66	9.35
367	28.0	2.60	2.50	16.0	1.311	5.3	21.47	8.01
386	53.0	2.31	2.50	78.0	1.268	2.4	21.13	0.32
387	35.0	2.58	2.51	39.0	1.417	3.4	19.99	2.60
389	40.0	2.54	2.49	44.0	1.045	2.7	21.13	0.76
396	47.0	2.55	2.50	56.0	1.300	2.3	13.05	9.09
398	38.0	2.64	2.50	34.0	1.339	2.5	20.07	9.30
406	54.0	2.18	2.49	99.0	1.081	2.4	20.36	1.54
407	18.0	2.65	2.52	71.0	1.950	1.5	21.98	2.94
408	40.0	2.66	2.52	24.0	1.165	2.8	20.67	2.85

416	65.0	2.53	2.50	87.0	0.984	2.0	20.39	1.33
419	64.0	2.67	2.50	20.0	1.351	4.4	20.30	6.76
426	63.0	2.52	2.51	81.0	1.119	3.2	19.99	0.18
429	40.0	2.64	2.50	32.0	1.901	2.6	20.78	11.58
436	50.0	2.46	2.50	41.0	0.671	5.5	18.49	0.01
437	39.0	2.39	2.49	65.0	0.942	5.4	18.11	2.64
438	36.0	2.60	2.47	27.0	0.871	6.8	17.53	0.01
506	83.0	2.49	2.51	98.0	0.677	3.7	20.46	2.37
507	62.0	2.58	2.49	48.0	0.888	1.7	19.30	3.37
508	27.0	2.57	2.46	31.0	0.776	4.8	22.59	15.24
509	69.0	2.48	2.52	20.0	1.328	5.1	21.32	12.99
516	55.0	2.48	2.51	9.0	1.169	6.0	19.92	7.58
517	72.0	2.55	2.50	69.0	0.902	11.3	19.00	9.01
518	51.0	2.62	2.53	74.0	1.958	2.7	19.91	6.98
519	52.0	2.23	2.47	37.0	1.078	3.1	20.78	3.66
526	61.0	2.59	2.49	10.0	1.454	3.6	20.25	23.06
536	52.0	2.52	2.51	21.0	1.457	3.1	20.49	18.72
538	68.0	2.53	2.51	84.0	1.148	1.0	20.18	0.73
539	68.0	2.64	2.50	74.0	0.828	4.3	20.03	0.01
567	10.0	2.44	2.52	71.4	1.072	1.6	20.93	0.40
568	41.0	2.50	2.50	70.0	1.286	2.1	21.13	5.10
569	41.0	2.59	2.53	87.0	1.072	1.6	20.58	0.91
576	0.1	2.49	2.48	15.0	1.317	2.0	20.74	0.74
578	0.1	2.57	2.47	0.1	1.386	3.5	19.19	5.92

(continued)

TABLE I-2 (continued)

Industry Code [a]	Unionization, X_2 (per cent)	Region and City Size, X_3 (dollars)	Location in SMSA, X_4 (dollars)	Establishment Size, X_5 (per cent)	Employment Growth, X_6 (ratio of 1960 to 1950)	Unemployment Rate, X_7 (per cent)	Annual Hours, X_8 (hundreds of hours)	Self Employment, X_9 (per cent)
906	0.1	2.53	2.49	75.8	1.210	2.5	20.61	1.63
606	4.0	2.54	2.50	10.2	2.076	2.2	22.89	21.93
607	4.0	2.62	2.50	13.4	1.171	2.2	21.38	13.27
608	4.0	2.64	2.48	6.8	0.650	3.2	20.61	24.74
609	4.0	2.46	2.51	7.3	0.790	3.9	21.98	25.17
616	4.0	2.29	2.50	4.6	1.089	3.0	22.47	20.67
617	4.0	2.55	2.51	22.9	1.350	2.3	21.30	9.03
618	4.0	2.56	2.53	11.2	1.827	1.9	21.75	16.45
619	4.0	2.45	2.53	11.9	1.065	1.8	22.84	14.05
626	4.0	2.56	2.51	11.9	1.198	3.6	20.90	16.93
636	11.0	2.45	2.48	1.8	1.014	3.3	19.60	28.20
637	11.0	2.43	2.50	0.1	1.014	3.3	22.75	21.47
638	11.0	2.55	2.49	59.1	1.263	3.9	20.32	11.35
639	11.0	2.47	2.50	13.4	1.578	4.2	20.55	18.12
646	11.0	2.54	2.48	10.2	1.010	3.6	20.08	34.63

649	11.0	2.45	2.51	2.0	0.836	3.0	22.04	28.13
656	11.0	2.41	2.50	0.9	1.506	2.8	23.30	24.07
657	11.0	2.38	2.50	0.1	1.383	4.0	22.87	45.64
658	11.0	2.47	2.47	0.8	1.272	2.8	19.07	36.06
659	11.0	2.42	2.48	2.1	1.065	6.9	21.32	35.29
666	11.0	2.31	2.49	0.7	1.066	1.9	23.51	33.73
676	11.0	2.41	2.51	0.8	1.118	4.0	21.16	20.98
678	11.0	2.51	2.48	0.1	1.060	3.3	22.05	47.83
679	11.0	2.50	2.49	0.1	1.239	3.3	20.34	33.57
686	11.0	2.49	2.50	0.8	0.847	2.5	21.40	46.93
687	11.0	2.42	2.48	1.0	0.774	4.8	21.97	27.82
689	11.0	2.50	2.48	0.3	1.149	2.9	20.95	36.41
706	0.1	2.54	2.49	35.0	1.636	1.2	20.54	5.67
716	3.0	2.62	2.50	22.9	1.663	1.5	20.35	24.68
726	2.3	2.56	2.51	35.9	1.415	1.1	22.10	19.09
736	11.0	2.60	2.47	35.4	1.115	3.0	20.31	41.86
806	0.1	2.69	2.50	25.4	1.162	3.3	19.27	29.33
807	0.1	2.63	2.50	21.6	2.568	3.9	19.78	18.56
808	5.5	2.44	2.50	0.3	0.771	4.3	21.46	33.15
809	0.1	2.44	2.50	0.9	1.192	3.9	19.73	36.32
816	0.1	2.40	2.47	0.1	1.197	8.2	11.25	5.28
826	20.0	2.46	2.47	22.9	1.118	6.7	19.54	25.37
828	15.0	2.50	2.47	5.8	0.893	3.8	21.29	23.17

(continued)

TABLE I-2 (concluded)

Industry Code [a]	Union-ization, X_2 (per cent)	Region and City Size, X_3 (dollars)	Location in SMSA, X_4 (dollars)	Establish-ment Size, X_5 (per cent)	Employment Growth, X_6 (ratio of 1960 to 1950)	Unemploy-ment Rate, X_7 (per cent)	Annual Hours, X_8 (hundreds of hours)	Self Employment, X_9 (per cent)
829	15.0	2.47	2.47	0.1	0.942	2.8	21.27	73.93
836	15.0	2.50	2.46	0.1	0.678	3.0	20.96	46.83
838	32.0	2.46	2.48	0.1	1.291	1.7	23.03	51.26
839	15.0	2.53	2.47	0.2	1.023	2.4	20.18	45.05
846	21.0	2.61	2.50	8.2	0.722	7.5	16.88	17.48
848	23.0	2.46	2.47	0.2	1.098	7.0	16.76	23.88
849	23.0	2.53	2.48	10.0	1.465	9.7	16.81	17.37
867	0.1	2.51	2.49	0.5	1.316	0.8	23.17	65.25
868	0.1	2.50	2.48	2.2	1.701	2.7	20.01	6.62
869	0.1	2.58	2.50	0.4	1.213	0.6	22.00	72.06
876	2.0	2.43	2.48	0.2	1.633	1.9	18.63	4.38
888	0.1	2.61	2.50	8.3	1.318	3.5	20.24	1.41
896	1.0	2.61	2.51	23.7	2.392	3.0	20.84	23.65
897	1.0	2.57	2.51	3.2	1.535	1.6	22.99	54.55
898	1.0	2.64	2.50	3.6	1.543	2.9	21.40	36.32
916	15.0	2.50	2.51	75.8	1.236	5.9	20.58	1.10
926	11.0	2.44	2.52	89.9	1.481	1.8	21.18	1.91
936	11.0	2.53	2.48	78.1	1.290	1.6	22.39	2.95

[a] See Table I-1 for industry titles

For retail trade, personal services, and entertainment and recreation, the ratio of the number of employees in establishments with 100 and more employees from the *Census of Business* to the same number from the BES was multiplied by the number of employees in establishments of 250 and more from the BES as a percentage of total employees plus proprietors from the *Census of Business*. This is equivalent to taking the per cent of employees in establishments of 100 and more from the *Census of Business* and then assuming that the ratio of employees in those of 250 and more to employees in those of 100 and more was the same as the BES found. This was done by detailed industry.

For wholesale trade, the same method was used, but the ratio of employees in establishments of 100 and more from the two sources was for total wholesale trade, while the per cent in establishments of 250 and over was by detailed industry.

For professional services and FIRE, the number of employees in establishments of 250 and over from the BES was used as a percentage of employed persons from the *Census of Population* 1/1,000 sample.

For government, the number of employees in establishments of 250 and over as a percentage of total employees from the BES was used.

In *Employment and Wages,* where figures were omitted to avoid disclosure the residual number of employees in the industry group for the employment size-class were distributed among the detailed industries in the same proportion that employees were distributed among the same industries in the preceding size-class. However, the following industries were assumed to have the minimum number for that class, since they would have less than that using the proportional method:

Employment Size-Class	Industry	SIC No.
250–499	Liquor stores	592
	Sporting goods stores	595
	Barber shops	724
	Garment alteration	727
	Misc. personal service	729
500–999	Liquor stores	
	Book & stationery stores	594
1,000 and over	Misc. repair service	76
	Investment companies	67

Where more than one figure within an industry was missing in the *Census of Business,* the residual number of employees for the industry were distributed among the employment size-classes in proportion to a

TABLE I-3

Zero Order Correlation Coefficients, Ten Industry Variables [a]

	Average Hourly Earnings X_0	Demographic Characteristics X_1	Unionization 20-60% X_2	Region and City Size X_3	Location Within SMSA X_4	Establishment Size X_5	Employment Growth X_6	Unemployment Rate X_7	Annual Hours X_8	Self Employment X_9
X_0		.8022	.3897	.4524	.6024	.3389	.2041	-.1761	.1582	-.0375
X_1	.8369		.0326	.2629	.4360	.1352	.2039	-.3490	.3919	.1253
X_2	.4011	.0641		.1952	.4635	.4870	-.0561	.3795	-.2329	-.3562
X_3	.4279	.2605	.1922		.2403	.3421	.2934	-.2505	.0986	-.1306
X_4	.6231	.4576	.4638	.2332		.4517	.0679	-.0197	.2051	-.2660
X_5	.4530	.1669	.5083	.3410	.5033		.0506	-.1398	.0276	-.6341
X_6	.2019	.1940	-.0821	.3273	.0605	-.0181		-.2560	.0506	-.0804
X_7	-.2761	-.3919	.3505	-.2303	-.0256	.0666	-.1979		-.4979	.0322
X_8	.3052	.4891	-.1854	.1179	.2324	.1360	.0411	-.4277		.2885
X_9	-.1719	-.0063	-.3699	-.1586	-.2898	-.5331	-.1653	.0719	.1420	

[a] Lower half: all variables in logarithms except unionization; upper half, all variables in regular form.

weighted distribution of the number of establishments in the employment size-classes. (50–99/100 and over = 2/1.)

For variables X_6 through X_9, the sources were as follows:

X_6 *Employment growth:* U.S. Bureau of the Census, *Census of Population: 1960,* Vol. 1, *Characteristics of the Population,* part 1, *United States Summary,* Table 210.

X_7 *Unemployment rate of males:* U.S. Bureau of the Census, *Census of Population: 1960,* Vol. 1, *Characteristics of the Population,* part 1, *United States Summary,* Tables 210 and 211.

X_8 *Average annual hours per employed male:* 1/1,000 sample.

X_9 *Self-employment income as a per cent of earnings:* 1/1,000 sample.

CYCLICAL FLUCTUATION ANALYSIS: SOURCES AND METHODS

This Appendix describes sources and methods used for obtaining monthly estimates of employment, output, and output per man-hour for the series discussed in Chapter 7.

Employment

Employment is defined as the number of wage and salary workers plus the number of self-employed workers. For wage and salary workers, the Bureau of Labor Statistics monthly employment series based on payroll data was used. This is published in *Employment and Earnings Statistics for the United States, 1909–66,* BLS Bulletin No. 1312-4. For the self-employed, we used unpublished monthly estimates of self-employment by industry, compiled by the Current Population Survey, Bureau of the Census.

The BLS employment series underwent a major revision in 1961 to reflect both the most recent industrial classification scheme and improved estimation procedures. Food store and automotive dealer employment were not revised prior to 1958. The old series for 1947–57 are not comparable with the new ones, as indicated by large discrepancies between the two for the 1958–60 overlap period (compare data in *Employment and Earnings Statistics, 1909–1966* with estimates in monthly issues of *Employment and Earnings* for the years 1958–60). Therefore, for both store types it was assumed that the 1958 ratio of the new series to the old series by month equaled the monthly ratios for each of the eleven previous years.

Self-employment in food, apparel, and automotive stores was estimated by applying the ratios of self-employed workers in each store type to all self-employed retail workers in Census of Business years to the monthly CPS self-employment in retail trade series. Ratios for every year in the period studied were obtained by interpolation between Census of Business years.

Output

With the exception of manufacturing, output is always given by deflated sales. Current dollar sales are compiled by the Bureau of the Census. All sales series used, except wholesale trade, are published in the *Survey of Current Business* of April 1966; *Business Statistics, 1961, 1959, 1957, and 1955;* and the *Survey of Current Business* of June 1957. The wholesale trade series is for merchant wholesalers only. It was assumed that the changes in total wholesale sales conformed to changes in this series. For 1948–55, wholesale sales were obtained from unpublished worksheets of the Bureau of the Census. Figures for 1947 were estimated by extrapolation based on data for service and limited-function wholesalers. (See *Business Statistics, 1951.*) For the remainder of the period, the source is the *Monthly Wholesale Trade Report.* For the years 1956–59, wholesale sales in the *Monthly Wholesale Trade Report* were multiplied by the ratio of annual sales figures in *Business Statistics, 1965* to annual figures in the *Monthly Wholesale Trade Report.* This procedure was employed to take account of the fact that the series was revised in 1961, but sales prior to 1960 were not changed with the exception of annual totals. (Compare data in *Monthly Wholesale Trade Report* with that in *Business Statistics, 1965.*)

Current dollar sales were deflated by price indexes (1957–59 = 100) to obtain constant dollar sales. Table J-1 shows these deflators.

TABLE J–1

Current Dollar Sales Deflators

Industry	Deflator
Retail trade	All-commodities component of the Consumer Price Index.
Food stores	Food component of the CPI.
Apparel stores	Apparel component of the CPI.
Auto dealers	A weighted average of the new automobile, used automobile, and tire components of the CPI. The weights were .5, .4, and .1, respectively.[a]
Wholesale trade	All-commodities component of the Wholesale Price Index.
Manufacturing	Manufacturing component of the WPI.

[a] For 1947–52 a price index for used automobiles was not available. Therefore, it was assumed that the new automobile index adequately reflected price movements of all automobiles in this period. This assumption was strengthened by the fact that few used cars were traded in these years. The tire index is published on a quarterly basis. Monthly figures were obtained by interpolation between quarters. A similar procedure was employed to obtain a new automobile price index between 1947 and 1952.

For manufacturing, output was measured by the manufacturing component of the Federal Reserve Board Index of Industrial Production (1957–59 = 100). This is given in the *Survey of Current Business* of April 1966, *Business Statistics, 1965,* and *Industrial Production, 1957– 59 Base.*

Output Per Man-Hour

Output per man-hour is defined, as real output divided by man-hours and is expressed as an index number with 1957–59 equal to 100. Average weekly hours are a weighted average of the hours of wage and salary workers and the hours of the self-employed. The weights applied were

TABLE J–2

Specific Cycle Turning Points

Series	Peaks	Troughs
Construction employment	12/48	1/50
	2/53	5/53
	6/56	6/58
	12/59	2/61
Manufacturing output (FRB index)	7/48	10/49
	7/53	4/54
	2/57	4/58
	1/60	1/61
Manufacturing output (deflated sales)	9/48	10/49
	7/53	10/54
	2/57	4/58
	1/60	1/61
Deflated retail sales	7/50	4/51
	3/53	1/54
	7/57	3/58
	4/60	4/61
Deflated wholesale sales	7/50	7/51
	7/53	1/54
	1/57	2/58
	2/60	1/61

the proportion of total employment accounted for by each group. Average weekly hours of wage and salary workers were given by BLS payroll data of hours of production workers. It was postulated that nonproduction workers worked the same number of hours as production workers. This corresponds to the supposition made by Thor Hultgren in *Cost, Prices and Profits: Their Cyclical Relations,* New York, NBER, 1965. For the self-employed, CPS estimates of the average weekly hours of the nonagricultural self-employed were used. It was assumed that the self-employed worked the same number of hours in every industry.

TABLE J–3

Average Rates of Change of Output During Business Cycles,
Selected Industries, 1947–65
(per cent per annum)

Industry [a]	Average Rate of Change in		Average Cyclical Change Net of Trend
	Expansions	Contractions	
Retail trade	5.0(0.2)	−6.5(3.0)	11.5(3.0)
Wholesale trade	7.0(1.1)	−10.1(2.0)	17.1(2.2)
Manufacturing (FRB index)	9.8(2.3)	−11.2(3.0)	21.0(2.9)
Manufacturing (deflated sales)	8.6(1.2)	−8.2(2.0)	16.8(1.9)
Nondurable manufacturing	6.4(1.6)	−2.3(1.1)	8.7(1.3)
Durable manufacturing	12.7(3.8)	−18.2(4.2)	30.9(4.3)
Food stores	4.7(0.4)	−0.2(0.7)	4.9(1.0)
Apparel stores	4.8(0.7)	−4.3(1.4)	9.1(1.6)
Auto dealers	5.0(2.9)	−17.6(8.9)	22.6(8.8)

Note: Figures in parentheses are average deviations.
Source: See Table 58.
[a] Figures for retail trade, food and apparel stores and auto dealers are based on turning points in deflated retail sales; wholesale trade, based on turning points in deflated wholesale trade sales; manufacturing (FRB index) and durable and nondurable manufacturing based on turning points in manufacturing production; and manufacturing (deflated sales), based on turning points in deflated manufacturing sales.

Appendix J

TABLE J–4

Average Rates of Change of Output Per Man-Hour During
Business Cycles, Selected Industries, 1947–65 [a]
(per cent per annum)

Industry	Average Rate of Change in		Average Cyclical Change Net of Trend
	Expansions	Contractions	
Retail trade	4.4(1.3)	−1.7(1.9)	6.1(2.3)
Wholesale trade	4.8(1.0)	−8.8(1.8)	13.6(2.4)
Manufacturing (FRB index)	4.9(1.7)	0.1(1.6)	4.8(2.9)
Manufacturing (deflated sales)	3.0(0.2)	1.7(1.1)	1.3(1.2)
Nondurable manufacturing	4.3(0.8)	3.2(1.0)	1.1(1.6)
Durable manufacturing	5.6(2.4)	−2.5(2.2)	8.1(3.8)
Food stores	4.0(1.6)	1.6(1.7)	2.4(2.9)
Apparel stores	3.7(1.2)	−1.8(3.4)	5.5(4.0)
Auto dealers	3.4(3.1)	−14.0(8.6)	17.4(8.2)

[a] For notes and source, see Table J–3.

AUTHOR INDEX

SUBJECT INDEX

Accidents, economic cost of, 121
Advertising, classification of, 15
Age
    of barbers, 108, 110, 115
    of beauticians, 110
    classifications, 220
    and employment, sector differences in, 11, 184, 185, 186
    and hourly earnings, 7, 68, 69, 130, 131, 136–137, 138, 221–223, 223–224
    and labor value, 120–121
    and technological change, 197
    See also Demographic characteristics.
Age-value profile, 121
Agriculture
    decline of, 19
    and Service sector growth, 25, 29, 31
    employment in, 1, 2, 14, 18, 19, 186, 207, 208
        by occupation, 36, 67
        rate of change of, 51
        by state, 24, 26–28
        in twenty OECD countries, 30–31
    growth of Service and Industry sectors relative to, 3
    hourly earnings in, 129, 129n
    labor's share of proprietor's income in, 49, 206
    output and input in, 209–210, 211–212
    output measurement in, 16
    output per man in, 5, 52
    and per capita income, 25
    rate of change of output, input, and productivity in, 55
    share of Gross National Product, 37
Air pollution, health and, 120
Alcohol, health and, 120
Alienation, 11
    and growth of Service sector, 189
Aluminum industry, employment in, 1
Annual hours, 252–258, 260
    and earnings, 149, 152, 154
Apparel stores, 79, 81, 84, 87, 88, 169, 173, 177, 233, 263, 265, 266
    output during business cycles in, 173, 177

sales deflators, 263
    See also Retail trade.
Australia, classification of Service sector in, 15, 15n
Austria, sector distribution of employment in, 30–31
Automation, alienation and, 11
Auto assembly plants, classification of, 15
Automobile dealers, 79, 81, 84, 87, 88, 169, 173, 177, 233, 263, 265, 266
    and rates of change of output during business cycles, 265
    real output of, 239–240
    and sales deflators, 263
Automobile industry
    employment in, 1
    productivity in, 194
Automobile repair services
    classification, 15, 206
    employment and intermediate demand in, 40, 41
Automobile repair shops, 79, 81, 84, 87, 88, 232
Average annual hours. *See* Annual hours.
Average hourly earnings. *See* Hourly earnings.
Average weekly hours. *See* Weekly hours.

Banking, 99
    classification of, 15
    productivity in
        and consumers, 195
        and demand, 197–198, 198n
Barber shops, 79, 81, 84, 87, 88, 109, 110, 111, 114, 232
    and beauty shops, 99
        and demand and productivity, 6, 197
        and labor quality, 128
        productivity studies of, 10, 107–115
        rates of growth of, 109
Barbers
    and business cycles, 160–161
    hourly earnings by class of worker and nativity, 114
    percentage distribution by age, 110
    percentage part-time, 111